Finding Meaning in Life, at Midlife and Beyond

Wisdom and Spirit from Logotherapy

David Guttmann

Social and Psychological Issues: Challenges and Solutions
Albert R. Roberts, Series Editor

Westport, Connecticut
London

Library of Congress Cataloging-in-Publication Data

Guttmann, David.

  Finding meaning in life, at midlife and beyond : wisdom and spirit from logotherapy /
David Guttmann.

      p. cm. — (Social and psychological issues : challenges and solutions, ISSN 1941-
7985)

  Includes bibliographical references and index.

  ISBN 978-0-313-36017-6 (alk. paper)

  1. Life. 2. Meaning (Philosophy). 3. Aging—Philosophy. 4. Aging—Psychological
aspects. 5. Existential psychology. 6. Logotherapy. I. Title.

BD435.G89   2008

128—dc22   2008020079

British Library Cataloguing in Publication Data is available.

Library of Congress Catalog Card Number: 2008020079
ISBN: 978-0-313-36017-6
ISSN: 1941-7985

First published in 2008

Praeger Publishers, 88 Post Road West, Westport, CT 06881
An imprint of Greenwood Publishing Group, Inc.
www.praeger.com

Printed in the United States of America

The paper used in this book complies with the
Permanent Paper Standard issued by the National
Information Standards Organization (Z39.48-1984).

10   9   8   7   6   5   4   3   2   1

This book is dedicated to Michal Yahalom, my partner for life, with a sense of gratitude for all the help she has given me in preparing the manuscript. This book is also dedicated to Mrs. Eleanor Frankl, Mrs. Frankl's family, and to the hundreds of students and practitioners I was privileged to teach about social work, gerontology, ethics, and logotherapy in many parts of the world during my thirty years of teaching, conducting research, and writing in the academe. I am glad to note that many of them became leaders in their fields of practice and serve with dedication and devotion in various services for the aged and other population groups. I also wish to dedicate this book to my children, family, and friends.

I wish to express my gratitude to the staff of the Library of Congress and the University of Haifa, Israel, for their kind and helpful suggestions and guidance, and for sharing their time and knowledge about using the most appropriate and relevant resources for this book. Ms. Elizabeth Yodim assisted me generously with the initial editing of this book before the submission to the publisher. My heartfelt thanks are due to the late Professor Albert R. Roberts, Series Editor, for his trust and encouragement. I am and will always be grateful to Professor Roberts. His death is a tremendous blow and loss to the entire social work profession, to his family and friends, and to me personally. He was particularly interested in the subject of this book because of his love of logotherapy and because of a family history that was full of hardship. Despite his family's hardship, he never lost interest in pursuing education and in transmitting knowledge to others.

My heartfelt thanks are also due to Debora Carvalko at Greenwood Publishing Group for all the help she has given me in the preparation of the manuscript for printing, and especially to Susan Yates for the excellent professional work she did in editing this book. I am truly grateful to all of you!

I wrote this book as part of a moral debt to my spiritual mentor and most esteemed friend, the late Professor Viktor Emil Frankl. He was during his life, and continues to be for me, a model of meaningful living in old age. Professor Frankl often expressed his wish to see his "brainchild"—logotherapy—expanded into many fields of science and therapy. I hope that with this book I have managed to fulfill his wish. I also hope that anyone who reads this book will find in it helpful suggestions, ideas, attitudes, and ways to make life meaningful in his or her second half of life.

Contents

Introduction

MEANINGFUL LIVING AS A CENTRAL CHALLENGE IN LIFE

Logotherapy concentrates on the age-old human quest to live a meaningful life. Created by Professor Viktor Emil Frankl, author of the best-selling book *Man's Search for Meaning*, logotherapy means psychological and spiritual therapy by discovering meaning in life. It combines psychological and philosophical attitudes to life with a methodology that emphasizes a deep commitment to humanistic values, respect for human dignity and freedom of choice, and the right to choose and form one's life so that it will be meaningful for him or her and for the society in which one lives.

This attitude to life emphasizes the importance of man's spiritual dimension and his quest for freedom, as well as personal responsibility for one's decisions and choices. Spirituality in its lay and religious sense is beyond the comprehension of the human being. It flows from hidden internal sources, nourishes one's soul and identity, and helps one to accept life with understanding and willingness. Spirituality helps to cope with losses that characterize human life mainly in its second half.

Today close to half a billion people in the world are sixty-five years old or more, and their numbers are growing steadily from year to year. In most developed (industrialized) countries, the elderly and aged constitute on average from ten to fifteen percent of the total population. The fastest growing group among these people are those seventy-five years old and over. According to demographers, gerontologists, and researchers in life sciences who study the subject of human aging in the world, these percentages will grow even larger during the first half of the twenty-first century and will have a dramatic effect on the welfare and well-being of the aged and on the provision of care, services, supports, and benefits, in terms of both quality and quantity.

In addition to the unprecedented growth of the aged population, longevity of life is also growing. Today it hovers around eighty years in the West and even more in Japan. Women enjoy a longer life span than men by five years on the average. How to turn the years in the second half of life meaningful is getting more and more critical for society and for each and every aging individual.

THE QUESTION ABOUT THE MEANING OF LIFE

The question about the meaning of life raises its head every time life reminds us of the fact that we will live in this world for only a short time, even if we have the fortune to live a hundred and twenty years, such as Moses in the Bible. This question returns and surfaces anew in times of crisis. Each human being that experiences some loss, becomes disabled due to sickness, accident, or act of terror, loses a beloved person or a cherished ideal that gave purpose and meaning to his or her life, or is unwillingly laid off work asks this same age-old question: What is the meaning of life? Each human being raises questions that emanate from this first one: Why survive? Why suffer? Why continue to live? Wouldn't it be better to finish life, while I can still do so, instead of continuing to suffer? Does life have any value at all when I will die in any case?

Questions about the meaning of life are characteristic not only of the old and aged, who are naturally closer to death than the younger generations and wish to know whether or not it makes sense to continue living when they are getting closer and closer to death each passing day, but also of the young. Doubts about the worthiness of life in this world full of dangers, violence, and aggression encompass all social classes and not only the poor, the downtrodden, the unemployed, and the sick. A life without meaning is a tragedy that can happen to the rich no less than to the poor. Crises can and do happen to all of us, irrespective of our social and economic standing in society. The crisis can center on a wide variety of factors, such as political, economic, religious, and social problems, and can paralyze a man's soul in whole or in part, depending on the severity the individual or society attaches to it.

It is imperative to help a person find meaning in life when they are living in an existential vacuum, which is a life without a clear purpose that would give it meaning. This is a goal in which everyone should be interested, because the young of today will be the old of tomorrow, and they too will face questions that press so heavily on the present generation of elderly: What is the meaning of my life? Did I do what was expected of me? Did I utilize the opportunities life threw in my lap? Did I cope successfully with the changes life brought to me? Was I aware of the fact that life has an end, that it is temporary, or did I waste the precious time given me?

UNIQUENESS OF THIS BOOK

Currently, successful aging is an art in itself, and each aging individual must learn its basics. This art is based on the willingness of the person involved to fully develop his talents and inborn capabilities hidden deep inside him—all the gifts he received from life in order to gain the main meaning of life—to become a real human being.

My main purpose in writing this book is to spread knowledge of the concept *meaning in life* among old and young people alike. I am convinced that we all need a strong philosophical and practical outlook on life, one that will guide us in dealing with the problems, difficulties, and crises that old age brings to most people. We must be armed with an ability to choose a perspective on aging that will nourish our souls and provide a spiritual anchor for facing and braving the vicissitudes awaiting us.

Another purpose for writing this book is to bring together the knowledge and experience I have gained during decades of teaching logotherapy and gerontology to students, practitioners, and the general public in many parts of the world. In my encounters with people I saw how eager they all were to acquire the wisdom and knowledge that has accumulated in both fields.

This book is different and unique in many respects from other books on aging. It is different by virtue of the fact that it does not inundate the reader with statistics. It does not deal with the subjects that one can usually find in most books in gerontology, such as life expectancy, illnesses in aging, services for the aged, social policy in aging, and so on. The differences between men and women in many areas of life in old age are not emphasized in this book. These subjects often repeat themselves endlessly. Thus there is a need to approach the subject of getting older from a different angle.

The emphasis of this book is on the value and importance of having a philosophical perspective on life in old age for meaningful living. Knowledge derived from philosophy, psychology, religion, and gerontology is presented with case illustrations to give the interested reader both intellectual pleasure and practical guidance. As far as I know, no other book on aging has both of these attributes, and no other book provides a philosophical approach to meaningful living in old age.

This book can serve those who are already aged and the pre-elderly—people in their forties, fifties, and sixties—equally well. This book can help them to make the necessary preparations to strengthen their mental and spiritual powers, talents, capacities, and resources for what will inevitably come, the trials and tribulations of life in old age. This book may also serve as an opportunity for new learning in old age.

Learning is a value that was recognized by the sages of all times. Learning affects not only the intellect but also the soul in the same way that forgetting does. The changes that life constantly brings in its wake necessitate learning and studying anew knowledge that has already been acquired in one way or another. Learning, as Socrates has said, is like being reborn.

I believe that my approach to getting older is one whose time has come. The more technical and machine-based the world in which we live becomes, the greater the danger is of losing its soul, and the greater the need is to strengthen the spirits of the people. This book could help students, professionals, and families of the aged not only to acquire a new approach to meaning in life but also to change their attitudes according to the spirit in which this book was written.

Gordon Allport writes in his introduction to Viktor Frankl's *Recollections: An Autobiography* (1997) that, according to a sentence attributed to Albert Einstein, the scientist stands before a dilemma: Either he will write in a theoretical language that is not open for laymen, or in a language that is popular yet superficial and that could be understood by everybody. However, this is not necessarily so. The obligation of the scientist is to write in such a way that both his colleagues and the educated public could use it. This obligation is valid for our universal heritage in literature, poetry, philosophy, and other treasures in the arts and sciences. I have tried to surface many pearls of wisdom from all of these areas in the arts and sciences about how to gain meaningful old age. My purpose was to offer a book that would entertain and provide knowledge.

MY WAY TO LOGOTHERAPY

Life, according to the Nobel Prize winner writer Shmuel Joseph Agnon, is a chain of meetings and departures. Each meeting contains many opportunities for discovering meaning in life. In 1984 I had a fateful meeting in San Francisco with Professor Viktor Frankl, my self-chosen spiritual mentor and since then beloved friend. He has influenced me to devote my life to spreading his theory, logotherapy, all over the world. Our wonderful friendship lasted until his death. This friendship continues with his family to this day.

In our first meeting Frankl was eighty years old, yet judging by his energy, enthusiasm, and youthful appearance, he could easily be mistaken for someone who was twenty years younger. He was the epitome of his theory. He was wise, witty, and above all had a sense of humor that enchanted me. Many years prior to our meeting I read his book *Man's Search for Meaning,* and I have used this important book in teaching a course titled Human Behavior in the Social Environment. This book had a deep impact on me and over ten million people who have read it, and I wanted to meet its author. When we met, I felt that I was standing before a unique personality, someone who could serve as a model for successful aging. Frankl has been my guiding light for meaningful living in old age ever since.

Part One

Theoretical and Philosophical Approaches to Meaningful Living

On Old Age That Steals on Us Fast

Gerontology is an area of scientific study of the aging process; a subject for teaching at various levels in higher education and informal settings; a professional work with individuals, groups, and communities; and the study of inter-generational relationships between old and young in a given social, cultural, and emotional environment.

As a relatively young science that has been developed especially within the past four decades, gerontology intends to understand, help, and prevent problems related to aging. Additional goals and objectives of gerontology are furthering the health and welfare of the aged population, explicating the needs of the aged, and offering ways to prepare for old age while in the middle of life.

Aging is an individual experience that each human being will experience if they are fortunate enough to live a long life. In the industrially developed countries of the world the majority of people enjoy an average longevity of eighty years. This length of life was unheard of in earlier centuries. Even in the first half of the twentieth century few people were fortunate to live this long. Despite this amazing longevity of life, many people among the aging population are still not psychologically and spiritually prepared for this period of life and negatively perceive old age without realizing the value of the gift they received from life.

The question is when do we realize that we have arrived at old age? To be an old man or woman is not a big deal. It is much more difficult to remain young in old age. In western countries millions of people try to remain young by means of cosmetics, plastic surgery, diets, and other artificial devices. However, as soon as one wipes off the cosmetics from one's face, looks into the mirror, and sees reality, one begins to tremble because behind the youthful appearance hides a figure that resembles more and more the picture of Dorian Gray.

People dependent on public opinion are willing to use anything to maintain the illusion of youth. They reject aging as a natural phase of life and fight against it unsuccessfully. They fight reason, logic, and biology. If they were more courageous and could say "I am old", they could get rid of their torment once and for all. Alas, they lack the power to say such words. We can, of course, understand them because in those countries to be old means being weak, useless, nonmainstream, and meaningless.

In a story by the French writer Guy de Maupassant (1850–93), a fifty-year-old man dresses and behaves as if he were thirty. During a dinner the hostess introduces her daughter, an attractive virgin fresh out of the monastery, to him. This gentleman succeeds in seducing this girl and takes her to his home. On the way to his bedroom, he looks at himself in the mirror, and the magic of the moment vanishes at once. He sees himself as he really is; a man with dull gray hair, deep black rings under his eyes, a bulging stomach and bent back, and he says to himself, "You are a has been, my dear." Now he is ready to forego the sought after pleasure and escorts the girl back to her home unharmed.

Many other people accept their old age with pride. Throughout history we see figures such as Plato, Voltaire, Goethe, Freud, Shaw, and Viktor Frankl, who in their old age performed great artistic and intellectual deeds and have achieved lasting fame. They should serve as models of successful aging for the young generations.

THE NEED TO FIND MEANING FOR THE SECOND HALF OF LIFE

If we could define aging by giving it a number in years, we would do well to begin with the second half of life, at age fifty for men and women. This number does not necessarily mean that each human being must be old at that age. Human traits are different from one individual to another. However, this number can symbolize a new phase in life that is open to new beginnings and new searches after meaningful living. Most fifty-year-old people would not voluntarily accept themselves as aged. This nonacceptance seems reasonable if aging is perceived as renouncing life. But if aging is perceived as a period of life in which one can enjoy life in all its richness and as a one-time only adventure, then aging could be welcomed and even sought after.

Unfortunately few people think and behave this way. For example, a scientist once decided to study the meaning of life. He took a randomly selected sample of some 3,000 people, whose names and addresses he got from the phone book of a large city, and sent these people a short letter containing one question: Why do you live? He expected to receive answers from less than ten percent of the respondents and was tremendously surprised when more than ninety percent responded. Many wrote that they were living and waiting for their retirement. Others wrote that they were living and waiting for the chance to take a trip around the world. Some wrote that they were waiting for their children to grow up. Still others wrote that they were waiting for something good to happen in their lives. In short, everybody was waiting for something.

The scientist became very sad when he read these answers and said to himself, "Isn't it pathetic that all these people let life pass in waiting?" He wrote back to his respondents, "The day is today! Dream if you wish, but do something to make your dream come true! The day is today!"

The following story about Abe (a fictitious name as all other names used in case illustration in this book from now on) is an example:

Abe, a man in his early sixties, came to me because he wanted treatment for the emptiness that had come over him in the past few years. He told me that he had been treated by various therapists and methods, including Chinese acupuncture, without success. He was still waiting for something that would bring an end to his suffering. He asked me suspiciously what method I used in my therapy; whether I used psychoanalysis or behavior therapy. I smiled in return because I remembered a story about Frankl. He had once been asked by a lecture participant to explain in one sentence the difference between psychoanalysis and logotherapy. Frankl said that he could do it, but first he wanted that person to explain to him in one sentence the meaning of psychoanalysis. This participant said, "In psychoanalysis the patient lies on a couch with the therapist behind his head, who must hear at times many unpleasant things about the patient." Frankl replied, "In logotherapy the patient may remain sitting erect but he must hear things which sometimes are very disagreeable to hear" (Frankl, 1962, pp. 95–96).

I said to Abe, "I use my own method." He seemed perplexed and asked, "You have no other method?" "No," I said. "I try to adapt myself to the special needs of the client. There are many methods in psychotherapy, but you can't help one with methods alone. But if you insist on a method then I tell you that I use logotherapy." I proceeded to briefly tell him the meaning of logotherapy. I said that in my thirty years of practice I had learned to find my unique way and to understand the client's language and world of concepts because only then could I help someone else find their unique way in life.

"Yes," he said. "I heard something about Frankl and the concentration camps. That's ok with me." He seemed relaxed and told me that despite his relatively good physical, social, and economic condition, he felt that something was missing in his life and could not find meaning and sense to his existence. He had circled the globe twice and worked as a volunteer in various organizations, but he could not find peace of mind. Something was missing and bothering him a great deal. I recalled a story by the Israeli writer Agnon about an old tailor that had to make a garment for the Lord. The garment was almost ready, but something was still missing. "That something if it exists," Agnon wrote, "then the garment is whole, and if it is missing, then the garment is not whole." That "something" means the accomplishment of the whole; because only the whole gives meaning to what man is seeking in his life.

The "something" that Abe was searching for was the meaning of his life. The lack of this "something" is what made his life empty and miserable. He felt that he was living in an existential vacuum without a clear purpose and goal. I told Abe that I could help him if he was willing to work hard and make some sacrifices. "What is it?" he asked. "What you feel is really important for you," I said. He was disappointed. "I thought that you would give me something else, perhaps some advice." "I don't have such things," I said. "In logotherapy we don't believe in the concept of instant therapy. There are no shortcuts. Man must work hard on himself to gain the necessary change. Logotherapy," I said to Abe, "is based on choice and responsibility, and these belong first of all to the client. The therapist can only help. He cannot make a decision instead of the client, for the client is the one who carries the responsibility for his choices and for his fate. If you want to live a meaningful life now, instead of living in the past, you must make an effort. First you should think about what activity is the most meaningful for you. After you invested your energy and soul in this effort, and made your discovery, then you are free to discuss the ways how to achieve your goal." Abe replied, "Do you mean that I have to change my habits; for example, to forego getting up late in the morning and spending hours in a café and many other things like these?" "It depends on you," I said. "You don't have to change a thing if you don't want to. You may stay in your misery and feeling of emptiness." "Good," he said. "I will consider your words. What do I owe you for this session?" "You don't owe me a thing," I said. "You owe only to yourself."

MEANINGFUL LIVING

What is meaningful living in the second half of life? How can we attain it? Can it be achieved by anybody or only by those with special qualities? Can we teach ourselves and others how to attain it? These questions are not at all new and original. They have existed since the dawn of human history and have occupied the thoughts of almost everybody, particularly philosophers, writers, and poets. These questions usually become stressful when it is rather late, when people are deep into old age. They are tied to the concept of the good life and human happiness.

Living a good life has always been the expressed wish of all people. Each of us has a vague idea of an overall goal in our lives. This goal was expressed by the ancient Greeks from the times of Socrates, Plato, and Aristotle, and up to the times of the Roman philosophers in the ancient Greek concept of *eudaimonia*, which is usually defined as happiness. This is the aim of all human pursuits, or the highest goal that a person can achieve by his or her actions, even in old age.

This idea was particularly well expressed by the famous Roman philosopher of antiquity, Marcus Tulius Cicero, in his delightful little book titled *De Senectude* or *On Old Age* (1909), which he wrote in 45 BCE. Cicero elected to present his philosophical attitude to meaningful living in old age through Marcus Porcius Cato, a character he took from Roman history. Marcus Porcius Cato, "the Elder" and Roman Senator, became famous in history for his oratorical skills. He used to end each of his speeches in the Roman Senate with the words "And Carthage must be destroyed."

According to Cicero, Cato lived for eighty-four years, an unusually long life in those days. Until his death he retained all his physical and mental powers, and did not think about his impending death. Thus he became a role model for the youth in Rome and continues to serve as such for the aged of today, especially for those who are afraid of the nuisance of old age and death.

Similar opinions about old age and the shortness of life were held by the Roman philosopher Lucius Annaeus Seneca, perhaps the greatest among the Stoics. He was born in 4 BCE. and died in 65 CE. Seneca was commanded to commit suicide by Emperor Nero on a false charge. He had a difficult life full of disasters and losses, but he never succumbed to the twists and turns of his fortune. He kept his stoic attitude toward life (of which more will be said later) until his last moment, saying, "Never did I trust Fortune (the goddess), even when she seemed to be offering peace. All those blessings which she kindly bestowed on me—money, public office, influence—I relegated to a place from which she could take them back without disturbing me" (Botton, 2000, p. 99).

ON THE SHORTNESS OF TIME

Seneca was deeply impressed by the philosophy of Cicero. He said that humans falsely accuse nature of giving them a short life unlike other creatures. The truth is that our lives are not short at all, but we shorten them by our own hands and waste our time without giving an account to ourselves, as if our lives are infinite and death has no rule over our existence. Life is long enough and sufficient for doing the most meaningful tasks if we use time wisely. Whoever wastes his time will perceive life as a passing moment even if he lives a hundred years. Living means understanding the value of life. The lingerer and the delayer waste their time in idle thoughts about the future without thinking about the present.

Many people begin to live their lives when the end is near. Chronological age does not guarantee a long life. It is only a reminder of the fact that one exists a long time. It resembles a man whose ship has been hit, instead of sunk, in a storm and tossed around in circles by the waves. He thinks that he has traveled a long way, but in reality he has only been going in circles. Such people note how quickly time passes only when they are in mortal danger. In these dangerous situations they are willing to make any monetary sacrifice to lengthen their lives, but in other situations they use time as if it were a commodity that can be replaced any minute.

Because time passes quietly and swiftly, many people mistakenly think that it is possible to postpone preparations for their coming old age. No wonder, therefore, that most people arrive at their old age as children—not ready, as if they bumped into it not realizing its nearness.

"Life consists of three parts," said the ancient Roman philosopher Seneca. "What has been, what is now, and what will be." Of these three parts only the past is secure, outside the control of fate, and unable to be hurt. What is, meaning the present, is always short and passing. If a man constantly occupies himself he will have no time left for mental tranquility.

If you wish to know how short life was for those who wasted their time on superfluous matters, for those who kept piling up more and more riches, pleasures, power and similar earthly goals, look and see how desperately they wish to lengthen their lives. Many such people try to cheat time by all kinds of lies and harmful behaviors and cling to an illusionary image of youth as if it were possible to cheat time. They wail that they did not live long enough because they did not have the time to accomplish their dreams or enjoy the fruits of their efforts. But those who were wise to keep watch on the passing of time and did not waste it are not afraid of the finality of life. They march calmly toward the finish. The life of the wise is long in terms of time because he can live hundreds of years in literary, philosophical, scientific, and religious creations. He is not limited as those people who always chase after honor, power, success, and riches. The wise can always meet good friends who have passed long ago through the great works they left behind. The wise can always engage in discussions with these people and enjoy their wisdom. These discussions and wisdom give the wise pleasure that is much greater in value than all those material and earthly matters.

INGRATITUDE FOR THE GENEROSITY OF THE AGED

Too few literary creations use old age as their topic. In folklore, for example, old age is not worthy of mentioning. Most children's stories end with the young living "happily ever after" to the end of their life as if they would never grow old. In many poems old people are compared to winter in which the leaves fall and the flowers of summer whither away. Winter hushes the songs of the birds, envelopes the heart in sadness, and freezes joy of life for the old.

Among the old people that literature has immortalized are Shakespeare's King Lear and Balzac's Father Goriot. Both of them are sad heroes that one can only pity. Forgotten by their children, they fight against their physical decay and emotional terror. They live a life of misery and want, poverty and lack of sustenance. All of their decisions serve as a warning of how not to get old! Both of them are illustrations of society's perception that aging is a calamity. *King Lear* and *Father Goriot* show us what happens to foolish old men that divide their wealth and means among their children long before their end and the price they pay for the illusion of being loved by their children.

In Shakespeare's play *King Lear*, the naïve king divides his entire wealth among his daughters long before his old age and death, and pays dearly for his mistakes. He trusts in the love of his daughters, but finds himself prey to poverty, destitution, and desperation.

Father Goriot, the hero in Balzac's book, is an old and sick man. He lives in a poor neighborhood in Paris at a cheap hotel for the downtrodden. Earlier in his life he was a rich industrialist who made his fortune during the French revolution. When his wife died, he spoiled his two daughters. He gave them a good and expensive education, married them to young noblemen, and gave his wealth to them. The only thing he asked for in return was human kindness. The daughters were ashamed of their father's poor background. They compensated their father by severing all connections with him.

Father Goriot in his hurt and despair left his business and went to live in that poor neighborhood in Paris. He gradually lost his fortune, and he even sold his last pieces of value to help his daughters pay for the losses of their husbands. When he became gravely ill, he asked to see his daughters. One of the heroes in the book, who lived in the same hotel, was sent to call the daughters to see their father before his death, but they shamelessly refused to see him.

These two masterpieces deal with intergenerational relationships. Despite the historical distance between these two great writers—Shakespeare lived from 1564 to 1616 and Balzac from 1799 to 1850—it seems as if the generations continue to behave in the same way. Children rob their parents and exploit the fact that old folks are willing to pay any price for the right to love them. Although King Lear in Shakespeare's story finally receives real love from one of his daughters, the father in Balzac's story, who sacrificed his entire wealth in order to make his daughters happy, is treated ruthlessly. Balzac's story comes to an inhuman climax when the daughters refuse to listen to the plea of the man sent by their father to come to his deathbed and do not participate in his funeral.

Today we witness the cynical exploitation of many old people, especially those who in their naivety behave as King Lear or Father Goriot. Despite the progress made in some welfare states in caring for the rights and well-being of old people, the family remains the most important informal support system for the old. Congress can make no laws about kindness, love, dignity, and honor for old folks. It cannot demand or command society to give emotional support and care to its aged members. Beyond the care of family, each person who has not reached the second half of life must make preparations for his or her old age in order to live comfortably and in security when the time comes. This is possible if the young understand that they have to save for the hard times, which include paying insurance fees for health care in the future and ensuring their rights to decent care in a nursing home.

LACK OF RESPECT FOR THE OLD

It is told of the king of Lydia, an important kingdom in ancient Greece, that when he was old and weak he traveled with his company to visit a city far from his capitol. The road went through a thick forest. Suddenly a ferocious lion jumped out of the bush with a tremendous roar and approached the company of the king. The king's frightened escort ran away trembling, and the king was left alone to face the lion. When he was about to be devoured by the beast, two young lads appeared and slewed the lion. When the king regained his voice, he blessed the young men and wished for them to die when young.

This story illustrates that old age was hard in antiquity even for a king—even if he did not have to suffer from hunger and cold as so many old people do in our days. The story also hints at the fact that when one gets old those who are supposed to take care of the king and provide security for him leave him to his fate, food for the lion. The latter symbolizes the forces of nature that overwhelm the old man and threaten to devour him. The king is left defenseless against these forces. He is too weak to defend himself. Old age is too burdensome and the lion is about to swallow him. This is why he gives that blessing to his saviors.

What bothers today's aged more than the length of life is the lack of respect for the aged by younger generations in many parts of the world. In the industrialized societies in particular, and even in the developing countries, the position of the old has deteriorated, and they are no longer perceived as the wise men or women in society. In earlier times respect for the old was regulated by religious and moral needs, as in the Fifth Commandment in the Bible. Even in the society of the ancient Hebrews that commandment entailed a reward, long life for those who fulfilled it, meaning that people had to be induced to adhere to this precept.

The respect accorded the old was based on the recognition that they possessed life experience and knowledge that was superior to that of the young. The respect was also based on the need for the old in certain occupations, such as arts and crafts, matters of family life, and in educating and advising the young. Today these functions are no longer necessary in our highly technological societies, and such knowledge is no longer recognized as a prized possession of the old. On the contrary, they have difficulty in keeping up with the rapid development in every field of science and technology, especially in electronics and computer-based technologies.

What bothers the aged in particular is connected to the devaluation of former traditions and norms. To be young, healthy, beautiful, and possibly rich, was most likely a human quest even in traditional societies, but today youth is overvalued. Consequently, many old people feel themselves unneeded and valueless in society. They have lost what can never be replaced: their youth and vitality. Many old people try desperately to cling to their lost youth by dieting religiously, exercising, and applying cosmetics. Many old people fail to accept the fact that time has passed and the future awaiting them is getting exceedingly short and frightening. Therefore each old person must decide how to spend their remaining years: whether in self-deception and in a compulsive holding on to what used to be, even when this feels impossible, or in accepting the inevitable, the coming losses and weaknesses, but also the new possibilities that are still open for finding meaning in life.

Many old people forget that they are first of all spiritual beings whose happiness and real wealth is measured in spiritual, emotional, and intellectual gains. The soul is the central factor in the life of each old person because the soul never ages. Although the body ages and declines, the soul remains young and continues to develop. True success in life is measured by spiritual yardsticks. Such success means giving to others, loving, sharing, and finding deeper meaning in everything we do.

WHY AGING IS PERCEIVED AS TROUBLESOME

Let us go back to Cato, as told by Cicero, who tells the young Romans seeking his advice that there are four reasons why aging is considered the most troublesome of the three phases of life: childhood, adulthood, and aging. The first reason is that it prevents us from continuing to engage in activities that we were used to doing. The second reason is that it weakens the body. The third reason is that it deprives us from enjoying all the bodily pleasures; and the fourth reason is that it is close to death.

It is interesting to note that in the past 2,000 years or more no real changes have occurred in the perception of aging as the most difficult and troublesome of the eight phases of life (Erikson, 1964; 1968). In 1975 the first survey about the attitudes of Americans to old age was published by the Gallup Poll. Its title was *The Myths and Reality of Aging in America.* Of the 4,254 respondents only two percent chose the sixties and seventies in a person's life as the best years, and one-third of the respondents claimed that these are the worst years for them.

As for the first reason why aging is troublesome, Cicero noted that those who deny the opportunities of the aged to do something great do not contribute much to clarifying this question. They resemble those who claim that the captain of the ship makes no contribution to its sailing. While the sailors are busy in all kinds of maintenance work that is necessary for sailing, the captain sits calmly and holds the steering wheel or helm. Although the captain is not doing physical work, his role is much more difficult and important than the role of the crew because he is guiding the ship and is responsible for its course and purpose.

Among the virtues that are characteristic of old age is mental tranquility. Many people and most philosophers perceive this as the greatest virtue of old age. The wisdom, steadiness of character, and right judgment that Cicero speaks about through Cato, are the actual and realistic expressions of that tranquility. It enables the old to have more patience toward themselves and others and to accept people as they are. This does not mean, however, that we must accept every bit of nonsense and show weakness in our old age. It means a correct judgment of what is and what is not possible to do or to gain. When people approach reality calmly, they usually become more evenhanded and objective.

Seneca saw similar traits in calmness and mental tranquility and emphasized that these are particularly important in old age. According to Seneca, lack of calmness, inability to concentrate on one thing or on one activity, and the need for constant changes are due to a lack of satisfaction with one's self. He advised his friend Serenus that to combat his inability to relax he must trust himself and work because nothing is more dangerous to a person than idleness.

Another virtue available to the old is a person's ability to love somebody. This love requires less selfishness and the ability to not take ourselves too seriously. We could also add that we should be grateful for the life we have already had, for the life that is perhaps ahead of us, and for everything we have received. We must learn to relinquish many things so that the greatest renunciation, life itself, will not surprise us.

ON THE NECESSARY RENUNCIATIONS IN OLD AGE

Aging requires us to make a choice. We can choose one of two ways of responding to a renunciation: either we perceive it as a loss and obsessively hold on to what is being lost, therefore increasing our suffering, or we accept it with understanding and love because we know that it is inevitable. Two other virtues in old age are modesty and lack of demands. If these two virtues are developed, the old person will be respected because instead of getting into arguments about what is lost and why, one can concentrate on giving something meaningful to oneself and to society.

As we age, we must learn to thank life not only for what it gave us so far but also for what is in store for us in the future. Gratefulness warms the heart and opens the door to a good feeling. We should be grateful for all the memories and for memory itself that is able to raise pictures and scenes from the past. These can flood one's soul with feelings of happiness.

This attitude to life was echoed some 1,800 years later by Schopenhauer. He was a philosopher who said that we must repeat what we have learned, reflect on the past, and raise it repeatedly to prevent its sinking into the depths of forgetfulness (Schopenhauer, 2001, p. 209).

When one reaches old age, one should take an inventory of his life. An old person should do a great cleaning job, preferably once a year, to get rid of all the superfluous junk that has accumulated so far, such as all the envy, desires for power and control, arrogance, conceit, hatred, and childish attitudes. This is the right time to say good-bye to all the excess baggage. Many times people say, "We can't take it along in the after life," but, as the saying goes, there is a great distance between what is said and what is done. Saying good-bye to this excess baggage permits one to live one's life with meaning. It enables one to choose what is meaningful over what is no longer needed. Beginning with the second half of life, we must learn to voluntarily leave behind objects, social status, and roles.

After age fifty one should heed the following advice: it is far better to enjoy and be happy with what one has achieved by his or her own effort than to poison one's soul and life by lamenting over what one will never get. The maturity of a fifty-year-old is being able to see the world as it is, in a new way and a new light—instead of the fog that has engulfed one's vision because of envy, yearnings, fears, and obligations. Thus one can learn an age-old truth: by being capable of renouncing everything, we will get everything (Nagy, 2000).

2

Spiritual Development

FREEDOM OF THE SPIRIT AS AN ADVANTAGE IN AGING

One of the advantages of old age is the spiritual freedom that can be acquired when people are willing to invest the necessary effort. It is a well-known maxim that nothing is given free in life, except a mother's love to her child. We need to train ourselves to be ready to discover meaning in life even in old age.

Spiritual freedom means less preoccupation with mundane matters and more involvement with what makes us spiritual beings created in the image of God. This freedom deepens the works of great artists, whose works have become more meaningful because their aging has brought greater maturity and wisdom. They usually are less interested in glorifying themselves, less drawn by their immediate instincts and urges, and more willing to make sacrifices to accomplish something meaningful. Spiritual freedom also means greater willingness to be frank and honest with one's self, less escape to illusions, and acceptance without mercy of one's faults and shortcomings.

There are several advantages to aging. Long life widens the opportunities for active living. The length of time lived permits one to develop and to refine one's talents and capabilities. It provides opportunities for sharing intellectual and material achievements with the younger generations.

Spiritual freedom means awareness of individual responsibility for one's deeds, good and bad. Personal responsibility is expressed in the wise use of time and resources for the benefit of society. An old man or woman should not become a burden to others. It is important to adopt a healthy lifestyle and to refrain from using substances harmful to one's health. Old people can change their behavior and habits—if they are willing to make the necessary effort. Change is open to everyone at any age as a human characteristic. Human beings must learn to change and adapt to the demands of life at each phase of development.

When a person approaches old age, he or she should get rid of the illusions that were an integral part of the younger years. This act is painful but necessary. It is hard to say to ourselves that we were wrong, that we made mistakes. We must realize what is beyond our strength. This learning is the last opportunity to get rid of all kinds of disappointments, envy, and hatred. When old people free their heart from these destructive elements, they can achieve a higher level of existence. Then they can look upon the world as it is, without envy, without sadness, without prejudice, and enjoy it to the fullest—despite its many shortcomings. Old people should learn to smile at life from the depth of their souls as a testimony to their inner peace.

The life of the great artist Pablo Picasso (1881–1973) can serve as an illustration to what has been said above. He lived ninety-two years, and during his long life he went through many changes that enhanced and enriched his art: as a young student he painted in the classical style of the great artists from the sixteenth century. In the beginning of the twentieth century he lived his "blue period" and afterward his "pink period."

In the 1920s Picasso was active in the cubist movement, and when the Fascists and Nazis came to power in Italy and Germany he began to paint in surrealistic and expressionistic styles. His fame and fortune grew with his aging. A testimony to his many talents can be found at his birthplace in Spain in the museum that houses his artistic creations.

Not every aging person is an artist, a writer, or a politician whose life can serve as a model for others. Ordinary people can also lead satisfying and rich lives if they keep an open mind and adopt practical wisdom.

As we age, we need to learn how to refrain from taking unnecessary risks. Each task or role offered to an aged person requires careful thought about the positives and negatives involved. Wise old people, for example, do not wait until their eyesight is so weak that they cannot see road signs or until their reflexes are so slow that they cannot respond quickly to sudden changes in traffic in order to refrain from driving.

The wise person listens to good advice, takes into consideration the feelings of others, such as the feelings of his family and kin, accepts and understands that he or she cannot remain young and independent forever, and is willing to live with the limitations that time and environment expect from him or her. The wise person does not try to escape into illusions. The noted psychologist Carl Gustav Jung, in *Memories, Dreams, and Thoughts* (1997), wrote about his old age in the following way: "I am satisfied with the way my life was structured. It was rich, and I gained a lot. How could I think that I would get so much? Everything that happened was things that I could not foretell" (p. 450).

ON WEAKENING OF BODILY STRENGTH AND LACK OF SENSUAL PLEASURES

The reason old age is considered troublesome for many people is that it is tied to the weakening of bodily strength. Cato has something important to say in this regard. Cato tells his listeners that old people should use what capacities they still have in whatever they do with all their might. Old people can remain active and nobody will prevent them from continuing to exercise their powers of intellect even in extreme old age. They still have enough strength to teach the young, to train and equip them for the duties of life.

Failure of the body's strength, Cato tells the young, is more often caused by the vices of youth than those of old age. A dissolute and intemperate youth hands down the body to old age in a worn-out state. Cato advises the young to enjoy their bodily strength when they have it, and when it is gone they should not wish it back. It is important to stand up to old age and compensate for its drawbacks by making an effort. We must fight it as we should an illness, for our bodies are like lamps: unless you feed them with oil, they too go out from old age. "The body is apt to get gross from exercise; but the intellect becomes nimbler by exercising itself" (Cicero, 1909, pp. 56–58).

Is it true that old age lacks all sensual pleasures? Cato replies that not only the body but also the intellect must be supported. Old people can have lots of pleasure from modest festivities, pleasant discussions and conversations with friends, and drinking and eating together with people of all ages, but these activities must be done in modesty and with restraint.

Cato prefers the intellectual pleasures to the physical or bodily pleasures as being more appropriate for the elderly. He praises in particular the pleasures of the farmer, which are not marred by any degree of old age because they deal with the earth and its productiveness, the planting and growing of vines. The production, cultivation, and growth process of grains, vines, vegetables, flowers, and fruits that grow in the garden or in the orchard can be observed and controlled to a certain degree, and can give more pleasure than all bodily enjoyments combined. These pleasures are available to many old people even today.

Cato emphasizes that neither white hairs nor wrinkles can at once claim influence in themselves; it is the honorable conduct of earlier days that is rewarded by possessing influence in the last days (Cicero, 1909, p. 69). Both old and young people today should take this advice to heart. There are aged people who get fretful, ill tempered, disagreeable, and avaricious. Cato stresses the point that these behaviors are the faults of character, not of the time of life, meaning old age. These faults are often the result of neglect, lack of respect, and the mocking of the old by the young. However, they can be softened by good character and good education.

THE BEST DEFENSE AGAINST THE TROUBLES OF OLD AGE

Cato's advice to the young to get passionately involved with life and to escape preoccupation with death is as relevant today as it was in his days. The best defense against the troubles of old age is active exercise of the virtues. If the virtues have been maintained at every period of life the harvest they produce is wonderful (Cicero, 1909, p. 48).

The words of Cicero, via Cato, with all their beauty of speech, richness of expression, poetic and literary strength, and wisdom, do not suffice for old people living in the modern world to know how to prepare themselves for their old age. They need knowledge drawn not only from philosophy but also from many other areas of life. They need knowledge that science and technology can provide them. But they also need knowledge beyond what is known and has been proven scientifically in the modern age. They need knowledge about the mystic of existence.

A virtuous life, according to Cato, is only part of the best defense against the troubles of old age. There are many factors in addition to moral virtues that presently make life more tolerable in old age. Chief among these factors is the machinery at home and outside that helps old people in their washing, eating, mobility, housework, and so on, thus making life relatively easy for most old people and accounting, in part, for increased longevity.

Advances in medicine and pharmacology to fight diseases and ailments associated with aging and the availability of knowledge about sanitation, hygiene, nutrition, physical exercise, sports, and use of leisure time, all contribute to the well-being, comfort, and ease of a growing number of old people, especially in the industrialized parts of the world.

Today there are many opportunities for old people to remain active, productive, and useful to society long after retirement, whether as paid workers or as volunteers. Old age subsidies and benefits given by the social security administrations of many countries now make the burden of living easier for more millions of old people than in any other historical era, even if there is a long way to go before a dignified old age will be assured for all.

PREPARATIONS FOR OLD AGE

To the advice given by Cato to the young in ancient Rome we may add ten commandments that modern gerontology has developed. These are geared toward achieving meaningful living in old age and, briefly stated, are the following: securing the necessary economic resources; safeguarding the waning physical, mental, and intellectual capacities; selecting the right time for retirement; strengthening social relationships to prevent loneliness; setting aside time for sports and exercise; selecting an option for meaningful work or occupation; securing sufficient knowledge about the use of modern technology; satisfying scientific curiosity and continuing one's education; satisfying the need for warmth, kindness, and sexual relationship; and serving society, rather than withdrawing from life.

These commandments are expressions of our human quest for security in old age. They reflect basic human needs in every part of the globe, and they are relevant and necessary for all old people in the historical times in which we live.

We can imagine different scenarios in our lives, such as our aging, and we are able to take steps to prevent the problems that are likely to happen in our old age as the life experiences of previous generations have taught us. Many people are making wise preparations for their future aging, especially in economic terms, which is a relatively easy thing to do if one begins it in the young adult years. These preparations generally include savings and insurance plans, and indemnities against illnesses, accidents, disabilities, and loss of life. There are others who maintain regular annual check-ups, eat healthy foods, refrain from smoking and from addictive or dangerous substances, exercise and engage in sports regularly, and think that they are making all the necessary preparations for their old age.

Although all the above preparations for old age are important and good, they are insufficient in themselves to provide a meaningful old age. If we do not make preparations for the time of the empty nest when the children are grown up and live away from home, we may pay a heavy price. The freedom that is sought after eagerly and suddenly arrives and is accompanied by an uninvited guest—the fear of emptiness. What previously gave sense and purpose to life has left. The routine order of daily life people were used to for decades has disappeared, and they are left with many empty hours.

There are aging people who sink into self-pity and reproach themselves, saying things such as "If I only were wiser" or "if I only did" so and so. And many others fall into depression or despair. Still others escape into passivity, become addicted to the television, refrain from mental activity, and accept their fates as a matter of fact. People whose lives centered only on daily routines, and who made no effort to combat this monotony or to go out into the wider world with its abundance of opportunities will find it difficult to make the necessary changes. They may erroneously think that it is already too late, and then they may find themselves succumbing to the inevitable. These are, alas, wrong and unhealthy ways of behaving that attest to a lack of preparation for their old age.

Each life event that happens without preparations hurts a lot. Whoever is caught by life unready risks negative results that could drive one to depression. Sometimes old age literally pounces upon a man, as it did upon Abraham in the Bible when he lost his wife and therefore his shield against old age.

When one reaches fifty, if not much earlier, one should begin to make necessary preparations for one's old age in three dimensions—physical, psychological, and spiritual, in its religious and secular sense—so that aging will not pounce upon one unprepared. This is the right time to begin imagining how one would like to arrive at old age.

Erik Erikson (1964), a disciple of Sigmund Freud, has remarked that life is built on "holding on" and "letting go." At each phase of human development we must learn what to hold on to and what to let go of and how. If one continues to hold on to things that one was supposed to let go of, continues to hold on to what is no longer relevant, and cannot renounce it, then one will not be able to accept his or her aging and fill it with life-satisfying content.

Before a person enters old age, it behooves him or her to learn which doors are still open and which doors are forever closed. For a young person it is almost impossible to imagine his or her old age. It is even more difficult for the young to make preparations for their old age at that time in their lives. Even students studying gerontology can hardly imagine themselves as old people. They resemble old participants in many studies who deny the fact that they are aged and insist that the others in the same age group are old.

An aging individual must learn what promotes his or her health and what poses great risks that need to be avoided. An appropriate diet and exercise can do wonders to preserve and even to enhance one's physical and mental well-being. Above all, older people must learn how to use their spiritual powers to gain successful old age. They must learn how to refrain from complaining and how to overcome frustrations that come inevitably with aging. An old man or woman should not become a nuisance to his or her social environment.

The following story illustrates this maxim. A man was invited to a party. He asked his wife to take his mother to a nearby café and to treat her to a light lunch. When he came back to the café, he asked his mother how she enjoyed the time with her daughter-in-law. The old lady said in a whiny voice, "I had a good time. I got a cup of coffee." The daughter-in-law became red in her face and asked, "And didn't you get anything else?" The old lady replied, still whining, "Yes, I also got a piece of cake." "And nothing else?" "I also had a roll with honey and butter." "Did you also get good cheese?" "Yes," said the old lady with a sigh. "And did you forget the fruits you got?" "Yes," said the old lady with a choking voice. "There were fruits too" (Nagy, 2000, p. 79).

Of course, not all old people behave this way, but they can become irritating, annoying, and ungrateful if they have not learned to be thankful for all the kindness bestowed on them. They need to defend themselves against the vicissitudes of life physically and mentally and to refrain from complaining unjustly.

The best and safest ways to prepare ourselves for old age begin in the early twenties of our life. Albert Schweitzer, the famous physician and winner of the Nobel Prize for peace, summarized this preparation in his book *Honor of Life* (1999). He wrote that his faith taught him to struggle and remain young in spirit, to refrain from being a "mature person" (meaning an old man) even in his old age (p. 235). Schweitzer reminds old and young people that life wishes to take away from us our belief in the good and the beautiful, in what is true. Life wants to rob us of our enthusiasm. But we must not throw away our ideals. True knowledge is in the power to rise above and beyond the disappointments.

"What is the greatest secret in life?" ask many old people today. Schweitzer replies that the greatest secret is to go through life without wearing out. One has to reflect about all the events that have happened and look forward in order to accomplish this feat (p. 236).

3

The Search for Happiness

The Dalai Lama (2001) has stated in his book on happiness that we all wish for something better in life, irrespective whether or not we have religious belief. Therefore the purpose of life is the search after happiness (p. 19).

The struggle to be happy, to enjoy lasting and fulfilling happiness in old age, seems to be never ending. We can differentiate among three kinds of struggle: nonvoluntary, partially voluntary, and positive. Of these, only positive struggle merits real attention, because it is a struggle that provides self-respect and compensates for depression, disappointment, loneliness, and illness.

Happiness is whatever confers well-being and good spirits. The attitudes that are the most likely to ensure happiness in later life are flexibility, self-respect, perseverance in a personal project, and knowledge of the difference between illness and aging. There are two kinds of happiness: short-term or instant, and long-lasting and fulfilling. Older people who developed a healthy attitude to positive struggle early in their lives and maintained it during their long lives, enjoy the latter (Gullan-Whur, 2002).

The problem with this approach to happiness is that not every older person is able to develop the necessary strength to engage in a positive struggle for happiness. Many people do not know what issues or situations in life are worthwhile to struggle for or what purpose is best for them to invest their waning energies in. Many people resign themselves to the less than happy circumstances of their lives. Moreover, each individual must find his or her own struggle that best promotes survival and happiness. What is important, therefore, is to let people accept that change is always possible; that they do not need to follow their life-long habits; that earlier attitudes to life, creativity, and happiness do not necessarily remain static, even in old age. Thus there is first a need to promote positive self-respect, by using talents and capacities in a socially accepted way, especially in the service of a great idea, and then to engage in the struggle for their fulfillment. This kind of struggle leads to the discovery of one's real self, the experience of symbolic growth, which, in logotherapy, is equated with peak feelings experienced during life events that are decisive for spiritual well-being and personal growth. What really matters in such a struggle is the impact on significant others and on the world.

Ignoring the symptoms of illness as long as they are not life-threatening, concentrating on new and rewarding activities, and denying age are other ways of maintaining a healthy and positive struggle for survival in old age. The German poet and philosopher Wolfgang Goethe wrote the second part of *Faust* while he was seriously ill and in old age. He did not give up the struggle to finish his masterpiece; he refused to succumb to the illness and continued to create and work until the very end of his life. Thus he turned a human predicament into a great human victory.

Albert Ellis (1998), founder of Rational Emotive Behavior Therapy and the grandfather of cognitive-behavior therapy, wrote *Optimal Aging: Get over Getting Older* when he was in his eighties. This work is a useful, witty, and valuable self-help manual for people, not necessarily only the old, who wish to lead meaningful and happy lives in their old age. Ellis developed twenty rules for optimal living in the twenty-first century (p. 271). He used Sigmund Freud's saying that the goal of all life is death but paraphrased it as the goal of all life is to have a ball. His book tells old people to concentrate on positive ways to create enjoyment in the second half of life.

A practical approach to optimal living is not enough for a happy life in old age. Many of the rules presented by Ellis and co-author Velten sound too idealistic and even somewhat preachy. A more balanced attitude to human happiness is given by philosophy.

Human happiness has constituted a philosophical problem ever since philosophy came into being. Each of the leading philosophers in the past 4,000 years of written human history had his or her own version and definition of this elusive concept. In antiquity, for example, the Greek philosopher Epicurus (342–271 BCE) equated happiness and joy with ethics. He said that each living creature tries to gain happiness, joy, and pleasure and to avoid pain. Someone who is able to nullify both bodily and mental pain has arrived at the happiness that is sought after by humans. Happiness oriented toward truth and justice can be attained, especially by the wise.

The great Roman philosopher Seneca (4 BC–60 AD) claimed that being dissatisfied with what one has will cause a person to remain miserable, even if he or she rules the whole world. Only the wise are happy with their lot, and every fool despises himself or herself. He also said that people ask for happiness throughout all their lives, yet few of them know the nature of this happiness and even less how to gain it. According to Seneca, the source of happiness is mental tranquility, which immunizes people against the upheavals of fate; this happiness is what the wise person senses when he or she lives in accordance with good virtues and morals (Seneca, 1997, p. 13).

Aurelius Augustinus (354–430 AD), who lived during the end of antiquity and is regarded by scholars of the Church as one of its philosophical founders, relied on ancient Greek philosophy to pave the way for the philosophy of the Middle Ages. His attitude to happiness was based on the belief that the way to happiness leads one to turn inside. The inner world consists of knowledge, understanding, and will—combined into one unit—as in the three sacred elements of Christianity. The truth dwells inside people and not outside them, Augustinus maintained. His ethics were based on the concept of love, which he equated with happiness. This happiness was not built on earthly riches, goods, and possessions but on love itself, on true love, on the love of God.

In the modern ages happiness was defined differently by philosophers and by religious leaders. John Stuart Mill (1806–73) was one of the leading utilitarian thinkers of his times. He defined the aim of a utilitarian attitude to life as the greatest possible happiness for the greatest possible number of people. He also thought that, as each human being is seeking personal happiness, so should each realize that personal happiness and welfare are dependent on the happiness of all others. An act is ethical if it results in advancing happiness and reducing pain and suffering. One needs to weigh not only the quantity of happiness created by the act, but its quality as well.

Friedrich Nietzsche (1844–1900), a great philosopher in the nineteenth century, related to happiness from an altogether different angle when he asked whether or not the final aim of science is the greatest measure of happiness and the minimum of sorrow. The answer given was that modern science can rob people of happiness and turn them into cold creatures. He believed that, one day, science would discover its ability to bring happiness. Then and only then would the stars shine even more (Nietzsche, 1997, pp. 53–54).

It is common to think that everybody wants to be happy, and everybody wishes to live a long life full of happiness. The proof of this statement is evident: at each birthday party, people are greeted with wishes such as "lots of happiness" and "may you live 120 years"—like Moses in the Bible—as though people could live life in a static situation of constant happiness.

The need for eternal happiness has its roots in early childhood, when the little child lives without responsibility, without differentiating between good and bad, without a sense of time. The small child does not know anything yet about life's temporality or about death, and thus life seems eternal. Bliss in early childhood—life without worry or much pain, life full of pleasure and joy—is perceived by many people in their maturity as their hearts' desire.

What is this happiness that people crave so much? Is it self-evident? Or is there perhaps some effort needed to reach it? Is it possible to gain it as a gift from fate? What is it made of? Is it control of others, or getting rich? Or is it dependent on living a modest life, yet with a sense of satisfaction with ourselves and with the world?

The Danish philosopher Søren Aabye Kierkegaard (1813–55) said that the door to happiness opens from inside out. When people try to force their way through it and to be happy by using all means, they only close the way to this door (1993, p. 64).

THE SECRET OF HAPPINESS

According to an Indian fairy tale, a little girl went on a walk in the field outside of her village many years ago. All of a sudden she saw a butterfly caught in the thorns of a bush of roses. The girl patiently and carefully freed the butterfly from the thorns and it flew away. A few minutes later there appeared a beautiful fairy who said: "You behaved very well when you freed the butterfly from the thorns and showed that you have a good heart toward all the creatures in the world. Therefore you can ask me one wish and I will fulfill it." The girl asked the fairy: "Teach me how to be happy all my life." The fairy whispered something in the ear of the girl and disappeared. And, from that day on, the little girl was happy all of her life, and nobody in the village knew her secret. When she got old and was about to die, the villagers came to visit her and asked her to disclose the secret of happiness; she said: "The fairy told me 'you will be happy so long as others need you.'"

A different attitude to happiness outside the world of fairy tales was exhibited by Albert Einstein (1934), the most important scientist of the twentieth century. In *The World as I See It*, his philosophical and autobiographical book, Einstein wrote that we are here on Earth for a short time, as a result of other people from whom our welfare and happiness stem and whose fate is connected to ours (p. 13). Since his childhood Einstein had despised banal goals, such as success and luxuries. Paradoxically, these are the goals that are equated with happiness and that motivate so many people in the world today.

The search for happiness as the most important goal in life is directly connected to the will to remain young forever, to remain beautiful and strong, whereas the bitter truth that life passes like a cloud is a reminder that nothing stays forever. This knowledge, whether clear and concrete or foggy and clouded, causes much anguish and disappointment. It forces us to cope with being transitory on the Earth. It forces us to accept the bodily, mental, and spiritual changes that old age brings to all of us, which nobody can escape. Unfortunately, many people hold on to their old-fashioned ideas about happiness as something that, once attained, lasts forever. The stronger this idea is, the more difficult it is to cope with the changes that time brings to us.

Despite the fact that we cannot generalize about the concept of happiness, it seems that, behind the search for happiness, stand two basic needs in humans: the need for self-actualization, which is so commonly accepted in the Western world, and the need for love in its broadest sense. As for the first of these two needs, each human being wishes to live his or her life with a feeling that he or she has achieved this dream and made life as meaningful as possible. Each of us wishes to love and to be loved, surrounded by good friends who love and care for us. Each of us would like to escape loneliness and social isolation. Each would like to remain independent, not to be swallowed up by the crowd. Each would like to maintain uniqueness. The life of each of us would surely turn miserable if these two needs were left unfulfilled.

These needs are closely connected; they complement each other and form a necessary synthesis for attaining happiness. The trouble is that we live in an historical time in which many people are mistaken and confuse healthy and constructive self-actualization with limitless egoism. Many people are addicted to materialism, an addiction that cannot ever be satisfied, and they live inside the illusion that material riches will give them happiness.

Many people perceive love in its narrow definition, as the satisfaction of their immediate sexual urges and drives. But—when people free themselves of the need to acquire more material resources, honors, social standing, and power that provide them with a sense of superiority over others and when they do not invest all of their mental energies in achieving fame and wealth but instead in attaining meaningful living and enrichment of their souls—they can get on the king's road that leads to both self-actualization and to love. But a precondition of the search for true happiness is that the search must begin in our hearts, in our souls, in our inner world.

THE SEARCH FOR HAPPINESS AS A SEARCH IN OUR HEARTS

Martin Buber (1878–1965), famous editor, translator, and essayist, one of the leading philosophers in the twentieth century, saw the search in one's heart as the first step in the process of change, leading toward becoming a real human being. In his lovely little book *The Way of Man according to the Teachings of Hasidism* (1976), he tells the story of Rabbi Zalman Schneur, a leader in this movement, who was jailed because of false accusations by his opponents.

One day the warden asked him: "How can we understand that God asks the first man, Adam, 'Where are you?' God who sees everything surely knew where Adam was, and thus he shouldn't have asked him at all." Rather than answering this question, the Rabbi surprised the warden with an opposing question: "Where are you in your world? Look here, you most likely have passed forty-six years, and where did you get in your life?" When the warden heard that the Rabbi mentioned his exact age, he said "Hurray," but his heart trembled (p. 10).

The Rabbi did not get into a debate with the warden; he raised his answer to the latter's question to a different and higher plateau by turning it around, as if the warden were asked by God "Where are you?" And, as the first man preferred to hide rather than answer the question and accept responsibility for his action, so do many people today prefer to escape this nagging question. Buber emphasizes that the purpose of this question is not only to discover whence one came, whither one goes, and to whom one will have to answer, as in Hasidic religious tradition. It is more important to remember that the main purpose of the search in one's heart is to give ourselves the chance to turn away from a certain path that leads nowhere and go back to the road to change—which is the point of the story. The purpose of the question "Where are you?" is to awaken people to the fact of their responsibility for their lives, to prevent them hiding, from giving their personal answers.

Buber says that everything depends on how people are able to cope with the question. Each person's heart trembles when he or she hears the question, but the system of hidings will help people to overcome this feeling, because the voice is not coming via thunder that endangers their lives. It is, rather, a quiet voice that is easy to drown (Buber, 1976, p. 12).

The search in one's heart is effective only when it leads to Buber's road to change; otherwise, it turns into something tasteless that only leads to self-torture, despair, and entanglement with the negative forces in human beings. To find this road, one needs to be ready to accept change and to turn away from the way already trodden. The trembling of the heart that Buber speaks about is equal for all who have faced the essential question of being in the world. For whose hearts will not tremble when they must struggle with the fact that their life may come to its end in an instant—even if they outwardly behave heroically, such as the warden in the story?

LIVING FOR OTHERS AS HAPPINESS

Most human beings approach their aging full of fear and even anxiety—about the future that threatens them and about the end that approaches with giant steps. Fear and anxiety exist even in the earlier phases in the lives of human beings, as the results of personality and genetic inheritance or of life experiences that demanded their price.

Many elderly people lived their lives as if for others, especially those who were unable to develop their own unique personality or those who were unable to live without their constant partner. They are full of anxiety about what may happen to them if they lose this partner: How will they be able to manage? What will they do with themselves? How many times do we hear old people living together for decades say that they cannot even imagine living without their better half? This dependency on another is similar to that of a small child on parents, especially on the mother. Such a child lacks independent life; his entire existence is dependent on the other.

Many older women, despite modern times and the achievements of feminism and equality between the genders, remain completely dependent on their partners for life and do not know how to take care of themselves without those partners. They may never have had a bank account, written a check, heard of the stock market; visited government offices, or bought something without consulting their partners and getting their permission. Their entire lives centered on caring for the children, the spouse or partner, and the household. They never gave a thought to what might happen in case of a disaster, such as the untimely death of that significant other.

There are many old people who find it difficult to bid farewell not only to loved people, but also to material possessions. They are caught in a panicky need to gain more possessions or in despicable miserliness. They think that their wealth will gain them additional life, and they live in a state of constant anxiety about the possibility of losing their fortune. The same applies to those who hold on to power obsessively and to the hypochondriacs who are preoccupied with their health. All these people exhibit fear of the future and inability to leave behind what has been gained graciously. These people may be characterized as living empty lives, without meaningful content.

Happiness is close to unhappiness, according to the historian Lukacs (2001). One can live and find happiness even in the worse circumstances, in the worse distress, provided that much effort is vested in the search for happiness. In order to be happy, people must renounce the easy way, which centers on the factors that make them miserable; they will soon discover all of the things that seem to be missing and to cause unhappiness. Yet, in order to be happy, one must gather all physical and mental powers and organize and plan life, because the search for happiness is a task that we accept voluntarily. And this is not easy. We need to think about what makes us happy. Most people, however, are too lazy to think about their own happiness, to think about what gives joy and pleasure, not to mention meaning, to their lives. Thus they refuse to think about their future.

During World War II, Lukacs (2001) wrote in his autobiography that, in the midst of hunger and bombing, misery, persecution, cold, and freezing weather, when he was hiding in a dark basement and was afraid for his life every minute, what kept him alive and even gave him happiness and faith for a better future—what prompted him to plan for that future—was hope, together with reminiscences about pleasant memories of his past life that gave him pleasure.

4

Meaningful Living according to Logotherapy

In March 2000 the findings of a survey entitled *The Myth and Reality of the Elderly Situation in America* was published by the National Council on Aging. Participants in the survey included adults aged eighteen or older. Its purpose was to discover whether or not there were changes in the attitude of the American public toward aging since the previous survey conducted in 1974.

Among the most striking findings of this survey were the following: Eighty-four percent of the participants said that they would be very happy to live until age ninety; forty-four percent of those aged sixty-five or older described the present years of their lives as the best ones. Moreover, even the oldest of the old, those in their late eighties or older agreed that these were the best years for them; sixty percent of elderly black participants and fifty-seven percent of their Spanish-speaking counterparts agreed with this statement.

The present life satisfaction of the elderly was far better than what was reported in 1974. At that time, only thirty-two percent of elderly participants thought that way. The meaning of these results, according to the president of the National Council on the Aging in America, is that the country has entered a new era in aging. This era may be characterized for millions by positive experiences and meaningful living until age ninety or older. This is an option waiting for the aged. But, despite all of the optimism from the results of this survey, we have to keep in mind that aging is a phase of life that is full of difficulties for millions of older Americans.

Today the attitude to the beginning of old age is different from what it used to be in the past. Many elderly find chronological age meaningless; only 14 percent of the participants in the present survey thought that a certain chronological age is an indication of aging. On the subject of retirement two central factors were mentioned by the participants: the amount of personal savings (sixty-four percent) and health (fifty-nine percent). The most frequently mentioned definition of the concept of aging was "a decline in physical abilities" (forty-one percent) and "a decline in mental capacities" (thirty-two percent). Many young people exaggerate the economic situation and loneliness of the elderly and refer to them as being severe problems, but loneliness among the young, aged eighteen to twenty-four, was found to be higher than among the elderly.

An interesting finding was related to the struggle among the generations for benefits and for economic resources. Contrary to the existing myth in American society that the elderly are in continuous conflict with the young for budgets and benefits given by Congress, the majority (ninety-two percent) of all age groups in the survey rejected the claim that "the elderly are greedy." The majority of the respondents (eighty percent) agreed that the elderly do not receive enough respect from the younger generations.

How far these myths are from reality can be seen by the answers that participants gave to the question: "Do you think that the government gives enough money for the aged?" Two-thirds of the respondents under age sixty-five rejected the idea that part of the Social Security funds earmarked for the aging should be given to children. The younger age groups thought that there should be a widening of medical benefits for the old folks and that they should include long-term and nursing care. Furthermore, they agreed on the need to train older workers in new technologies to enable them to continue working beyond the present age of retirement.

As for the fear of crime against older people, the survey has shown a marked improvement in this area compared to the results of the previous survey in 1974. In sum, it is safe to conclude that the majority of the more than thirty million Americans aged sixty-five or older lead meaningful lives, at least in the material sense. Nevertheless, the question of what to do about those whose lives lack meaning should be raised.

PSYCHOLOGY OF THE HEIGHTS

Aging persons in modern society face a difficult problem even when they do not have an economic problem. They crave happiness and life satisfaction but lack guidance about how to achieve them. On one hand, they have lost their natural and healthy instincts that guide animals in their behavior. On the other hand, those who lack strong religious belief have lost the traditions and values that guided the attitudes of their forefathers. They find themselves empty-handed, worrying about what to do. What should they choose? Many people choose conformism; that is, they do as others do, or they succumb to totalitarianism and obey the commands and the demands of others instead of acting according to their own conscience and outlook on life.

Modern men and women lack a *Guide for the Perplexed* (Maimonides) on how to live in the rapidly changing world. They ask why they have come to this world and how they can maintain normal living despite the cruelty, terror, hatred, and wickedness that exist in the world. They search for a way that will help them discover meaning to their lives and strengthen them in the spiritual sense. One such way is offered by Professor Viktor Frankl in logotherapy, which he has created, developed, and spread throughout the world for more than sixty years.

WHAT IS LOGOTHERAPY?

Frankl (1962) has referred to logotherapy as a theory of motivation—a way of thinking and a methodology combined. The aim is to enable clients to discover meaning in their lives—rather than to satisfy their drives and instincts, as in psychoanalysis (p. 103).

In every theory of psychology the essence of a human being is central. This essence refers to a mental picture of what characterizes an individual, and this picture helps explain the theory and the therapeutic method that emanate from them. For Sigmund Freud biology was a determining factor in the evolution of humankind. This is why Freud concentrated his work on biological, sexual, and libidinal urges, drives, and instincts that influence human existence, especially in the early phases of human development.

Frankl emphasized the adult phase of development, during which spiritual determinants are more decisive than biological ones. According to Frankl, the human spirit is the only healthy nucleus found in even the sickest individual.

In all of Frankl's works a struggle to make the concept of meaning clear and understandable in the modern world is apparent. This struggle is not limited to the concept of meaning alone but encompasses all of the systems of people's relationship with themselves and with the meaning of their existence. According to Frankl's biography (Klingberg, 2001), at the age of four Frankl was already wrestling with the question of the meaning of life, and his struggle continued throughout his life. At age seventeen (Frankl, 1995, p. 36) he tackled the question in a lecture entitled "The Meaning of Life," given at the Volkshochschule in Vienna (People's College). On this occasion he presented the audience with two main points that were later developed into his theory of logotherapy: first, life does not answer our questions about the meaning of life but rather puts those questions to us, leaving it for us to find the answers by deciding what we find meaningful; second, the ultimate meaning of life is beyond the grasp of our intellect but is something that we only can live by, without ever being able to define it cognitively.

When criticized about his system of logotherapy as being basically a case history of his own neurosis, similar to those of his predecessors Freud and Adler, in *The Unheard Cry for Meaning* (1978), Frankl said that he was not entitled to speak in this context, but, as far as logotherapy was concerned, he would gladly confess that as a young man he had to go through the hell of despair over the apparent meaninglessness of life. He added that he wrestled with it, as Jacob did with the angel, until he could "say yes to life in spite of everything," until he could develop immunity against nihilism.

More than twenty-seven years ago, noted psychologist Irvin Yalom (1980) said that logotherapy is basically religious, and, for this reason, it speaks mainly to the common people in the street. What then is logotherapy?

Logotherapy is therapy for the sick, support for the sufferer, education for the confused, and philosophy for the frustrated. Logotherapy includes and deals with the biological, psychological, and spiritual dimensions of a human being. And all of these dimensions come together and are expressed in the functional dimension.

In addition to treating those suffering from neuroses that originate in the spiritual dimension, logotherapy has developed methods for working with clients who suffer from phobias in their sexual behavior, have incurable diseases, or lead empty and meaningless lives. Logotherapy can also serve as a complement or supplement to conventional methods of psychotherapy for addicts, victims of accidents, the physically disabled who have lost limbs, and others, especially in cases in which the losses are accompanied by a lack of meaning in life (Guttmann, 1996, p. 6).

Frankl's main aim in creating logotherapy was to make psychotherapy more human and to offer it as an additional way of looking at the world, both philosophically and in therapy. Logotherapy has a universal message and mission—namely, to counteract any tendencies to reduce human lives to tiny cogs in a large machine. This mission was what Frankl saw all of his life as his major reason for being in the world.

Logotherapy's basic assumptions stem from anthropology, the view of human nature; philosophy, the view of the world; and psychotherapy, the concept of therapy. Its major concepts—freedom of the will, will to meaning, and meaning of life—were based in no small measure on the philosophical writings of Schopenhauer and Scheler, two German philosophers whose works appeared mainly in the first half of the nineteenth century. For example, *Freedom of the Will* was one of Schopenhauer's most important books.

FREEDOM OF THE WILL

Frankl built the theory of logotherapy on triangles: three life events influenced Frankl about the importance of the meaning of life and brought him to develop logotherapy.

The first event was his arrest by the Gestapo, along with that of his entire family—parents, brother and newlywed wife—who were all taken to the concentration camp in Terezin outside of Prague.

The second event happened on the way to Auschwitz, when he had to give up the manuscript of his first book on logotherapy, later known as *The Doctor and the Soul* (1986).

The third event occurred when he was marching to work along with the rest of the prisoners at the concentration camp and discovered to his surprise that his wife existed inside his soul. At that moment he understood that, even in the most horrible physical and mental conditions, people can feel, even for an instant, joy from the very thought and reflection on a loved person.

These three events were linked in a symbolic way to the three triangles of the concept of meaning in logotherapy. The first of these triangles deals with the concepts of freedom of the will, the will to meaning, and the meaning of life.

Freedom of the will is the opposite of fate. Even in the concentration camps there was a measure of freedom: the freedom to choose one's reaction to the living conditions. The prisoners in the camps had to undergo a transformation from independent people who were free to make decisions about the circumstances of their lives into creatures who were forced to deal with the most inhuman, primitive, and degrading conditions possible. It is no coincidence that many of the prisoners suffered from an intense feeling of inferiority in the face of their sadistic tormentors.

Many prisoners succumbed to despair or fell into apathy, and many died for lack of meaning in their lives. Frankl consoled his suffering fellow prisoners by emphasizing that there was a meaning to their sufferings. And this meaning was that someone was observing each one of them—expecting them not to frustrate him or her and expecting them to bear their suffering proudly, not letting anyone trample on their human dignity—and that each of them would know how to die as a human being.

Frankl saw that even Sigmund Freud was wrong in his theory of human behavior: he had assumed that people left without food for days would become alike, that the hunger would diminish their differences until they disappeared. In the concentration camps of the Nazis, the opposite was true. Some prisoners behaved according to Freud's assumption, but others were willing to share their last piece of bread with their fellow prisoners. Frankl concluded that people are capable of sinking to the bottom of the abyss, to the level of animals, and to commit horrible and evil sins, but they can also become like angels and elevate themselves above and beyond all imagination and attain a purified level of spiritual existence.

The concept of meaning in life is also divided into three components. These constitute the second triangle and refer to the three values that can help people discover meaning in their lives: creative, experiential, and attitudinal values. These are discussed at length by the author in *Logotherapy for the Helping Professional: Meaningful Social Work* (Guttmann, 1996). The third triangle is composed of attitudinal values, such as the attitude to suffering, guilt, and death.

Frankl raised the question: How is it possible to refer to a human being in his or her totality? He emphasized that the individual should not search for an abstract meaning to life. Each one of us has an occupation or mission in life to do something concrete, something that only he or she can and should do. And, in this something, he or she cannot be replaced by anyone else, in the same way that his or her life cannot be replaced by another person's. Therefore the role of each human being is unique, in the same way as the opportunity given for its fulfillment is unique to each person (Frankl, 1962, pp. 108–109).

THE INFLUENCE OF ALFRED ADLER ON THE DEVELOPMENT OF LOGOTHERAPY

According to Frankl's autobiography (1995), he was influenced in his youth by the founder of the school of individual psychology in Vienna, Alfred Adler (1870–1937). One of the basic assumptions in Adler's psychology was that people exist in a given world, in which they are a tiny but necessary cog, and that, in their interactions with the world, they must fulfill three obligations. Achievements in all three areas of obligation result in a sense of meaning and self-respect; failure means suffering from various ailments and disorders.

In *The Meaning of Life* (1996), Adler claimed that these three obligations confront three central roles that one cannot escape in life: maintaining relationships with other human beings, finding some occupation for a livelihood, and engaging in a loving relationship to propagate humankind. These roles are connected as one unit and anchored in the fact that each one is dependent on human society, on the cosmos, and on the other gender. Positive fulfillment of these roles provides one with a happy existence in the world.

We may imagine these roles as a test of a problem in mathematics. The greater the mistake is that a subject is making in solving the problem, the greater is the mistake in life. There is also the danger that the mistake will get one into difficulties in life. Yet, this danger remains hidden as long as one does not experience some tragic life event, as long as life does not test his or her ability to carry a burden. The following is an example.

Recently I met Mr. Blum (false name), aged seventy-eight. He said that his beloved wife had become ill with cancer during the past year and had a heart attack too. Now he must try to learn the roles that his wife did for him, to be the supporter and encourager of the family. The illness of his wife opened the eyes of Mr. Blum. He saw that he failed to provide sufficient emotional support to his wife when she needed it. If he would have done so, he could have found deeper meaning to his life and felt greater satisfaction. The discovery gave him an opportunity to correct his way and to find a new meaning in life.

One can learn from this case that each difficulty that life poses, each question that life asks, is a chance to engage in a new search for meaning and an opportunity for finding it—even at age seventy-eight.

Adler's attitude to the roles just described reflects his theory of psychology. Accordingly, every effort one makes to overcome deficiencies is actually an attempt to gain greater security. Adler saw each individual as a unique and creative person, blessed with various degrees of creativity. People have different goals and purposes in life, yet the meaning of life is created by working toward the welfare of others.

Adler maintained that human beings create lifestyles based on the interpretations that they give to their hereditary inclinations, to the opportunities that arise in their lives, and to the goals they set for themselves to achieve. These lifestyles combine the three human dimensions of body, soul, and spirit and lead toward a final aim and purpose. They can be characterized by dependence either on feelings

of inferiority or pursuit of superiority as a compensation for feelings of weakness. They may also involve pursuit of excellence and can enhance feelings of security and self-respect.

Achievements in the three areas of life—friendship, love, and work—contribute to self-respect. The appropriateness of the goal of human life was perceived by Adler on the basis of a double criterion: whether or not individuals use them to enhance their self-respect and advance the life and prosperity of the society in which they live and work, that is, whether or not individuals have a deep sense of responsibility toward society.

A mentally healthy individual maintains well-developed social interests, exhibits more optimism and bravery, and is willing to accept more responsibility than an unhealthy one. Such an individual works more diligently and industriously to advance the welfare of the community than does a neurotic. Adler made positive comparisons between his individual psychology and religion. He claimed that both of these refer to the wholeness of the soul in a loving community. People can discover meaning in life through religion, which gives strength and enhances love for the social interests of people.

Adler wrote two books toward the end of his life that dealt specifically with the subject of meaning. In 1931 he published *What Life Should Mean to You?* and, in 1933, *The Meaning of Life*. In the latter he said that we live in a world of meaningful relationships. We never have interests only in facts; we refer to the facts only when they have some meaning for us. Our reality is based on the meaning that we assign it (Adler, 1994, p. 7). Adler's attitude to life and meaning was later incorporated into Frankl's logotherapy.

Adler was aware of the human weakness to postpone thinking about the inevitable. He said that, as long as the sailboat of one's life is going straight, one does not ask these questions.

An illustration of this idea is the story of Mr. Green, aged seventy, who came to talk with me. He has built his life on the honor that he received as the president of a certain organization and was absolutely certain that, as a result of his diligence and loyalty to his work, he would be able to stay in this position for another decade. "And all of a sudden a young man came and deprived me of the honor I built by great effort. He made various manipulations with the members of the board and succeeded to push me out. Now I have nothing to live for." "Are you sure?" I asked him. "Is it true that you have nothing to live for? Is your life meaningless just because you are no longer the president of this organization?" He seemed embarrassed because he didn't expect this answer. He hesitated a minute and then said: "Perhaps there are things that I can do in another organization."

JUNG'S APPROACH TO MEANING IN LIFE

The Swiss psychologist Carl Gustav Jung (1875–1961) referred to the problem of a meaningless life by saying that absence of meaning in life plays a crucial role in the etiology of neurosis. Jung saw in neurosis a suffering of a soul that has not discovered its meaning; he said that a third of the cases that he treated were not suffering from any clinically definable neurosis, but from the senselessness and aimlessness of their lives (Jung, 1954, p. 83).

Jung placed great emphasis on transforming a human being into a unique and independent personality by the development of inner strengths. When Jung reached his fifties, he began to claim that the second half of life, from year thirty-five and older, serves different purposes and goals than the first half of life. This assumption is supported by his own life: until the age of thirty-five, Jung worked mainly with severely psychotic patients. Later he decided that he did not feel himself strong enough to treat such people and began to work with mentally healthy individuals, searching to find their unique way in life.

Jung has maintained that the first half of life is devoted mainly to success in social and economical endeavors—marriage, occupation, and in raising children, whereas the second half of life must be successful in cultural achievements and accomplishments. According to Jung, women should not "roll down the curtains" just because they pass their age of fertility. He saw in the second half of life a gift from nature and said that, in the middle of life, after people have reached the peak of their efforts and built the work of their life, they have the freedom to look back and to question how their life has been shaped: they begin to search for the real motivation to their existence and to discover their authentic self and uniqueness. The discoveries that they make about themselves are possible only when they are willing to pay a heavy price, because they may cause great commotion. The following is an example.

A client in his fifties told me—when he began to perceive that it was getting late for him to achieve what he wanted all his life, that is, to devote himself to his hobby and become a singer in the opera: "Until now I was a slave to my commitments to work and home. Yet even if I didn't do a thing to fulfill my dream, I thought that I have the necessary talent. Now I see that I made a mistake. It is difficult for me to admit that I was wrong, that I made a mistake. It is hard for me to accept this fact, but I have no choice. I went to see a music teacher. He gave me a serious test and said that I could sing in a choir, but I could never be a soloist in the opera, not even in his own choir. I look back upon my life and see that I missed the many opportunities life gave me to fulfill my dream. This insight gives me shivers. Can you feel how hard it is to forego a dream?"

It is impossible to solve great problems in life once and for all. One cannot discover a meaning that will be valid in every minute of life, from childhood to old age. My client will have to find a new dream to fill his life with meaning or new ways for making his old dream come true. The meaning of life can never be achieved in a static answer to the question that life poses to us. It requires hard and consistent work. It arouses in us a spiritual sense and prevents us from sinking into foolishness or being fossilized.

Jung has shown that, in the second half of life, people wake up and feel their powers and capabilities that were neglected, as did my client. Aging individuals may achieve greater spiritual development by gaining understanding of their past, dreams, way of life, and the meaning of their life events. They understand anew what these events symbolize for them, and they can thus gain greater satisfaction and happiness, by accomplishing their dreams and by finding new meaning to their life. "Life has posed for me a question," Jung said, "and I had to answer to the best of my ability" (p. 451).

Jung perceived the world into which we are born as rude, coarse, rough, and obscene, but nevertheless containing divine beauty. According to him, what people wish to believe is dominant in the world depends on their mood: meaning or its lack. Jung knew that, in terms of metaphysics, life is lacking meaning and yet is full of meaning and hopes; in the end, meaning will gain and win (p. 451).

WHAT LIFE DEMANDS FROM ME: MEANING OF THE MOMENT

In each moment we are requested by life to respond to the meaning offered by some life event and to realize the meaning potential hidden in that moment. We should ask "What is life demanding from me now, at this moment?" Meaning, Frankl stresses, comes from "getting out of ourselves" toward purposes and goals, ideals to achieve and to serve, and people to love.

When human beings cannot discover, recognize, or accept meaning, they find themselves in an "existential vacuum." This vacuum cries out to be filled. Those who cannot fill their lives with some meaning are apt to pay a price, in the form of psychiatric symptoms, such as deviations from the social norms that are commonly accepted in a given culture. These symptoms are expressed as addictions to dangerous and harmful substances, violence and aggression that, in their worst excesses, can lead to what Frankl has termed "existential neurosis." This malady is characterized by suffering, anxiety, and depression.

The meaning of the moment is transitory: it cannot be repeated, postponed, or delayed. Life forces it on us whether we like it or not. The meaning potential is always present in a given situation. We are only required to discover it and to act toward its realization.

Each situation in an individual's life is unique. It cannot be substituted for by someone else's. Nor can someone else take on our lives and problems. We all live in a given historical era, with its specific requirements and opportunities—not only for need fulfillment, but for meaning fulfillment, too. Every moment that we live or every time that we encounter a unique situation requiring a decision offers us an opportunity for finding meaning. Yet, whether or not we respond to the call of life depends entirely on us. And the way that we respond to this call decides whether we use or miss the unique opportunity for finding meaning to our existence—or whether our lives are "full of vanities," and not really different from that of the animals, as Ecclesiastes says.

A relevant illustration is taken from the life of Frankl, as told by his granddaughter at the conference on logotherapy held in Madrid in 2005: "My grandfather was forty years old when he was freed from the last concentration camp he stayed at that time. He returned to Vienna and found that there was no one waiting for him.

His home was destroyed by bombings. All his family, his parents, his brother, and his wife were killed in the Holocaust. He was lonely and forlorn, without a home and penniless. He was depressed and destitute and had thoughts about suicide. Then he remembered that what kept him alive during his three and a half years in four concentration camps, aside from his hope to see his family, was the manuscript he wrote about logotherapy. If he would commit suicide, then the chance for his 'brain-child' to see the light will be lost too. He gathered all his physical, mental, and spiritual strength and instead of sinking into self-pity, he began to work furiously on the manuscript he managed to reproduce in his mind. Thus he began to find new meaning in life."

The meaning of the moment changes from one minute to the next, from one individual to another. The same situation may have a different meaning for a different person in the situation concerned. The situation itself is the same, but each individual is different; therefore, each perceives the same situation in accordance with his or her own perception, need, feeling, and understanding, which is projected onto the situation. Our task is to find the unique meaning that a particular situation offers us. Sometimes behind the trivial things hide great opportunities for meaning fulfillment. They seem to be hidden from the human eye, yet they exist.

Our conscience reveals the one thing that is required to actualize the meaning in a specific situation. This is the meaning of the moment. This unique thing that ought to be cannot be comprehended by rational terms or by universal law. It can only be experienced intuitively. It is our inner voice, our inner monitor, which needs to be heard and heeded to attain inner peace. This capacity can be used to the fullest when a concrete choice has to be made, such as between placing an incapacitated parent in a nursing home or caring for him or her at home until death.

SUPRA-MEANING AND MENTAL HEALTH

A famous actor happened to visit an exclusive resort. The owner was very proud of this actor's presence among his guests, so he begged him to perform after dinner. To the owner's surprise, the actor agreed and said that after dinner he would recite chapter twenty-three in the book of Psalms. When the dinner was over, the actor stood up and delivered a most profound act. When he finished, he got a standing ovation.

Among the guests of the resort happened to be a once-famous old cantor, and the owner asked him too for a guest performance. The old cantor climbed slowly on the stage and said that he would recite the same Psalm. In a faltering, stuttering, tearful voice, with his eyes lifted to heaven, he began: "The Lord is my shepherd, I shall not want . . ." and, when he finished, there was a great silence, but every eye was wet with tears.

After the evening performances were over, one of the guests went to the actor and said to him: "Perhaps you can help me. I don't understand what happened here tonight. When you recited the prayer, everybody cheered, but when the cantor recited the same prayer, everybody cried. I can't understand the difference."

The actor replied: "I think I can. You see, I know how to act, but the cantor knows the Master."

This episode illustrates Frankl's attitude to the subject of "supra-meaning." Frankl (1962) believed in a world beyond the human world, one in which the question about the final meaning of suffering will find an answer. This meaning Frankl called the "supra" or "ultimate" meaning (p. 118). Therefore, in logotherapy, Frankl speaks of another dimension in addition to the biological, psychological, and spiritual: this dimension is supra-meaning.

Frankl devoted two of his books to clarifying this dimension. The first, published in 1985 as his dissertation for the PhD, was *The Unconscious God: Logotherapy and Religion*. The second, *Man's Search for Ultimate Meaning*, was completed close to his death in 1997 and contains most of what appeared in the first one with the exception of two chapters: one about new research in logotherapy since 1975 and one about the search for the final meaning of life.

As an abstract concept, ultimate meaning is difficult to grasp, yet its existence is evident. We just have to look around in nature and the cosmos to see that there is order in the world, on our own planet Earth and beyond in infinite space. How did this order come about? How does it work? How does it affect the lives of the people on Earth, their individual and collective destinies? These are some of the questions that the greatest philosophers, thinkers, humanists, and psychologists have asked and continue to ask from one generation to the next. No one has real answers; no one has seen this supra-meaning with his or her own eyes (unless they were prophets). And yet there are opportunities in life for us to experience something extraordinary that reaffirms the existence of that special dimension: peak experiences.

People are capable of glimpsing for a fleeting moment the mysteries of nature, of feeling exultation, and of sensing a beauty that cannot be expressed in words. For some individuals these moments can be provided by music, for others by the arts, and for still others by nature. This is why we speak of a divine gift, as in the music of Mozart or Beethoven, or as a result of a special encounter with another human being. In all such instances we feel elation, a wonder that can give us a fleeting insight into the great force or order that moves this world. Frankl (1986) said that belief in a super meaning, whether as a metaphysical concept or in the religious sense of God, is of the foremost psychotherapeutic and psycho-hygienic importance. Such a belief adds immeasurably to human vitality. To such a faith, nothing, ultimately, is meaningless (p. 32).

Frankl (1985) was aware that not every person can grasp a meaning beyond the physical or psychological world. Therefore he used the concept of ultimate or supra-meaning to convey something that is not comprehensible with our presently available scientific means. Nevertheless, even those who do not believe in God are aware that such a superhuman dimension exists. Frankl maintains that to be human means to relate to something different from us or, to say it better, to someone different from us. We are directed toward the world beyond ourselves, and in this world we wish to fulfill meanings. And this is possible only if we can transcend ourselves. This is why the essence of human existence is self-transcendence.

We cannot understand the supra-meaning contained in human suffering, because thinking about it does not suffice to grasp the purpose of that meaning. Supra-meaning is not a matter for thought, but for belief. We cannot perceive it intellectually, only existentially, outside of our experience—that is, by faith. We cannot break the dimensional barrier between the human world and God's world, but we can come close to the supra-meaning by a faith, one in which belief in existence "out-of-this world" serves as a mediator. Therefore we cannot speak about God. We can speak to God by prayer (*The Will to Meaning*, p. 173).

For a religious person, the supra-meaning is vested in God. Belief in God is a private matter and a personal value. Good therapists must make a conscious effort to enter the value-world of their clients, to use their knowledge in a responsible and intelligent way to help with spiritual problems. An illustration of such help was given by Frankl when he encountered a rabbi from Eastern Europe who had lost his first wife and six children in the Holocaust. This rabbi was in despair because his second wife was sterile and thus he would have no son to say Kaddish after his death. Frankl asked him whether he hoped to see his children in heaven, whereupon the old rabbi burst into tears and confessed that the true reason for his despair was his fear that, as a sinner, he might not be assigned the same place as his martyred children.

Frankl (1962) asked the rabbi if it was not conceivable that this was precisely the meaning of surviving your children: that you may be purified through these years of suffering so that, finally, you too may become worthy of joining them in Heaven. Is it not written in the Psalms (56:8) that God preserves all of your tears? The old rabbi found relief through the new perspective that Frankl had opened before him (p. 120).

Frankl emphasizes that we should not limit our perspective to the biological dimension; instead, we should widen our horizon by including in it a higher dimension. Thus we learn that a higher dimension exists, even if we cannot see it, because it does not appear in the lower dimension. This is a matter of faith: that something exists on a different plane from the one to which we are accustomed and perceive as based on our biological development. We cannot refer to it as if it were the same thing that we know in our biological and psychological dimensions. With the following story, Frankl (1997) illustrated this mistake in the thinking of those who cannot perceive the difference. A small boy said to Eleanor, Frankl's wife, that he already knew what he wished to be when he grew up. "And what is that?" asked Eleanor. The boy replied, "Or I will be an acrobat in the circus, or I will be God" (p. 147).

What about someone who does not believe in God? Does such an individual's life have a supra-meaning too? Is there such a thing as a nonreligious person? Frankl (1997) claims that, as early as age fifteen, he arrived at an operational definition of God. Accordingly, God is the partner of our most intimate reflections and thoughts. When one speaks completely alone, in all sincerity, the one to whom he or she turns can rightfully be called God (p. 151).

Frankl was convinced that a religious sense exists in all human beings. Sometimes this sense is buried, and sometimes it is repressed in the unconscious. Therefore even someone who is not religious in the broadest sense of this term can find supra-meaning no less than the believer in God. Faith in God is either without qualification, or it is not faith at all. A weak faith resembles a weak love: crisis and tragedies weaken it, but a strong wind and enthusiasm inflame it. Those who survived the Nazi concentration camps were divided into two groups: believers and nonbelievers in God, and the number of the believers whose faith increased was much higher than that of the nonbelievers.

When Frankl was asked in an interview on the occasion of his ninetieth birthday whether he himself was religious, he answered: "I don't feel debased or humiliated if someone suspects that I'm a religious person. If you call 'religious' a man who believes in what I call a Super-meaning, a meaning so comprehensive that you can no longer grasp it, get hold of it in rational intellectual terminology, then one should feel free to call me religious" (cited by Matthew Scully in *First Things*, April 1995, p. 43).

5

Guiding Principles of Logotherapy

Logotherapy's principles express its founder's philosophical attitude toward life. Their aim is to help perplexed people in the modern world learn how to live meaningful lives—including midlife and beyond.

THE FIRST PRINCIPLE: FREEDOM OF WILL

Life has meaning, as long as one is conscious, in all circumstances. One can choose an attitude toward what is happening to one as a result of outer and inner forces. This principle was validated by the life experiences of Frankl and his comrades in the concentration camps. There it was shown without doubt that one's chances to bear horrible conditions and survive are greater when one has some value that gives meaning to one's survival. Frankl used to cite the philosopher Nietzsche's contention that if one knows the why of his suffering, he can bear almost any how.

One can find meaning in life even in the most difficult circumstances. A friend of mine told me about a seventy-nine-year-old man he met in a hospital. This patient knew that he was about to die in a matter of weeks from heart disease, but when he felt strong enough he asked himself what he could do to help others whose condition was worse than his. How could he ease their suffering? He would go from bed to bed, talk with the patients and encourage their spirits. That was the meaning he found in that place and time of his life. Although there was nothing he could do to change his fate, or the fact of his impending death, this did not prevent him from living a spiritually fulfilling life.

A meaningless life is like death. An old woman was depressed because she had no children and thus she thought that her life had no meaning. Guttmann (1996) cites a therapeutic discussion Frankl had with this old woman when she was close to her death. He succeeded in making her aware that a meaningful life is not dependent on having children. Many famous personalities didn't experience the pains and pleasures of raising children, yet they were aware of the meaningfulness of their lives. What is important for an aging person is to achieve something that can give sense to his or her life. That old woman had loyally served the family she worked with for many years. She had suffered a great deal as a lonely person, yet had shown courage in the way she managed her pain and sorrow. When she heard and realized that her life had meaning, she died peacefully, proud of her achievement (pp. 57–60).

Meaning is a potent force in each and every phase of our lives, irrespective of our physical, family, occupational, or mental condition. Therefore, it makes sense to search for meaning in every phase of life, even close to death. There is always some choice one can make, even in the worst situation. One needs to be aware of one's choices and weigh them according to the importance of their meaning for one's life. This is a very important principle, especially for the widows and widowers who find themselves in the situation of Abraham in the Bible, of whom it is said that old age literally jumped on him when he lost his beloved wife Sarah. While not every widowed man can remarry as Abraham did, each widower or widow can decide not to succumb to despair and find his or her way by saying "yes" to life.

Human beings have the basic freedom to find meaning in life. In each problem that one faces there is a measure of freedom to choose the most meaningful response to the situation at hand.

Recently I met a colleague, a fifty-year-old woman who told me how she used this principle. When she was forty years old her husband disappeared, together with the family's savings. He left a huge debt and the burden of caring for their four small children on her alone. "At first," she said, "I developed psychosomatic reactions and fell ill. I couldn't function at all. I thought that my life had ended. This situation lasted for three weeks. I was immersed in my sorrow up to my neck. But one morning I felt that I must make a decision: To remain psychologically disabled for life, or to begin a new life. I chose the second option. I collected all my spiritual strength and overcame the obstacles. Today I am independent, strong, and successful, and my children are proud of me."

THE SECOND PRINCIPLE: THE DEFIANT POWER OF THE HUMAN SPIRIT

The defiant power of the human spirit is very important for survival even in old age. Frankl coined this term to emphasize the human capacity to not succumb to destructive internal or external factors. We are not supposed to meekly accept what life brings us, especially not disasters that fate deposits at our doorstep. We can revolt against them and turn our defiant power into a tool of survival at any phase in life. The woman in the case description above is a good illustration of this power. Two additional illustrations are presented below.

A forty-seven-year-old woman told me that she had a similar experience. She was born and raised in Eastern Europe, in a small village where traditionally the man makes all the decisions related to the family's economic situation. "When he left me for another woman," she said, "I didn't know how to write a check. I had to learn many things about financial matters and simple accounting. I was so used to the decisions of my husband that I didn't think independently. And all of a sudden the responsibilities fell on me. I suffered a lot because of my helplessness, until the change came in the form of a dream.

"One night I dreamt that I was in a lake without a boat, sinking into the water and close to drowning. There were no people around the lake that I could turn to for help. I collected all my strength and began to swim until I got to the shore. When I woke up I understood that the dream came to tell me that I must begin to swim, or I would sink and die. I made a decision not to become a victim and started to swim. Today I am standing on my feet independently, and am happy with my life."

The second case illustration is Joe, my childhood friend. I encountered Joe after decades in which we had not seen each other. When we were children we studied in the same class. He told me that he became head accountant in a large factory and is now retired. I remembered that as a child he had great difficulties with mathematics and couldn't solve most of the problems we got as homework. I even helped him many times with these problems. And now he tells me that he was head accountant. When he saw the surprise on my face he laughed, and said that his father and the math teacher said to him quite often that he would never succeed. He agreed with that assessment, until one day he decided to show them that they were mistaken. He worked very hard and succeeded in making progress in an occupation that is built on knowledge of mathematics. He used the defiant power of the human spirit that was embedded in him and succeeded beyond expectations.

THE THIRD PRINCIPLE: THE THREE HUMAN DIMENSIONS

Human beings have physical, psychological, and spiritual dimensions. People should never be referred to as "nothing but." That is, they should never be reduced to just one of the dimensions listed above, or seen as machines in need of repair. A therapist who relates only to the psychosocial dimension diminishes the dignity and self-respect of a human being.

Simon, a fifty-four-year-old man, had suffered from high blood pressure for the past eight years. The first level in his treatment concentrated on his physical condition. Simon's resistance to other medical intervention was overcome by biofeedback: He found that his blood pressure was connected to the psychological tension he experienced in his work as manager of the savings department in a large bank. When various tests supported this finding, the second phase in his treatment began. This phase concentrated on finding ways to reduce his high blood pressure through relaxation and autosuggestion. These gave him mental tranquility and a more lenient attitude toward himself. After this phase in the treatment was successfully completed came the time to inquire about the concept of meaning of his life, his goals and plans.

A therapist who refers only to the psychosomatic aspects of his patients reduces their value as human beings and hurts their self-image. Despite the great strides made in medicine during the past few decades, recognition of the importance of the spiritual dimension's influence on mental health is too slow, or missing to a large extent.

THE FOURTH PRINCIPLE: THE HUMAN SPIRIT IS THE HEALTHY NUCLEUS IN EACH HUMAN BEING

According to logotherapy, someone can be sick in his body, or in his soul, but not in his spirit. We saw a moving illustration of this maxim in the story of the individual with heart failure, who helped terminally ill patients by encouraging their spirits; and also in the story of the woman whose husband left her and she fell into despair—until she decided to make a change in her life.

Logotherapy maintains that the human spirit is free and is not chained to an individual's body or soul. Consequently, a person is free to choose his or her reaction to what happens to him or her.

THE FIFTH PRINCIPLE: MAN CAN RISE ABOVE AND BEYOND HIMSELF

The uniquely human ability to rise above and beyond physical or mental limitations by virtue of love for the sake of another person in need is the fifth principle. People are capable of performing great feats by tapping into their spirit, such as donating a liver or a kidney to a sick daughter or son, or excelling in science, in arts, and in sports when physically disabled.

For example, a sixty-year-old woman donated one of her kidneys to her sick daughter despite the risk to her own health. This daughter endured dialysis for many years and underwent two unsuccessful kidney transplant operations. The kidney she received from her mother gave this daughter a new lease on life for several years.

THE SIXTH PRINCIPLE: WE HAVE THE CAPACITY FOR SELF-DETACHMENT

The sixth principle states that we can refrain from constant preoccupation with ourselves through humor and laughter. We are capable of using these tools to deal with human weaknesses in a humorous way without being too serious. Frankl turned the two human capacities, *self-transcendence* and *self-detachment*, into important therapeutic devices in logotherapy.

(These concepts will be dealt with in detail later in this book).

THE SEVENTH PRINCIPLE: WE LIVE IN THE PRESENT AND SHOULD LOOK FORWARD TO THE FUTURE

Our existence in the present is determined not only by our past, but also by what we wish to become in the future. We are able and willing to make sacrifices only when we know that these are necessary for achieving something meaningful for us. We should not live in the past, but concentrate on the present and look forward to goals we wish to accomplish in the future in order to live meaningful lives.

For example, Mrs. Smith, age fifty-eight, became suddenly unemployed after thirty years as head of a boarding school. She had two options: To enjoy her new status and refrain from additional work, or to gather her strength and begin building a new career. She decided to use her life experience, talents, and capabilities in voluntary work with refugees. She defended her choice by saying three simple words: "They needed me."

THE EIGHTH PRINCIPLE: EACH MAN IS UNIQUE AND IRREPLACEABLE

Each individual is unique in the world and cannot be replaced by someone else. Many old people have accepted the popular saying that, "The cemeteries are full of people that cannot be replaced." They forget that each human being is essential and irreplaceable; if he or she were not, there would have been no need for him or her to exist in the world.

Our uniqueness in the world is expressed by our contribution to its welfare and preservation; by our creativity and attitude to life; in the way we live and maintain relationships with others; in the way we carry our pain and suffering; in the way we use the opportunities that life tosses at us; and in how we deal with feelings about guilt and death.

We sense the meaning of our lives when we feel our uniqueness. Each one of us is unique and no one can be replaced by someone else. For example, I knew an artist, a painter who struggled with various materials for years until he was able to develop his unique technique and style. Some of his students tried to imitate his work by using the same means, but their works lacked the uniqueness of their teacher.

One can be unique not only in the creative arts. One's relationship to the social, physical and interpersonal environment, to family, friends, and colleagues, to religion and country are unique to one. Finally, even the search for meaning is unique. Frankl emphasized that one should not search for an abstract meaning to life. Each individual has a unique mission on earth and must perform this mission to the best of his or her ability. One cannot be replaced in this task by someone else, for only he or she can perform it.

THE NINTH PRINCIPLE: MEANING IS SUBJECTIVE AND CHANGING

Each and every situation in life presents an opportunity for discovering meaning. The individual decides whether to use or to lose the opportunity inherent in the situation to find that meaning. This meaning is subjective; we cannot buy it, and we cannot transfer it to others. Each person must discover the unique meaning of his or her life, for life brings to all of us many opportunities for finding the unique meaning of our existence.

Seventy-eight-year-old Mrs. Brown, a strong and courageous woman, cared for her bed-ridden husband for six long and painful years. The physical and mental care for her husband gave meaning to her life during those hard times. When her husband died, she felt a great emptiness within herself and tried to overcome this void and to fill up her psychological battery by escaping to a life of leisure and entertainment. Mrs. Brown visited museums, theaters, concerts, the opera, and the movies, and went from one party to the next. There were no free nights. All these activities were in vain because she could not find the mental calmness she was seeking, and life seemed empty and meaningless to her. When she changed her lifestyle and began to work as a volunteer in a nursing home, she felt that she had come home and was living again. Suddenly she found what she was searching for. This discovery gave new meaning to her life.

THE TENTH PRINCIPLE: THE MEANING OF THE MOMENT

It is important to emphasize once again that the meaning of the moment is not always clear and evident to us. We must be patient in order to discover it. We must make an intellectual effort to catch it. Missing the opportunity to find meaning in what life throws our way results in sadness, and sometimes even despair that may accompany us throughout life.

Let us take seventy-one-year-old Mr. Miller to illustrate this principle. He told the following story to his therapist: A friend of his was about to retire from the company where the two of them had worked for many years. This friend came to consult with Mr. Miller before going to the personnel department where his pension and future benefits would be decided. Mr. Miller was very busy with some matter that could not be delayed, and told his friend to come back the next day. His friend did not show up the next day. He disappeared forever. Mr. Miller forgot about this incident until he himself was standing before the director of the personnel office to discuss his retirement and the same thing happened to him. Then he understood that life gave him an opportunity to help someone in need, but he did not grab it. He missed the boat.

THE ELEVENTH PRINCIPLE: WE ARE RESPONSIBLE FOR OUR CHOICES

Responsibility is the ability to respond to the demands of life in a given moment. Logotherapy, as opposed to various theories still in vogue today, emphasizes that we must take personal responsibility for our deeds and mistakes in life. We are always responsible for the choices we make, for good or bad, and are not supposed to hide from this responsibility by blaming others for our failures. Mr. Miller from the previous example was responsible for not using the opportunity life gave him to assist a friend. He could not project his guilt feelings onto his friend who didn't come back the next day. And he could not blame his work that kept him so busy that he forgot to deal with the request of a friend in need. If he did so, he could find some temporary relief from his feeling of guilt, but then he would not make any progress in finding meaning in life.

Choices are present in every situation. We only have to be aware of these choices and weigh them according to their meaning for our lives. Frankl emphasized that personal responsibility is the cornerstone of psychotherapy. According to logotherapy, in each and in every situation in life one always has what Frankl called "response-ability." One can respond to a concrete situation by using one's freedom of choice. That freedom is available to everybody. Frankl has illustrated this freedom with his own life experience. In 1988, when he received an honorary doctorate from the University of Haifa in Israel, he told the audience that when the Nazis entered Vienna he was thirty-three years old and served as director of the neurological department for mentally ill patients at the Jewish hospital. The Nazis agreed to leave him in that position, but on one condition: if he tried to escape, they would send his old parents to a concentration camp.

One day he received an urgent message to come to the American Embassy in Vienna for his visa of entry to the United States. He had only twenty-four hours to do so before the visa would expire. Frankl had waited many years for this message. Now he found himself facing a serious dilemma: Here was an opportunity to go to America, to publish his book on logotherapy and spread its message to the world. On the other hand, if he did so, his old parents would be left to their fate. He was torn by this dilemma and tried to find the right answer. He took off his yellow Star of David, hid it in a briefcase, and went outside the hospital to find a quiet place for musing. He found refuge in a church, but after an hour or so of sitting there, he could not arrive at a decision. Brokenhearted, he went home to his parents. When he entered the apartment, his father came to welcome him. He showed him a piece of marble he had found in the ruins of the old synagogue in the city. On this piece of marble there was a golden letter in Hebrew, *Kaf*—the beginning letter of the Fifth Commandment: "Honor thy father and thy mother."

At that time, Frankl said, his dilemma disappeared and the sense of responsibility won. Frankl perceived in an instant that this was the sign sent from heaven he had been waiting for, and he decided to stay with his parents, to share in their fates.

Frankl insisted all his life that we are responsible not only for ourselves, but also for our deeds, for our loved ones, and for our sufferings. There are two kinds of responsibilities: inner and outer ones. Outer responsibility is tossed on us by an outside authority, such as the law, or the state, the family, or religion. Inner responsibility stems from within, from our spirit. Meaning is not projected from the outside. It is gained from this freedom of will.

THE TWELFTH PRINCIPLE: SPIRITUAL TENSION

Tension and stress are part and parcel of human existence. These are the two main enemies of human existence in modern times. According to logotherapy, one does not need equilibrium or homeostasis to prevent tension. One needs *noetic* or spiritual tension to attain personally important goals and objectives in life. We all need this tension in order to live our lives in such a way that it will be meaningful to us. The spiritual tension is a potent force in achieving important goals. It keeps us ready and willing to do something for our well-being—rather than letting ourselves sink into apathy, the mortal illness in old age. To illustrate:

James, aged sixty-two, was happy when his request for early retirement was approved by the Board of Directors in the insurance company he had worked for during the past twenty five years. He was full as a pomegranate with plans about all the fun he would have with his wife. And indeed, according to his plans, the couple went on a long trip around the world. Yet, after their return home, James became nervous and grouchy, could not relax, and felt that his life had become empty. James would use the disappointment with himself as a weapon against his wife, and she was thinking about divorcing him.

There are many people like James who, in their second half of life, wish to retire as early as possible. They dream of wonderful trips around the globe. They dream about lying on the beach, enjoying the sun for hours, in an endless chain of spring-like days somewhere on an island in the Pacific Ocean. And when their plans are finally fulfilled, they find themselves disappointed. The magic of travel and time spent lazily in daydreaming suddenly disappears, and boredom, nervousness, and grouchiness fill their place. They feel as though they were cheated by life. The freedom from the tensions in their former work does not produce the rest they sought. That tension, which Frankl has called *spiritual* or *noetic tension* (from the Greek word *noos*, meaning spirit), is a healthy tension. It is the opposite of homeostasis, or balance in psychoanalysis.

Mental health, Frankl maintained, is based on a measure of tension between what has been already achieved and what one wishes to accomplish. When one has fulfilled a certain goal, this tension comes and reminds one that the time has come to search for new goals and objectives that would fill one's life with meaning. One does not need a state of nirvana, a tensionless state. One needs to be motivated to find new goals and to struggle toward accomplishing them.

THE THIRTEENTH PRINCIPLE: DISCOVERING MEANING IN LIFE IS NOT A GIFT, BUT AN ACHIEVEMENT

An individual does not know his or her limitations as long as life does not force him or her to test them. It is impossible to give meaning to other people. Each human being must discover his or her personal meaning according to his or her understanding, abilities, and efforts. We can only help someone to make the necessary steps that would lead that individual to discover meaning in his or her life. The logotherapist serves only as a teacher or guide for this purpose.

For example: A young man in his forties was suffering from self-deprecation. This man had a dream that wires popped out of his heart, and all his efforts to push them back were in vain. He told the therapist about his failure, and compared the wires to a spider's web that engulfed him and made him immobile. He was afraid to do anything to change this situation, for he didn't believe in himself. The therapist helped him to make a change in his attitude toward himself by emphasizing his achievements along with his failures; achievements that no one could take away from him. The emphasis on the achievements–rather than on the failures–helped the client to see himself in a new and different light. He received support from an authority. The therapist urged this man to take responsibility for his life in the present, rather than dwelling on the past. This young man told the therapist that there were people in his life who had helped him to get out of difficult situations. The insight this client received from the therapeutic dialogue made a turn in his life: He found meaning in the effort that he would have to make to fulfill his dream—to free himself from the spider's web in which he was entangled, without fear of failure.

THE FOURTEENTH PRINCIPLE: A POSITIVE ATTITUDE TOWARD LIFE

Personal and spiritual growth and development are the results of change. This change is expressed in one's positive attitude to life. Therapy is needed only when the change is not accompanied by a feeling of growth.

THE FIFTEENTH PRINCIPLE: HAPPINESS IS A BY-PRODUCT OF MEANING IN LIFE

The last principle for meaningful living states that life does not owe us pleasure, but only meaning that we must find. Happiness and pleasure, wealth and power, and all other worldly benefits are by-products of finding meaning in life.

At the World Congress for Logotherapy, held in 1984 in San Francisco, Frankl was asked by one of the participants what is the meaning of his life. Frankl answered without hesitation: "To help other people discover meaning to their lives." Frankl was not interested in money, in luxuries, or pleasures, not even in enduring fame. Frankl was interested in living a meaningful life. Like King Solomon in the Bible, Frankl asked for wisdom to help people whose lives were lacking in meaning.

6

The Courage to Be Authentic: Philosophical Sources of Logotherapy

After discussing the principles of logotherapy in the previous chapter, we shall dive into their depth and examine them in their philosophical sources.

The problem of human existence is age-old, and so is the philosophical attitude toward this problem. This problem takes on special importance in the second half of life when we become aware—more than in the previous phases of life—of our impending death, and try to understand whether or not there is a meaning to life and existence, and how this existence will be perceived by the generations to come. The problem is that few people are capable of living their lives in such a way that their values and creativity are combined with enthusiasm, dedication, and joy that help in overcoming despair and preoccupation with thoughts of death. Most people, particularly old people, live their lives on a low spiritual level and allow time to carry them. They live for the moment without asking themselves, "Why?" This kind of living is like living in a vacuum, and it lacks meaning.

NIETZSCHE AND LOGOTHERAPY

As we have seen, the meaning of an individual's life cannot come from the outside. Meaning is always an internal journey, an internal search. This idea was taken from the philosophy of Nietzsche and from his attitude toward human behavior.

Friedrich Nietzsche, an eccentric genius who lived in the second half of the nineteenth century—from 1844 until 1900—was unique among the great philosophers of modern times. His literary style too was unique, and his clear-wittedness and originality were phenomenal. His importance in philosophy is commonly accepted today. In *Ecce Homo: How One Becomes What One Is* (1997a), Nietzsche praised himself unashamedly and predicted that his fame would spread in the world a hundred years after his death.

His prophecy has become reality. Nietzsche said that whoever takes one of his books in hand will feel that he or she has been given the most precious gift that can be given to man (p. 55). Nietzsche had a special relationship with another great philosopher, whom he considered almost equal to him, Schopenhauer. In his recently published book titled *My Sister and Me* (2004), Nietzsche wrote that his place in history is almost secure, but when he remembers Schopenhauer, who was a whole person despite his faults, more attentive and madder than Nietzsche could ever be, he cannot forgive him (p. 117).

This original philosopher revolted against all the previous philosophies and commonly accepted social mores that had influenced mankind for long centuries prior to his appearance on the scene of world history. Nietzsche assumed that the development of science and critical thinking in Western history and civilization led to the loss of mankind's ability to believe in what is beyond reach—meaning the concept of God—as the basis for life. Nietzsche expressed his philosophy in a series of publications that were unique and stunning in terms of their ideas, richness of opinions, deep knowledge of history, mythology, poetry, music, and intellectual thought. Nietzsche emphasized that concepts such as world order, God's will, and reason are nothing more than the creations of human thought. They have no power over our lives and cannot tell us how to live our lives. He tried to shape a vision of healthy life. Accordingly, he said that people could gain such health when they are willing to forego their belief in those antiquated and outdated concepts.

Nietzsche was also the first psychologist in the modern sense of this term. There are many thinkers who consider Nietzsche the first psychoanalyst in the Western world. His importance for logotherapy is even greater, for he laid the foundation for the theory of mankind's spiritual motivation in life. Although Freud thought that our behavior and basic motivation in life are vested in the will to experience pleasure and Adler thought that it was in power and in ruling others, Frankl perceived human motivation as being centered on discovering meaning in life. This idea was actually taken from Nietzsche's attitude toward human behavior.

Nietzsche has shown in his writings how dependent we became on the values that were created by our values. We are not able to move without them in our daily lives, for without them we have no yardstick by which to judge the quality of our actions. Therefore we are limited because of them. This paradox in Nietzsche's attitude toward values forces us to think, and to find our place in the world of values without getting towed away to nihilism.

According to Nietzsche, it is not possible to accomplish a work of great art without experience. Nor is it possible to attain high social standing immediately; nor to become a great lover at the first attempt. In the pause between failures and subsequent successes, in the gap between what we wish to become one day and what we are today, must come pain, anxiety, jealousy, and humiliation. This attitude toward the present and future is one of many ideas Frankl has incorporated into logotherapy.

How can one recognize the healthy individual? It is in the way this individual influences our senses with the pleasantness of his or her appearance and ways. Such a person is hard, yet noble, as if carved from a fine tree, finds medication and cures to all problems, turns each obstacle to advantage, for what does not kill him or her, strengthens him or her. Such a person does not believe in sin, or in misery; knows how to manage himself or herself and others; knows to forget, and is strong enough to turn everything in his or her favor. From these aphorisms we can deduce what Nietzsche would have said about finding meaning in the second half of life.

FREEDOM TO CHOOSE

In addition to the philosophers of antiquity and the modern era, Frankl was heavily influenced by the philosophy of Nietzsche. Consequently, Frankl incorporated many concepts of this great philosopher into the theory of logotherapy, such as the attitude toward health and sickness. Nietzsche built his philosophy on saying yes to life, and so did Frankl. And it is not just coincidence that Frankl's most famous book, *Man's Search for Meaning* (1962), was originally titled in German *Trotzdem Ja zum Leben Sagen* (1982), in English: "Despite Everything Say Yes to Life." Nietzsche used the term "despite everything" in his book *Thus Spoke Zarathustra* in order to denote his attitude toward life; accordingly all portentous things are created by this "despite everything."

For Frankl this "despite" was expressed in the unconditional acceptance of life, for only while living can one create experience, transcend difficulties, and acquire meaning. Frankl's experiences in life strengthened his concepts and ideas regarding human existence in the world. Frankl always emphasized one's spiritual commitment to life, to one's role and purpose. What human beings give to life, and the way in which they deal with the problems and difficulties that life poses them, determine the meaning of their lives. A positive attitude toward life and its acceptance without reservations, despite any condition or price, resembles old Jewish traditional values which perceive life as sacred. The sanctity of life is expressed in the saying: "Who saves one life—saves a whole world."

Nietzsche and Frankl held similar attitudes about freedom and choice. An individual is perceived by both philosophers as one who craves freedom as he or she craves air to breathe; one who is capable of choosing his or her way in life. In all of Nietzsche's philosophical works one can see how historical and biological factors work as if behind mankind's back, and influence the decisions of people without their being aware of it. Even when the limitations are perceived and identified, there remains the belief in one's ability to rise above one's condition and to be the master of one's fate. The choice that exists in any situation, according to logotherapy, has its source in Nietzsche's concept of philosophy.

Frankl emphasizes that choice is available to us in any situation, even in those that seem to be hopeless and offer no chance of survival or success. We can always say "yes" or "no" to what happens to us and to what stands in front of our eyes as a matter of choice. Nietzsche demonstrated this ability of one to choose how to spend one's life in his own life-long struggle with the many illnesses that befell him, until he succumbed to an incurable mental illness from which he suffered ten years without respite.

Freedom for Frankl meant taking personal responsibility for the results of one's actions. Frankl objected to collective conventions and conformity to social pressures, and emphasized that freedom results from a deep commitment to life. Real freedom exists only when one is aware of the choices and the options, when one willingly accepts the responsibility for the choices made and for their results.

THE COURAGE TO BE AUTHENTIC

Bertolt Brecht (1898–1956), the well-known playwright and poet, demonstrated the attitudes of Frankl and Nietzsche toward freedom, choice, and responsibility, in his short story "The Undignified Old Lady," in which he tells about his grandmother. She was seventy-two years old when his grandfather died. The grandfather owned a print shop in the small town of Baden in Germany, in which he worked along with two helpers until his death. The family lived in a dilapidated house. Grandmother took care of five children and cooked and washed for the few boarders who lived with the family. She worked very hard for many years.

When the grandfather died the only child who remained in the same town was the youngest, and it was he who supplied the information about grandmother's fate to the rest of his brothers. He reported that grandmother decided to curtail her family obligations to the bare minimum and refused to move into the house of this youngest son. She did not join any club or social circle in the town either. Instead, she used to visit the shoemaker's shop. It was said that he had traveled in the world and drank a lot. Grandmother would sit in the shop, listen to the stories and sip a little red wine. She also stopped cooking for herself and ate at a small restaurant, and when the priest came to ease her loneliness, she would invite him to go with her to the cinema. Furthermore, grandmother regularly visited the horse races. She secretly took out a second mortgage on the house, and nobody knew what she did with the money. It seems that she gave most of it to the shoemaker, who moved to another city after her death and opened a larger shop.

Brecht tells in the story that his father, the youngest son, found that in the last half year of her life, grandmother took liberties of which most people in the town were completely unaware. She would get up in the middle of the night and enjoyed strolling in the empty streets. She was not lonely at all. When she died sitting next to the window in her favorite armchair, only a young and mentally limited girl was with her. Grandmother lived seventy-four years, and had a long life full of hard work and suffering until she reached age seventy-two. But in her last two years of life she tasted freedom and enjoyed her life to the fullest.

Courage as a unique human virtue is among the four cardinal virtues the ancient Greek philosophers regarded as essential for anyone interested in serving the public. This courage is unlike the one exhibited in the battlefield; it is unlike courage forged by lack of any other choice but to fight for the principles and values that are most important to one. This courage means taking full responsibility for the decisions one makes and for the actions one voluntarily accepts.

Like Sigmund Freud, who was expelled from the Prussian Academy of Sciences and was not allowed to teach at the University of Vienna in Austria due to his ideas about human sexual behavior being the major motivation in life, and yet continued to develop his psychoanalysis without fear; and like Nietzsche, who showed extraordinary courage in the face of the Church by clinging to his philosophical belief, and who despite his illness and economic difficulties did not waver, Frankl too was blessed with this unique trait and virtue. Thus he can serve as a model for any man, old or young. The courage of Frankl never left him and was expressed in many areas of his life. This courage—more than any other philosophical concept—Frankl borrowed from Nietzsche for the development of logotherapy, and he demonstrated it in his life.

Frankl's courage was expressed early when at age sixteen he rebelled against a chemistry teacher's assertion that human beings are no more than machines with internal combustion. Frankl's protest at that incident later became the cornerstone of logotherapy. Frankl fought all his life against any attempt to reduce and rob somebody of human dignity by stating that a person is no more than a machine in need of repair—whether in medicine or in psychology.

His courage led Frankl to the development of logotherapy as a theory of motivation in human behavior, separate and different from the theories of his teachers Freud and Adler. Frankl admired both of these men, was influenced by them, and learned much from them in medicine and psychiatry. He never forgot the debt owed to these men by the scientific world, and always emphasized that it was Freud who laid the foundations for modern psychology and psychotherapy, while Adler made contributions to both. Nevertheless, Frankl had the courage to depart from their theories and to establish his own approach to human behavior.

Frankl's *height psychology* is a testimony to this courage. As indicated before, climbing in the Alps strengthened his natural tendency to look upon men and women as spiritual beings whose central will is to carry out an idea, a mission for the attainment of which they were born. Realization of ideas or a mission is possible only in the spiritual dimension, in the notion of freedom, and in the knowledge and awareness that a person is not chained in spirit; that there are peaks in development one can yearn for; and that a person has powers that enable him or her to conquer any peak. This is why Frankl placed these human traits at the center of logotherapy.

Nietzsche's influence on Frankl is evident in the latter's attitude toward religion. Frankl wrote a doctoral thesis to explain the logotherapeutic use of concepts, such as the *spiritual unconscious, conscience,* and *medical ministry.* Contrary to Nietzsche, who negated religion, Frankl saw religion positively, as a necessary power for good mental health.

ON FOLLOWING A CLOUD

Frankl compared the uniqueness of an individual's way in life to the Biblical story about the wanderings of the Hebrews in the desert after the exodus from Egypt where they were slaves. *God's cloud* that led them there was used by Frankl to illustrate the goal that should lead those who follow it. And in the same way that this cloud was different during the day and at night, when it became a pillar of fire, so are various events in life and the problems with which one must struggle. Yet God's cloud had another characteristic: it was always above and in front of the heads of its followers, and it could not be reached. People could only follow it, and get close to it, if not physically then mentally. For this cloud symbolizes the spiritual dimension with which one is blessed and by which one is able to work wonders. This approach to one's spiritual dimension has important implications for mental health, and Frankl made good use of it in the methodology of logotherapy.

Frankl adopted the view of Goethe, the German poet, writer, and philosopher, who said that if we wish to help someone who is in distress, or suffering from a conflict or a dilemma he or she cannot solve, we should not look upon him or her as he or she is now, but should approach him or her as he or she could be in the future. Changing one's attitude toward self and the world is possible by use of the spiritual dimension. People are blessed with the ability to take a stand against the circumstances of life, fate, genetic inheritance, education, and all other influences in their long years of growing up. This applies especially to people who suffer from illnesses. They should be reminded that only their bodies are sick, not their spirits, and they can always take a stand against what ails them. They can choose their attitude toward the circumstances of their existence.

PAIN, BOREDOM, AND HAPPINESS

Arthur Schopenhauer, the German philosopher who lived between 1788 and 1860, and who is generally regarded as the greatest pessimist of all the philosophers, doubted the great truths that encompass the entire human race. He fought valiantly against the moral and intellectual fatigue of mankind, and related to human existence as a mistake, of which he said, "Today is bad and each day is getting worse, until the worst will happen" (cited by De Botton, [2000], in *The Consolations of Philosophy*, p. 171).

Schopenhauer exhibited a negative attitude toward life, a view which logotherapy rejects. In his view, life lacks meaning; life is a web of despair, and meaningless, and therefore the best answer to such a life is suicide. Behind this pessimistic approach to life were a series of failures in relation to his early philosophical works and in love. His pessimism about life was peculiar considering that, according to his biography, at age seventeen he inherited a large fortune from his father and he never had to work for a living. Although he could have lived a life of leisure and indulgence, he preferred loneliness to the company of others. Only in the last decade of his life did he gain the fame which he so desperately yearned for. But even this unexpected success did not change his attitude toward life. He remained convinced until his death that human existence is an incorrigible mistake.

Schopenhauer's philosophy may be seen as a reflection of the aesthetic and intellectual currents of his time, while his pessimistic outlook on life is tied to events he experienced and which influenced his philosophical system. In his philosophy, *will* and *idea* are central concepts, and his major work centers on both. According to Schopenhauer, the more a human being is conscious about life, the more he or she is able to recognize that life consists of suffering. The will is directed toward satisfaction and expansion, yet both are doomed to failure. Life is not meant to be enjoyed, but to be endured and ended. One can choose one of two alternatives. One can look upon the will positively, with a clear mind, and accept life as it is, with all that has happened in it and will happen in the future. This attitude toward life is echoed in the work of Erik Erikson (1959) with respect to the last phase of life, meaning old age, and its requirement that we attain wisdom.

Schopenhauer arrived at his general philosophical position early in his life, and all his works are further developments of the same basic initial ideas. He insisted that will is more basic than thought in both humans and nature. His *will to exist* was adopted by Frankl, along with the concept of the will. Schopenhauer also maintained that one can attain moral goodness by unselfish compassion for others. This concept lies behind the *appealing technique* in the logotherapeutic treatment of depression and despair, for example, when all other means are useless.

Schopenhauer wrote a book late in his life in which he in fact negated his own philosophical theory. The book was called *Life Wisdom* (2001). Despite the fact that he did not perceive this work as his most important one, the picture that emerges in it regarding life is quite positive. In this book Schopenhauer claims that he is using the term "life wisdom" in its inner meaning. This meaning is expressed by the art through which one shapes one's life; through which one makes one's life happy and pleasant. This book also contains an important chapter on the differences among the various phases in a person's life, making it particularly important for modern gerontology in that it shows the way to attain a happy life. This happy life is one that, even after careful, rational, and cold consideration, is preferable to nonexistence. This is life we hold on to for itself, not only from fear of death, and therefore we would like to see it as being infinite.

Schopenhauer emphasizes that we spend the first half of life longing for happiness that cannot be achieved, and the second half worrying about disasters. In that phase of our lives we already understand that happiness exists only in our imagination, while suffering is real. While in adolescence and in young adulthood life seems long and projects forward and far away, in the latter years life is perceived as short, and gets shorter with each passing year.

One understands the shortness of life only after one gets old. Until age thirty-six, which for Schopenhauer symbolized the middle of life, we live from the *interest*, for the force of life we use renews itself again and again. Later on we begin to use the *capital* too; at first in small sums, then at a faster tempo. The same holds true for our spiritual energy and for its elasticity; these are abundant in the first half of life, until age forty at the latest, and from then on they diminish slowly and gradually. Yet there is compensation for this loss—knowledge and experience—which in the second half of life grow and become richer.

Schopenhauer claimed that the first forty years give us the text of life, and the next thirty years (today forty or even fifty) the explanation of the text. This explanation reveals the meaning of our lives. Only in old age is one really able to understand oneself, said Schopenhauer, but on one condition: That one is absolutely sincere with oneself. The old individual frees himself or herself from the illusions of the young, is able to judge the true value of things, and recognizes the insignificance of material things. He or she ceases to be amazed from what is going on in the world, and stops believing in happiness.

Many people pursue all kinds of roles, honors, and social status in the second half of life, stating that these provide sense to their lives, while actually they are running away from boredom. When these people get old, they are unable to pursue these same enterprises. They feel boredom and emptiness. People who develop their spiritual powers find themselves free of boredom all their lives, including their old age in particular.

At the other end of that experience are pain and suffering. Like boredom, suffering and pain are two experiences very likely to be encountered in old age. Spiritual powers help in the struggle against boredom and against certain kinds of suffering. Yet these are not enough. There is a need for economical resources too. Whoever lives in poverty and destitution is at times helpless to rise above the pain and suffering in his or her circumstances.

Schopenhauer was aware of the contradictions between his high philosophy, with its negation of human existence, and this book in which he relates favorably to life in this world. But he also hastened to emphasize that all of his assumptions are temporary and far from being whole, for the subject cannot be dredged to its very bottom.

Following the ancient Greek philosopher Aristotle, Schopenhauer too divided human life into three parts: external things, the psyche, and the body. Differences in the fates of human beings he based on three things: The personality of a person, including his or her health, beauty, mood, moral character, understanding and education; his or her wealth and resources in the broadest sense; and his or her role. Of these Schopenhauer referred mainly to the last, the role of a person. Schopenhauer saw in this role the reflection of a person in the eyes of others, as they imagine this person in their mind's eye and their opinion of him or her. These are expressed in the honor, respect, status, and good name accorded to that person (2001, p. 7).

According to Schopenhauer, the character of an individual is the result of nature's creation. This character affects our happiness or misery more than the qualities of personality and wealth. For the one's character stems from one's inner self—not from outer factors. These factors influence one's behavior indirectly. The essence of the world in which one lives is perceived differently by each human being, exactly as one intellect is different from another. Therefore one person perceives the world as poor, dull, meaningless, and flat, and another as vibrant, exciting, rich, interesting, and meaningful. One lives in one's conscious world and cannot hide from it. It is impossible to help someone from the outside. This assertion is problematic for those psychotherapies that are built on the assumption that an individual can be helped by raising the unconscious content of his or her mind and thus influencing his or her conscious behavior.

In terms of our happiness in life, Schopenhauer says that personality is the most important factor, for it is not subject to fate and is efficient in any circumstance. Personality cannot be stolen, and therefore its value is absolute and not relative, as is the value of the other two factors mentioned above, wealth and resources. Only time has some control over the powers of body and psyche. Personality, however, is a gift of nature that remains constant throughout life, and the only thing we can do about it is to use it for our greatest benefit. We must therefore develop our personality gradually but steadily, support its most noble goals and objectives, give it the highest status, the most appropriate occupation and the life style of which it is worthy, and refrain from anything that goes against it.

Schopenhauer (2001) has also emphasized that one's happiness has two relentless enemies, pain and boredom, and that there is a connection between the two: In the same measure that an individual succeeds in escaping from the one, he or she gets closer to the other. Our lives are in perpetual motion between these two poles. Sometimes the motion is strong, and at other times it is weak. In terms of the external aspect, need and lack cause pain, while abundance and security cause boredom. Thus we see the poor in an eternal struggle with need and pain, and the very rich groups in society in a despairing struggle with boredom (pp. 23–24).

According to Schopenhauer, only those who can rise above seeing the world as full of suffering can triumph over it. When one sees the world for what it really is, one learns to renounce all strivings and will. Then the individual is blessed with grace, which Schopenhauer believed to be equivalent to salvation.

Frankl emphasized that the boredom Schopenhauer spoke about has an important role. Boredom is a warning bell. It exists in order to allow us escape from lack of activity, and to identify meaningless situations in our lives. As in biology, where pain warns us that something is wrong in our body, so boredom warns against something that is not in order in our mental and spiritual life.

STRUGGLE FOR SAYING "YES" TO LIFE

Existentialism was born during the Second World War and flowered afterward when Europe, destroyed by the war, experienced hunger, the collapse of traditional values regarding family life and morals, and when life seemed absurd, for all the previous ideologies were then found to be empty of value and meaning.

The central questions people were asking at that time were the same ones that are asked each time a great calamity falls upon society: Why survive? Is life worth all this suffering? Is it not better to commit suicide? In the second half of life we may find ourselves in a similar situation when we must retire from work against our will and lose livelihood and social status; when our health deteriorates, the self-image is hurt and we feel superfluous in the world.

I met Elisabeth, aged fifty-two, in a major city on the West Coast. She was afraid that her fate would be similar to that of her mother, who struggled with pain and torment for years and died of breast cancer. Elisabeth began to study medicine to overcome her fear, but was not able to deal with her lack of hope. She left her studies and tried to forget about cancer; even managed to cheat herself for some time, but all her struggle was in vain. When she found symptoms of cancer in her body, she was forced to realize that the cancer had struck her too. The discovery of this illness tormented her a great deal. Elisabeth asked herself again and again: Why survive? Why suffer? Is there any hope for recovery, or that some new medication would wipe out cancer? Is it not better to die now and avoid additional suffering? A while later she began to think about suicide in earnest. And indeed, after a few years I heard that she ended her life tragically.

The case of Elisabeth is not unique. Recently I heard about the suicide of a sixty-eight-year-old man with many accomplishments who was struck by Alzheimer's disease. This man too preferred to commit suicide rather than become a burden on his family.

Albert Camus, the writer and philosopher known for his books that stress the absurdity of life, gave a positive answer to these questions. Camus said that by accepting the absurdity called life, and by willing it consciously, one is able to overcome one's fate. In his important work *The Plague and The Myth of Sisyphus* (1991), Camus presents a tragic and absurd hero. Sisyphus was condemned by the gods to roll a stone up to the top of a hill forever; upon reaching the top, the stone would roll back and he had to start working again and again endlessly. The gods thought that this punishment of Sisyphus, who betrayed their secret and rebelled against their will, would break his spirit, for there is no worse thing then work without hope and utility. Yet, the gods were mistaken. Sisyphus's spirit did not break! He won a moral victory!

The torture of Sisyphus by the gods seems inhuman and terrible, and yet Camus says: "At the moment this man is returning from the top of the mountain I see him walking erect and with measured steps toward the torture whose end he will never see, and every time he leaves the top of the mountain he transcends his fate. He is stronger than the stone that he must push upward" (p. 124).

Camus emphasizes that this myth is tragic because the hero is conscious of his fate. Sisyphus is aware of his situation and thinks about it when he descends from the hill. This is the time when his tragedy begins. Despite his blindness, he is aware that each atom in this rock, each drop of mineral in the mountain creates a world in itself. The struggle on the way to the top of the mountain is enough to fill his heart with joy. Sisyphus bursts into a roar: "All these suffering, my advanced years and greatness of my spirit bring me to conclude that everything is good" (p.125).

According to the theory of logotherapy, the struggle to achieve meaning in life is the most important struggle. There are many aging people who cease to continue the struggle, and now they expect that someone else will give meaning to their lives. But life empty of content is no less hard than the life of Sisyphus. Even if the struggle means suffering, pain, and disappointment, these strengthen the spirit. As long as one struggles, one is alive emotionally. One gets more mature, more seasoned, and richer spiritually by the struggle. Sisyphus found meaning in his suffering, and that meaning gave him the strength to carry on his suffering and to find a few minutes of grace.

THE IMPACT OF SCHELER ON LOGOTHERAPY

The philosopher Max Scheler (1874–1928) had a major impact on the development of Frankl's logotherapy (Frankl, 1985, p. 17). This philosopher is known as one of the founding fathers of modern phenomenology. Scheler influenced many other thinkers and philosophers in the twentieth century, particularly Martin Buber, Gabriel Marcel, and Ludwig Binswanger.

Scheler (1973) foresaw a harmony between God, the self, and the world. This harmony enables the human spirit to collaborate with personal freedom and responsibility. Scheler's philosophy emphasizes that meaning exists in investigation of the *noos*, or spirit in ancient Greek, and this spirit pushes one to discover how to become a human being, one that carries values. His philosophy is realistic, for it puts the burden on the shoulders of the self and on one's place in the world.

The worldview of Scheler was elective. He maintained that the world is perceived by people in a special way, subjectively, and any division into levels or dimensions, such as the biological, psychological, and spiritual, which is regarded as scientific pluralism, misses the mark. A human being, according to Scheler (1960), is one unit that cannot be divided, and when we relate to one or two levels or dimensions, we disregard a person's existence. Scheler also claimed that one lives in all three dimensions together (body, soul, and spirit) and is therefore free to discover how these dimensions function together and create the personality and its relationship to the world. Frankl adopted this approach of Scheler's to life and to an individual's place in the world.

In Scheler's view, a person is not a substance or an object, but the concrete unity of acts. A person is essentially both an individual and a member of a community, a view Frankl accepted and incorporated into logotherapy. The unity of the three dimensions creates harmony. Freedom and responsibility are expressions of this harmony. The essence of a person, according to Scheler, is not vested in his or her will, nor in his or her thinking, but in love. Humans are loving creatures. The idea of God is the major value. Therefore love of God is the highest form of love.

In his approach to the spirit of an individual, Scheler differentiated between control and guidance. The spirit does not control one's actions and decisions, but rather guides one. The spirit helps to express intentions, to select and to decide in what to invest one's strength and resources. Experience gives validity to life and is necessary for judging the authentic intentions of an individual.

Scheler was influential in Frankl's attitude toward the concepts of *fate* and *destiny*. Fate for Scheler was a given of life that is blind to values, and limited to those events in our lives that are determined by our character traits. In contrast, destiny is not what happens to the self, but an integral part of selfhood. The differentiation Scheler made between fate and destiny was used by Frankl to explain logotherapy's attitude toward destiny, because it is tied to the way we respond to what happens in our lives.

Another concept which Frankl adopted from the philosophy of Scheler is *creative tension*, an expression of the human spirit, which Frankl turned into noetic or spiritual tension. It is based on the understanding that the human spirit serves as guide, rather than control, yet it needs tension to create something. The spirit is the dimension which enables one to make choices and to express intentions, while the tension pulls one not to succumb to the temptation of homeostasis, or balance, between the physiological and the psychological dimension that Frankl calls stability without growth.

Scheler was also influential in Frankl's adoption of the concept of the individual as *bearer of values*, a person aware of his or her own self-worth and of the value of others.

Scheler and Frankl agree that the noetic or spiritual dimension is the key to self-understanding. Both agree that this dimension serves as the internal quality that makes a person. They also agree that sometimes this dimension is blocked or ignored, yet it cannot become sick. In their view, one's ability to rise above and beyond oneself in special circumstances and situations for a loved one, for an adored person or ideal, is an aspect of the spiritual dimension. This dimension enables one to attain a perspective on life and its purpose. Finally, both of them agree that the spiritual dimension gives strength to live life creatively and to discover meaning.

Conscience is the central part of the spiritual dimension. An individual can remain free to hear or to ignore the voice of conscience. The individual is unique, say Scheler and Frankl, because he or she carries the capacity for good or bad. One can decide to elevate oneself to the level of saints, or to sink to the level of an animal. Furthermore, conscience serves as a tool for the progress of mankind.

One's ability to transcend oneself is another concept shared by Scheler and Frankl. It is through self-transcendence that one attains both perspective and direction for life. Self-transcendence is expressed through a task worth doing and/or a person to love, and these two correspond with Scheler's concept of *ordering of love*.

Scheler considered people not only as thinking beings but also and most importantly as loving beings. Therefore, wherever a person's heart pulls him or her, there he or she finds the center and essence of things. Frankl added that only the search for meaning can lead an individual toward meaningful living. As a result of this search, one's heart can accept the past, live a responsible life in the present, and plan the future realistically and with optimism.

CHOOSING ONE'S UNIQUE WAY IN LIFE

Existential philosophy sees the birth, life, and death of a human being as basic situations. These are equal for all human beings: We are born, we have to work for a living, we have to live in a world with other human beings, and we have to die. Yet these basic situations are personal and we cannot make generalizations about them.

The purpose and the essence of one's life are not given by an authority, such as God or Nature. Each one needs to define who he or she is by his or her own actions. We are born into a world that we didn't choose, and we must define our identities and our basic characteristics in the way we live our lives. Human beings determine their destinies. They create themselves. They are responsible for their lives, for they have free wills. This freedom enables them to decide how to deal with the social and biological conditions in which they live.

Since we are creating ourselves, we must take full responsibility for our actions and for molding our lives. Logotherapy places personal responsibility in the center of its theory. Accordingly, one must take responsibility for one's existence. The emphasis on personal responsibility is the opposite of the exaggerated freedom of choice that is characteristic of our times. This freedom has resulted in a chaos of values, since it was not followed by personal responsibility for one's actions.

An individual's uniqueness is expressed in the personal goals that he or she chooses for himself or herself; in his or her imagination and creativity, that are always unique and cannot be mimicked by someone else; in his or her love for other human beings and for ideas and spiritual creations; in his or her humor; in the way he or she takes responsibility for his or her actions; and in the measure of his or her pity and compassion with which he or she behaves toward people that hurt him or her.

BUBER'S PHILOSOPHY AND INFLUENCE ON FRANKL'S LOGOTHERAPY

Martin Buber was one of the leading philosophers in the twentieth century. His relationship to human behavior is detailed in his famous book *I and Thou* (1994). Human relationships attain their validity in the emphasis on *we*. By the relationship between *I* and *thou*, an individual arrives at a higher dimension of the self, at his or her spiritual dimension. When this happens, then we speak about *self-transcendence*, which is one of the major logotherapeutic concepts coined by Frankl. Logotherapy has adopted Buber's philosophical relationships to human beings, and particularly his emphasis on face-to-face and direct relationships in which the parties to this relationship are perceived as equals.

Buber gave a poetic description of this relationship in his book titled *Between Man and Man* (1975). In this book, Buber describes a dream that kept returning to him in exactly the same way, sometimes after years. He called this dream "the double cry." The dream happens in some cave or building made of clay, or in a dense forest. In his dream, he is struggling vigorously with a small animal and suddenly everything becomes quiet, and he stands alone and cries out. This cry sounds the same every time and turns into a poem or song, and when it ends his heart stops beating. But then, from a great distance, another cry comes closer to him, a cry similar to his own, and this cry is not an echo. This cry appears as a long series of questions. Each time the cry is different, and each time it is new. And when the cry is finished, he is stricken with the knowledge that it now happened. It happened now, only now when there was an answer to his cry.

After he had dreamt this dream in exactly the same way many times, Buber had a dream that started as usual, but later was different from his previous dreams: There was no reply to his cry. Buber explains the lack of answer by his waiting for the answer. Until this dream he had not waited for an answer. The answer came by itself. Now that he waited for the answer, it refrained from coming. And then something happened. He opened his entire being to space; he opened himself to all senses and perceptions. And then the cry appeared all over without sound. It didn't come. It was there, and let itself be felt, let itself be heard. Buber describes how he heard this cry in all of his being, in all of his entity, and it was more whole than ever. And when the dream came to its end, and he finished absorbing it, he felt more secure than ever before, for "now it has happened" (pp. 1–3).

The uniqueness of the individual must be preserved in old age too, and even in death. It is told of Rabbi Bunam, one of the most famous Hasidic rabbis, that when he was old and blind he said, "I would not like to change places with Abraham, our forefather. What good would happen to God if Abraham was blind like me, and Bunam would become Abraham? Instead, I think that I have to try to become a little more like myself."

Frankl related the same idea when he maintained that there is no need to search for an abstract meaning in life (Frankl, 1962). Each human being has a concrete and unique task that requires fulfillment. And in this task he cannot be replaced by someone else. No other philosopher could describe this idea better than Hillel the Elder, who lived some two thousand years ago and said, "If I am not for myself—who is for me? And if I am only for myself—what am I? And if not now—when?" Frankl used this maxim of Hillel to stress humankind's uniqueness and ability to elevate human existence to a higher level.

7

The Concept of Meaning in Religion and Literature

"What is the meaning of our existence, and what is the meaning of the existence of all living creatures?" asked Albert Einstein (1934) in his autobiography. To answer this question, he said, means to be religious. "You ask: Is it reasonable at all to ask this question? And I answer you: He who finds his own life and the lives of other people lacking meaning is not only unhappy but is hardly fit to live." (Einstein, pp. 13–14)

Questions about the meaning of life were always problematic. They provoked, and still provoke, heated debates among scientists, philosophers, and religious leaders. The need to understand the essence of our existence in the world remains as strong and urgent as it did in the distant past. The difficulty in understanding the essence of our existence is related to our inability to see life as one link in a chain that can be compared to other links. It is not surprising therefore that many people turn to religion as the source of welcome relief from the doubts they experience about living and the value of life in general.

JEWISH RELIGIOUS ATTITUDES TOWARD MEANING OF LIFE

One harsh winter evening two students of Jewish religious studies arrived at a small town in Russia. They asked the passersby, "Where is the ritual bath?" They were told that there is such a bath in town, but that it is built at the foot of a steep hill and now in this freezing weather the road to the bath is dangerous and nobody uses it, except an old man that goes there each morning. The two students did not believe this story and decided to see if it was true. The next day they got up and saw that indeed an old and weak man was going down the slope with sure steps. They could hardly follow him and fell frequently on the ice. When they arrived at the bath, they asked the old man, "How could you go so safely on this road?" The old man said, "If man is connected to what is above, he can hardly fall on what is below" (Jacobson, 1995, pp. 231–232).

The late Rabbi Menachem Mendel Schneerson, the foremost Hasidic leader in the Jewish world, said that religion and science can dwell together because both may be regarded as motivating forces in life. He also emphasized that there are two forms of faith. One is of the children and the ignoramus. For them, faith is blind. It needs direction and it serves as support because of their weakness. The other form is the faith of those who have already come a long way in life and have gained an understanding that there is an obstacle that cannot be passed without faith. Rabbi Schneerson said, "If we are searching for the truth then we have already laid the foundation of belief in God. Yet, like in all dynamic relationships, the process of search is long and hard" (Jacobson, 1995, p. 194).

According to Rabbi Schneerson, there are two approaches in the search for truth: The human search via science and the search via God. There is no question that the universe is guided by logic. At the outset, man begins searching for truth from the outside in, trying to understand various phenomena and then piece them together like a jigsaw puzzle to make a complete picture.

"Scientists and philosophers peer through the outer layers of the universe to discover the forces lying within. What we are all actually searching for, whether or not we acknowledge it, is God, the hand inside the glove. But if we choose instead to search for the truth from the "inside out," looking directly through the eyes of the creator and abiding by His laws, we begin to gain a more complete understanding of how the world operates and why" (Jacobson, 1995, p. 194). True science and true religion are two sides of the same coin.

There is a strong connection between science and belief in God. Rabbi Schneerson had high esteem for the way science has dramatically improved our living conditions in the material and technological sense. However, he emphasized, we must understand that science is basically a search and not an absolute method of knowledge.

Science is based on a number of theories that can be used for good and bad. Therefore, meaning in life must be based on morals and creativity. The search for a deeper meaning of life beyond the material encompasses millions and millions of people all over the world. It does not matter how happy, capable, rich, or talented we are. Sooner or later we have a need to discover the deeper meaning of life.

Many elderly and young people live in a historical era in which material things are more valuable than spiritual things. Many people have no idea about God and what He demands from us. We have a lot of free time, but we fail to fill it up with spiritual content and meaning. It is difficult to find wise guidance because all the teachers, politicians, and parents are helpless when confronted with questions about the meaning of life. Rabbi Schneerson said that man can never be happy if he does not nourish his soul as he does his body (Jacobson, 1995, p. 3).

Once a man came to him and complained about the lack of meaning in his life. This man told the Rabbi that he had a good and healthy family and a successful professional career, but at the end of the day he felt empty and lonely.

"Are you leaving time for your soul?" asked the Rabbi.

"How could I find time for my soul when I am so busy with my work and my family?" answered this man.

"There is an old saying," said the Rabbi, "that when two men meet this means two souls against one body. Since bodies are centered in themselves by nature, they cannot unite their strengths—each one pursues after his physical needs. The souls, contrary wise, are not egoistic by nature, and therefore when two men combine their strengths, their souls unite" (Jacobson, 1995, p. 3).

This story implies that in the second half of life it is important to leave time for spiritual activities. For a religious person such activities may be studying the Holy Scriptures, devoting himself to literature or music (sacred and secular), or doing some other leisure time activity that occupies the spirit. By gradually engaging in such activities, one prepares himself for the years after retirement when the habit gained would give pleasure and satisfaction to one's life.

To live a meaningful life, according to Rabbi Schneerson, means to pierce the hard layers of outside material that cover one's heart and join the inner energy. This is not a simple or easy task because the body acts via its senses and the soul by more refined, noble, and gentle spiritual powers. These cannot be measured or weighed because man has many mysteries that oppose scientific measurement. The body tries to hold us to the earth, but the soul has power to lift us up, beyond the earth and beyond material existence.

A beautiful illustration to this idea was given by Jacobson (1995) in the name of the Rabbi:

> A rabbi when he was a young boy, played with his friends who climbed on a ladder. All the little children were afraid to climb to the top of the ladder except this boy. Later his grandfather asked: "Why you were not afraid when all the others did?" The boy said: "When they climbed up, they looked down. They saw how high they have arrived and were stricken with fear. But when I climbed, I looked up and saw how low I still was, and this motivated me to climb higher." (Jacobson, 1995, p. 7)

The meaning of life in Jewish religious perspective refers to one's standing before God and one's consciousness about this standing. This consciousness is the content and essence of religious belief. That belief, said Professor Leibovits (1999), answers the following question: What is the meaning of life? It claims that in man's life, irrespective of its length, and only in his life, can man accomplish the ultimate purpose of his being in the world. This purpose or essence is serving God (p. 21).

Rabbi Nachman of Breslau (1772–1811), the leader of the Breslau Hasidic movement and its spiritual guide, was known for his mystical approach to the sacred texts in Judaism. Rabbi Nachman was also a spellbinding storyteller, one who invented great and mystical stories about all kinds of people. His doctrine reflects man's longing for a better world. Rabbi Nachman sought substance and meaning to life. As a Hasidic rabbi he felt himself at ease with the common people, and could be equally at home with the downtrodden and the scholar. Rabbi Nachman compared this world to a narrow bridge that had a deep abyss on each side. In order to cross that bridge safely, man has to be equipped with a strong faith and a heroic soul.

Life, according to Rabbi Nachman, contains many troubles, and lots of depression, sadness, ups, and downs. One who has faith spends his life in happiness because when things go well and he has what he needs he feels good. And even if the opposite is true it is still good because he is sure that despite his misery God will take mercy on him in the future and will end his days happily (Raz, 1986, p. 43).

A religious and philosophical attitude toward life could serve people entering the second half of life, in which questions about the worthiness of life become more urgent than before. Carl Gustav Jung, the psychoanalyst, said that the life of a man is built on two parts: One part from luck and the other part from absence of luck, and we don't know ahead of time which part will fall in our lap when we pass age fifty. We must be ready to accept the good and the bad.

GREAT WRITERS' ATTITUDES TOWARD MEANING IN LIFE

People and lives have meanings. These meanings are expressed in literature and poetry in countless ways, but we are the ones that make the interpretations of their behavior. We give meaning to their thoughts, feelings, characters, personality, and so forth. Fiction and poems formalize the means by which we answer how we make and lose meaning. We differ in our perceptions of the meaning in a work of fiction. One reader is unlike another reader when it comes to eliciting the meaning intended by the author of the work. It is hard to decide what was really meant in the text because each work of fiction is dependent on the cultural, linguistic, and personal vocabulary of its author, and these factors can be interpreted in many ways.

Each of the great writers from antiquity to the present had his concept of meaning in life, and each of these writers approached this subject from a subjective perspective. For example, the old philosopher in Thomas Mann's (1955) *The Magic Mountain* is different from the old hero in Roman Gary's (1980) *King Solomon's Dread*. Whereas the former is satisfied with philosophizing about the meaning of life, the latter acquires his meaning by performing many good deeds for people in social and economic disadvantage. The same applies to the hero in Hemingway's *The Old Man and the Sea*. His meaning in life comes from an eternal quest for a great catch and from his struggle with the sharks that rob him of his triumph. Nevertheless the old man has no bitterness in his heart. The old man accepts his defeat and goes home to rest and prepare himself for the next fight for survival in the cruel sea.

In Kundera's (1990) *Immortality*, the heroine that comes to see the old poet and philosopher Goethe is driven by a need for meaning in her life, and she acquires some of it vicariously from the great poet. In Goethe's *Faust* (Part 1), (Gray, 1965) the aging professor realizes that he has missed the real meaning of life—love, pleasures, and happiness—when he sacrificed his youth to study. Faust is willing to sell his soul to the Devil in order to gain back what he missed, only to find out that these delights cannot serve as substitutes for a spiritually meaningful life.

Hrabal (2001), the great Czech writer of our time, wrote a delightful autobiography—*Memories of a Class Repeater* (2001)—when he was in his eighties and close to his death. Hrabal wrote that from now on his way in life would be backward. "I had enough with all the information! Now I want to know who I am. Why am I here? What for? Where am I going? And from where did I come? Who stands beside me and who is against me? What is above me and what is below?" (p. 284)

Hrabal presents in this book the simplest and most difficult questions in life. These are questions that each person must answer alone. These are questions that each person must answer candidly, deep inside one's soul. These are questions that are impossible to escape. They always appear, whether one is conscious or fast asleep.

Leo Tolstoy, the Russian writer, held a unique attitude toward the meaning of life. In *The Death of Ivan Illich* (1992), originally published in 1886, we can witness his philosophy that even in the face of death the life of a man can be meaningful. In Tolstoy's book, death and insight appear simultaneously. The hero is a high-ranking clerk in the government who discovers that the life he has had until he became terminally ill was meaningless.

Tolstoy wrote, "The life of Ivan Illich was simple, ordinary and terrible" (p. 193). "And he knew that he was dying. In his depth of soul he knew that he was dying, but he did not get used to the thought. He simply didn't understand, and could not perceive that it is possible" (p. 225).

The dying man remembers only the happiness and love he has had. His pains disappear the minute he stops holding on desperately to life. Through his suffering the hero gains insight and develops far beyond what was expected of him by his immediate environment. Ivan Illich becomes a man with inner greatness; and this greatness of soul nullifies all that has been done until then and makes his life meaningful. In his death, Ivan Illitch becomes a man who is able to transcend himself and turn his suffering into great human achievement.

The heroes in Shakespeare's play *King Lear* (1947) and Balzac's book *Father Goriot* (1991) are sad figures in their old age. They seem to live a pitiful life, forgotten by their children—except when the latter are in need of money and power—isolated and cast away, and weak in body and spirit. They present an ugly picture of aging, and their fates are even more depressing. One can deduce from their travails that there is no greater calamity in life than old age. They are a far cry from those old and much respected philosophers of antiquity, so beautifully described by Cicero (1909), who attracted the youth by their wisdom and life experience as a magnet attracts iron. Plato would have liked such people as leaders and rulers in his ideal state because old people are interested in safeguarding their moral virtues and standing for what they have fought for and suffered for all their lives. They know, with few exceptions, that there is no time left for new ventures, whereas it is easy to destroy the existing ones that have been accumulated.

In *Souls on Fire*, Elie Wiesel (1993), winner of the 1986 Nobel Peace Prize, refers to the question of the absurdity of living by saying that man can take a stand toward the world and toward life through irony and humor, or in other ways. Wiesel presents the following Hasidic story to illustrate his approach to meaning:

> A Hassid came to see Rabbi Menachem Mendel of Kotzk and complained: "Rabbi, I have terrible thoughts lately." "What are those," asked the Rabbi. I am afraid of mentioning them," said the Hassid. "Nevertheless, tell me," said the Rabbi. "Sometimes I reflect that God forbid there is no law and no judge." "So, what do you care," said the Rabbi. "If there is no law and no judge," cries the Hassid, "then what purpose is there to life and to the world?" "So what do you care if the world has no purpose," said the Rabbi. "If the world has no purpose," said the Hassid, "then there is no sense to the Torah, no sense to life, and this, Rabbi, I mind very much." "If you mind this so much, then you are a good Jew, and a good Jew may have such thoughts," said the Rabbi.

If life is meaningless, objectively speaking, then we should turn the search for meaning inward. The reasonable thing to do is to care for what gives us meaning inside. Life has meaning as long as we discover its meaning for ourselves by engaging in meaningful activities that give purpose and taste to life. Even if life is absurd, as some existentialist philosophers claim, man does not necessarily need to be absurd.

In terms of logotherapy, awareness about the search for meaning is connected to the concept of responsibility. Logotherapy emphasizes the importance of here and now in existential philosophy for meaningful living. One should not waste time in futile reflections about days past because these prevent one from doing the unique task of one's life. A life without meaning is punished by feelings of emptiness, disappointment, and suffering. Logotherapy claims that there is always a choice in each life situation. An individual can choose what is really important for him, and do what his choice demands from him. Man is free to find his own way in life. Logotherapy rejects a deterministic attitude toward life. If we accept such an attitude, then our lives will pass in despair.

8

Life as a Task

It is written in the book of Job (5:7) that man was created to toil. Humans must be productive; otherwise, their lives remain empty and meaningless. All human beings have to work, even older people. They also need to remain productive throughout life. An old man must work and toil even if this toil is not linked to earning a living.

Life is a task by which each human being can realize his or her potential for meaningful living. A most moving proof of this maxim is given by Bohumil Hrabal, the Czech writer and winner of the Nobel Prize for literature, in his book *Too Noisy Silence* (1994). This book, published in the author's old age, presents a man who works with a hydraulic press—alone in a damp, poorly lit basement—for thirty-five years. His job consists of transforming all kinds of waste papers, using the hydraulic press, into huge bundles that he decorates with paintings of the saints, which have been thrown away along with other waste paper.

The story unfolds during the communist era in Czechoslovakia. Hantya, the hero, develops a deep love for the old machine and for the literary classics in world literature that have been thrown into this basement as waste paper. Hantya saves these from destruction and oblivion, fills his small apartment with these books, and carries on a brilliant discussion with the characters in them.

Hantya finds special meaning in this work by turning the poor, grey, depressing conditions and loneliness of his work and life, even the noise of the machine, into extraordinary experiences. In his imagination, Hantya creates a wonderful world, a world full of meaning, beauty, and enchantment. Thus he is able to detach himself from the depressing reality that would otherwise close in on him; he is able to elevate himself above the conditions and circumstances of his life and to discover the treasures that hide in the mountains of waste paper falling down from the overhead hole into which the trucks unload their cargo. Hantya finds meaning in life by discovering a rare book that he is able to save.

Hantya describes this work, this task, and this way of life as follows: "Like a beautiful little fish that appears suddenly in the muddy water, so does a rare book appear glistening in the waste papers surrounding it. I turn my eyes for a moment blinded and afterward I fish it out, wipe and dry it with my apron. I open it, sniff the text a little, read the first sentence my eye fells upon, and I put it along with the rest of my treasures in the box" (p. 9).

Reading classical literature opens a new world for Hantya, one filled with wisdom and beauty. After the day's work is over, he carries the treasure back home, full of expectation that in the evening he will discover something of himself that he did not know (Hrabal, p. 14).

Hantya accepts his life with love, lives life the way he wants, and takes responsibility for his choices. Hantya is content with himself and with his actions, an exemplification of what Frankl (1962) emphasized: that meaning can be found in any situation or circumstance if one is open to receive it.

When we acquire awareness about our task in life, we also acquire a value that is important for our mental health. There is nothing more important than this awareness, because it enables us to cope successfully with the difficulties, disillusions, pains, disappointments, frustrations, and hardships that happen along our way in life. Every person who has survived a life-threatening illness, who was a captive or a prisoner of war, or who suffered yet survived life in a concentration camp or in a ghetto by the strength of his or her spirit, would most likely say that the source of this strength was the knowledge that there was a role for waiting to be filled. Therefore, these individuals had to find the courage and make every effort to survive, to carry all of the burdens and pain. For only that knowledge and work toward its fulfillment can make one able to withstand the vicissitudes of life. In this connection, Frankl (1986) liked to cite a famous saying of the philosopher Nietzsche: "Whoever has a reason for living endures almost any mode of life" (p. 54).

IMPORTANCE OF THE TASK

The importance of human beings' task in life, which is waiting to be met, is vested in turning the "why" in life into a "how." If people have a clear goal that they wish to achieve with all their hearts, they most likely will bear the "how"—even if it is very difficult—and the larger the place is that the "why" occupies, the more the "how" fades away in the background.

Coping with difficulties makes one's life meaningful. In this respect, said Goethe, the great philosopher, poet, and humanist: "You ask what your role is? And how can you know yourself? Not by observation or by contemplation! Try to do your role and learn what is hidden in it. And what is your role? What the day demands from you" (Frankl, 1986, p. 79).

In the lectures that he gave all over the world, Frankl used to repeat another idea from the philosophy of Goethe: that we should not accept people as they are, because then we only spoil them. Instead, we should relate to them as if they are the way they should be. Only in this way can we bring them closer to their goal.

The task of human beings is vested in the attitude to work: the urge to work and to accomplish something in the world is a most important part of life. The task of humans in the world is exemplified not only by their work but by the way that they live. All through life, people have to develop virtues to elevate them from the biological and animal characteristic of their existence to the spiritual one. Living life according to virtue is the best proof that we are capable of overcoming our weaknesses and shortcomings and of rising above ourselves for the sake of other human beings or of certain ideals.

Tension and stress are integral parts of life. Spiritual tension strengthens people and helps them in their quest to live their life as it should be, rather than as it is. Thus, what is called self is the struggle and the tension not to remain the same all through life—which, in any case, is impossible—but the need to become a personality, someone willing to wrestle with the tensions that determine one's place in the world. This wrestling is continuous, without end, similar to that of Sisyphus. And one's life story is the proof of what has been achieved in this struggle.

Our existence always points to the future; we are always interested in achieving something. Our deeds in the past may be seen as successes or failures. Our existence in the present is determined not only by our past but also by what we wish to become in the future. We are not supposed to inquire or to dig too much into the past. It should only be dealt with as the safest thing that we have; nobody can take it away from us.

The past has already been lived. Therefore we should only take out of it what has given us meaning and has enriched our lives to help us, in the present, to gain strength for successful coping with the demands of life. The past not only contains what has been good and pleasant and given meaning to our lives, but it also enables us to learn from the mistakes we made and to search for ways to atone for them in the present. We are able to mend our ways and to exploit the experience gained to create something positive in our present lives.

The essence of existence is to grow beyond one's self. People are closeted in a narrow world and cannot perceive what exists beyond this world. Yet, in this world, there are opportunities to make life meaningful. One can realize values, both immediate and eternal. These values seem to be waiting for the individual to come and grasp them, to use the opportunity for their realization. If one misses what life is offering, the opportunity passes and is wasted and the values remain unrealized.

PERSONAL RESPONSIBILITY IN TASK FULFILLMENT

In *Reflection on My Eightieth Birthday*, Bertrand Russell (1956) wrote that, when he reached eighty, he felt that the bulk of his work was done. Yet he still wanted to achieve two goals that he had longed for since his youth: to find out if anything could be known and to do whatever he could to make this world into a happier one (p. 220).

This quest from the famous scientist-philosopher seems especially relevant today. Russell wrote of completing the bulk of one's work at age eighty, which leaves a good number of years of constructive work beyond the customary age of sixty-five as a time of life for taking leave of one's major life accomplishments. Russell echoed ideas that many elderly people sense: the need to come to terms with one's age, to make peace with oneself, to accept responsibility for things that happened in one's life, and to recognize the significance of one's contribution to others. This quest is basically spiritual.

Retirement at age sixty-five (earlier or a bit later) is a relatively recent phenomenon, especially in its institutionalized form. Most people tend to associate retirement with physical and emotional deterioration, followed by decreased morale. The combination of these factors often results in low satisfaction with life and increased vulnerability to stress. The fear of retirement is related to the difficulty of accepting change in the accustomed ways of perceiving and dealing with the world.

Being uprooted from the world of work may impede successful adaptation to retirement. Those who are forced to retire on a small pension experience a drastic reduction in their standard of living, and some may experience poverty for the first time in their lives. Those who do not develop interests outside of work during their preretirement years usually do not adapt satisfactorily. Often they based their self-worth and identity on the status of work and the virtue of productivity and therefore find it difficult to justify a life of leisure activities.

Some people recognize the task that life demands of them and are willing to realize the value attached to the temporary situation, and yet they perceive their lives as lacking essence. These people are unable to explain to others why they feel that way. Ordinary people are far from prophecy and consequently cannot foresee what the future holds for them. And perhaps this is for the better; if humans were blessed with the ability to foresee the future, they would relate to it completely differently than at present. As long as they are unable to predict their future, they cannot judge it and say that life is worthless.

In *The Doctor and the Soul* (1986), Frankl tells a story about a black man, condemned to a life sentence, who boarded a ship for prisoners in Marseille. On the way to their destination in the open sea, a fire broke out and, when this man was released of his chains, he saved the lives of ten prisoners and was pardoned. But if he had been asked in Marseille while boarding the ship, whether or not his life had any meaning in his situation, he would surely have shaken his head in negation (p. 56).

Each person must fulfill a role in life in accordance with his or her concrete situation and personal knowledge and must try to respond to the concrete demand of life. There is no sense entering into abstract questions about the best step that one must take in order to respond to this demand of life, because it is impossible to define such a step. Instead of concentrating on abstract ways, people should take concrete steps, with the intention of doing what is expected of them to the best of their ability.

People must take personal responsibility for their one and only life and for their unique role, their personal mission, on the Earth. People who find themselves lacking this cognition become weak and vulnerable in difficult situations and then resemble a mountain climber in the Alps who gets stuck in dense fog, cannot see the goal in front of him, and is in danger of collapse and loss of his strength. But, when the fog lifts and he can see a shelter in the mountain that he can reach, his strength is renewed and he is able to continue his effort.

In *The Doctor and the Soul* (1986), Frankl wrote about one of his clients who told him that she could not find any sense to her life and did not want to get well. If she had an occupation or role that could give her satisfaction, "everything would be different." For example, if she were a doctor or a nurse or a scientist discovering some new and valuable medicine, she would be happy. "I had to educate her," says Frankl, "that it is not the occupation that is important, but how we fulfill our roles" (p. 128).

Meaning is not dependent on a concrete role, but on ourselves, in what we are doing in our unique existence and in the unique opportunities, given to us by our work, to make life meaningful.

This client of Frankl's did not understand that the work of a doctor or a nurse can be boring and very unpleasant at times. What makes the work of the therapist valuable in the eyes of the clients is not necessarily the professional knowledge that the therapist has. This knowledge is taken for granted by the consumers.

The doctor or the nurse who remains a decent human being despite all limiting circumstances is truly valued. And in order to be such a person, the therapist must fill his or her role with human content. Exhibiting kindness toward the client, caring for his or her well-being, and giving a smile and a kind word has no economic value, only a human one, give life its meaning and uniqueness. Despite the value that people place on the work role, this client needed to understand that work is just one of the roles in a person's life by which meaning can be found and that she could realize her uniqueness in many other ways.

THE FUNCTIONAL DIMENSION

In *The Will to Meaning*, Frankl (1985) describes only one among the four wills that motivate humans to act according to some of the greatest psychologists. For the Russian psychologist Pavlov (1881–1939), the most important was the will to survive. Pavlov developed the concept of conditioned reflex in his famous experiments with dogs. Sigmund Freud (1856–1939) considered the will to pleasure as the most important. Alfred Adler (1870–1937) regarded the will to power and superiority as the guiding wills in human existence. These three wills show what is common to human beings and to animals, namely that these center on the biological and the psychological dimensions.

Viktor Frankl (1905–97) maintained that the will to meaning is unique to human beings, because it expresses the dimension of the human spirit. This dimension is not a means for gaining something, nor is it a by-product of the gain, such as gaining power for the sake of superiority, but it is the central aim in life.

Hiroshi Takashima, a Japanese physician, has presented a fourth dimension: the functional dimension. Takashima has successfully incorporated and employed Frankl's theory and method of logotherapy in his medical treatment and has shown the benefits accrued to medicine and to the individuals concerned from this approach. According to Takashima, in diagnosis and treatment, we have to consider all four dimensions.

In *Humanistic Psychosomatic Medicine* (1984), he wrote that sickness can begin in one of the four dimensions and influence the others. For example, an ulcer can be an organic illness and cause disturbance in the functional dimension. A correct diagnosis of the dimension in which the illness originates is necessary, along with an assessment of how the rest of the dimensions are affected. Thus there is a need to combine psychotherapy, medications, and logotherapy (meaning-oriented psychotherapy) to modify a client's attitude toward his or her illness.

Takashima used the metaphor of an orchestra to illustrate his approach to medicine and to the four human dimensions: he compared the instruments of the orchestra to the somatic dimension and the technical skill of the musicians to the functional dimension. The musicians' minds were analogous to the psychological dimension, and the conductor symbolized the spiritual dimension, because the conductor translates the spirit of the composer to the orchestra (Takashima, p. 24).

Takashima included in his book many cases to illustrate the working of the functional dimension. I have selected one that is characteristic of his attitude, as a physician, toward people in his care. In this case, he tells about a manager of a supermarket and coffeehouse who turned to him for help, complaining that he limped on his left leg. This limping had started three months ago, yet it was confined only to his workplace. Outside the office, he could walk without limping, climb steps, and take part in various sport activities. Only in his work during the day did he limp.

This patient was seen and tested by many doctors, including psychiatrists and neurologists, and no evidence was found of physical or neurological factors or causes for the limping. Takashima asked the patient when the limping had started. He answered that it was when his boss has reprimanded him because of a mistake he made. When he returned to his office after that, he bumped his left leg against a chair and fell; all of the treatments that he received were of no avail.

Takashima asked the patient to walk for a while in his presence, and the patient indeed limped with his left leg. "Then I said to him," Takashima tells, "try to limp on both legs." "No jokes," said the patient, and he did not try to limp. Instead, he walked well—without limping on either leg. This patient saw that, when he tried to limp on purpose on his right leg, he could not limp on his left leg. Then he tried harder to limp on his left leg, but he couldn't. Takashima asked this patient to return to the office and try to limp on his left leg on Mondays, Wednesdays, and Fridays and on his right leg on Tuesdays and Thursdays. The patient laughed. Several days later he phoned Takashima and told him that he was sorry that he could not fulfill the doctor's order, because he had forgotten how to limp (pp. 91–92).

This was a case of functional disease with an unknown cause, yet it was treated successfully with Frankl's paradoxical intention, a method of treatment that Frankl described and presented in detail in a chapter of his first book, *The Doctor and the Soul* (1986, pp. 221–252).

In our times many people in their second half of life live only for the hour: they tend to see the concept of here and now literally, as a call to grab as much from the pleasures of life as possible. These people live a life of care for their wealth but forget to care for their time. Their money cannot help them when the time comes to depart from this world, and their days are not returning as they wish. But those who make the necessary effort and find meaningful tasks for themselves, those who occupy themselves in activities that bring joy to others, see a blessing in their work and gain satisfaction and happiness in their lives.

9

On Fate and Meaningful Living

If fate overcomes you, don't run away! Don't throw away your armament, and don't search for shelter, for fate will get you everywhere. Instead, search for a place and for a task that will be useful to others. (Seneca, 1997, p. 22)

Fate has always been and continues to be a much-discussed subject in philosophy, poetry, literature, and music, as well as in science and religion. Many of the greatest creations in these human endeavors were devoted to fate's intervention in human life and affairs. Two of the most famous musical creations, for example, are Beethoven's *Fifth Symphony*, generally known as the Symphony of Fate, and Verdi's great opera *La Forza del Destino*, or the Power of Fate.

In literature the fate of the hero or heroine is imagined, yet his or her actions resemble real-life behavior. Fate is directed toward some purpose, which may or may not be understood or perceived by the individual as fate.

Fate is an important factor in the lives of millions of elderly people, for some of whom fate is part of the cultural heritage by which they try to explain to themselves and others the important events that happened in their lives.

The concept of fate and its influence on human behavior is presented in this chapter via the scientific work of Lipot Szondi, the Hungarian-born psychiatrist and scientist who developed the theory of fate analysis and used it in his therapeutic work. Logotherapy's attitude toward fate as a philosophical and a psychological concept is also presented via the writings of Frankl and others.

BIBLICAL AND LITERARY ATTITUDES TOWARD FATE

In its many forms and expressions, fate appears more than seventy times in the Bible (in the Old Testament). In its original role, fate constituted small pieces of stone with a number on top that were cast to make decisions about the fate of something or someone. Thus, for example, the division of the land among the twelve tribes of Israel after its capture from the Canaanites by Joshua was done by casting fates (Joshua: 8–12).

Fate occupies a central subject in two of the twenty-four books in the Old Testament, in the books of Jonah and Ester, and it signifies a double role: on the one hand, fate shows how insignificant humans are against the power of God, and, on the other, fate is clothed as chance happening to someone.

In the book of Jonah, fate is mentioned in various contexts. First, the sailors cast fates to see who is guilty of causing the storm that threatened to sink their boat, in which Jonah wished to escape from the mission that God gave him to fulfill. Fate appears to Jonah a second time when, instead of being drowned in the storm, he is swallowed by a great whale. When Jonah is tossed from the whale's belly onto the land, he fulfills God's command, but even then he must first taste suffering in order to understand that his protest against God's command is useless: human beings are only tools in the hands of God and their revolt against the fate meted out to them will not help them.

Jonah's story is just one illustration of the concept of fate. Another is told in the book of Ester: Haman, chief advisor to the king of Persia, casts a stone (fate) to decide on which day of the month the Jews of ancient Persia will be killed. Fate, however, intervenes and turns his wishes upside down: Rather than killing all of the Jews as he has intended, he is hanged, along with his sons.

Sometimes fate serves a different purpose from the one originally intended. The Bible uses the Hebrew word *inah* (coincidence), as in the case of a murderer who happened to kill someone by chance or mistake because God had chanced it to happen. The ancient people of Israel were aware of this turn of fate and erected special towns and places where such a murderer could find refuge to save his life from vengeance by the family of the murdered man.

In the book of Judges there is a story about Yiftach, the Israeli general, and his vow to kill the first person he met if he came home victorious. He meets his own daughter. This story is another example of the double meaning of fate in the Bible. In the cases of Jonah and Yiftach, the reader cannot escape the feeling that fate makes a mockery with them. Fate in its biblical use gives a reason to achieve something or some purpose. But this purpose is hidden from the one who serves as the subject of fate. Heroes in the Bible do the very things against which they are warned and consequently pay the price.

Fate is used in literature much as in the Bible. In a book by the Israeli writer Meir Shalev, the hero is running away from the fate that he knows awaits him. He is afraid that he will die young and in strange circumstances, like the men in his family. Fate intervenes at times in human life and shakes people up with such a force that afterward their whole life and attitude to the world are changed. This is what happens in Thomas Mann's *Magic Mountain* (1955), in which the hero, stricken with tuberculosis, is living in a sanatorium away from reality and slowly sinks into a dream world. He awakens only when the World War I shakes him up and puts him back on his feet and face-to-face with reality.

What then is fate? Is it chance or is it ordered by some power? Is it possible to control fate, to predict its course? Perhaps human beings have no power against it. These questions keep nagging not only the heroes in the Bible, in literature, or in operas, but they concern psychologists as well.

The psychoanalyst Carl Gustav Jung referred to fate in two of his books. In *On the Paths of Our Depths* (1993), Jung wrote: "what is decreed of man is an irrational factor like the power of fate that presses on us to detach ourselves from the crowd, to be independent and not to follow the paths known to the herd. For a man with real personality always has a mission; He believes in it" (p. 29).

In his old age, Jung wrote *Memories, Dreams, and Thoughts* (1997), his autobiographical book, and made references to fate. Jung wrote that, when he worked on his family tree, he saw his partnership with fate become clear to him. This partnership bound him to his ancestors. Jung said in this book that he frequently imagined a karma, or impersonal fate, that passes from parents to children; he added: "I have always felt that I must answer the questions fate put before my ancestors, or that I must finish things they did not have the time to complete" (p. 283).

FATE IN THE THEORY OF SZONDI

The subject of karma (fate) and collective fate that passes through generations, according to Jung, was investigated and developed into a psychological theory of motivation by the Hungarian psychiatrist, therapist, and researcher Lipot Szondi.

In 1986, at the age of ninety-two, the Jewish Hungarian psychoanalyst Lipot Szondi died. Known all over the world as the founder of the theory and method of fate analysis, an independent school within depth psychology, Szondi was one of the great personalities who have enriched our knowledge of the human psyche. Szondi made highly significant contributions to understanding the motivating forces behind human behavior. As a product of the former Austro-Hungarian Empire, born in 1893 and raised in Hungary, Szondi worked furiously in Budapest until 1944, survived the Holocaust, and lived in Switzerland from 1945 until his death. His institute and worldwide center for training in the method of fate analysis still operates outside of Zurich.

Like Frankl, Szondi was a physician, a psychiatrist, and a psychotherapist. He worked with patients who suffered from various disturbances in their behaviors. In *Fate Analysis and Self-Disclosure* (1996), Szondi summarized his scientific career by the question that many people asked him: "Why is a scientist in the natural sciences and a physician perceiving something as mythical and mysterious as the fate of an individual as a medical and psychological problem?" "We cannot dissect it after death, or treat it by medicines or operations," Szondi answered, "I had a different opinion. I maintained it all my life and it always remained with me. Even as a young man I saw that decisions and choices were directed by the family or by the genetic inheritance and this choice shapes fate" (Szondi, p. 5).

Szondi's interest in fate analysis began early in his life, seventeen years before Sigmund Freud published his essay "Dostoyevsky and Patricide" in 1928. At that time, in 1911, Szondi was an avid reader of the novels written by this famous Russian writer, and he asked himself: "Why did Dostoyevsky choose murderers and saints to serve as heroes in his books?" His answer later served as a breakthrough to his new theory of psychoanalysis. Szondi found that Dostoyevsky knew how to describe the souls of his heroes and their inner worlds, because he himself carried, as genetic family inheritance, the same traits and characteristics, and Dostoyevsky projected these traits onto the heroes in his books. Szondi also assumed that great writers include in their books the genes that they inherited and the contents of their instinctual worlds, without being aware of this unconscious process in their writing. Szondi was so convinced about the truth of his new theory that he had the courage to publish it. The responses that he received were almost equally divided: there were those who perceived his theory as true, and others who rejected it as complete nonsense.

A similar thing happened to Szondi's famous book, *Analysis of Marriages*, which was published in 1937. At that time he was already convinced that the responses to this book were connected to only one thing, namely, that this book touched on something deep and basic in the soul and psychological makeup of human beings. Therefore he decided to develop his discovery further and to devote his life to the theory of fate analysis.

Szondi's initial feeling about Dostoyevsky was verified in 1947 when the French author Henri Troyat published his biography on Dostoyevsky: Troyat showed that the family of Dostoyevsky, which dated back to the sixteenth century, included many soldiers, priests, and judges, but also thieves and murderers.

The same thing happened to Szondi with Balzac, in whose books one can find a murderer who serves as a literary expression of Balzac's own family unconscious, which is discussed in more detail later in this book.

There were other incidents in Szondi's own family, such as the sickness of his mother and eldest brother, as well as in the families of his patients, that strengthened Szondi's belief in his assumptions about fate. His older brother served as his model. This brother studied medicine in Vienna but didn't finish his studies because he married a blond German Aryan woman, became a father, and remained unhappy all of his life.

Szondi participated as a frontline medic in World War I and was almost killed when a bullet hit the spade in his backpack. He decided that his escape from death was a sign that he must finish his studies in medicine and help the sick and the suffering. Afterward he arrived at a military hospital in Vienna with an infection in his liver. There he met a blond Aryan woman and fell in love with her. One night he woke up in great anxiety because he dreamed about his family discussing the unhappy life of his older brother because of that unfortunate marriage. Szondi woke up with the feeling that he was going to repeat the mistake of his brother. He wanted, however, to live his own fate, rather than to repeat what had already happened. This was the moment when Szondi resented his genetic fate and decided to choose his selected fate instead. Following this incident, he began to develop his concept of the family unconscious.

Another incident that strengthened Szondi's decision to study fate's influence on human behavior was connected to one of his patients, who brought his wife to Szondi for therapy because of the fears she had that she might poison herself and her family. Szondi told the husband of this woman that her case was rather similar to that of an older woman who had been in therapy for many years because of the same fears. When Szondi described her physically, the husband exclaimed that she was his mother. Szondi was disturbed by the question of why this man had chosen a woman with the same family history and fears. The answer that he arrived at only strengthened his resolution to develop his theory further.

SZONDI'S SCIENTIFIC WORK

The scientific work of Szondi encompassed two main periods: First, from 1936 until 1944 in Budapest, Hungary, Szondi concentrated his efforts on developing the theory and method of fate analysis. In the second period (1945–1954), the question of whether it is possible to direct fate was posed. Szondi was interested in seeing how fate analysis could be used for therapeutic purposes. This second period in Szondi's scientific activities laid the basis for the new *anancology*, or theory of fate analysis, which was further developed during Szondi's lifetime into a theory of psychotherapy.

Between 1934 and 1936, Szondi had undertaken his own fate analysis. During that time he originated the concept of the family unconscious, which consists of the following: in the unconscious, as important factors for existence, are models of ancestor figures that direct the fate of the offspring by force. Szondi called this factor forced fate. It comprises the family unconscious of the offspring many generations later. The family unconscious contains the aspirations of the ancestors. The opponent of the ancestors is the ego of the offspring, which can take a stand. The ego is capable of choice, despite the interest of the ancestors. This choice forms the basis for the concept of freely chosen fate. Szondi called this ability of the human being to choose his or her fate directed fatalism. He also made this ability the cornerstone of fate analysis.

In ancient Greek fate is *ananke*, which has two meanings: a limit on freedom due to some outside force—in this sense, fate means suffering or worry—and blood relations, such as the family. Thus fate includes both force and family. Until the end of World War II, fate had been investigated scientifically during two periods. In *Fate Analysis* (1996), Szondi reported a case of fear about poisoning one's family, as previously presented, in which he was not content with the customary answer that it was just a matter of coincidence. Szondi asked himself the question: "Why did that man fall in love with that particular woman and not with somebody else?" And the answer that he found became the basis for his major work. Additional choice-related questions were derived later when fate analysis was reinforced by thousands of cases offering evidence for his approach.

In the concept of the family unconscious, Szondi investigated the opposing interests of the ancestors and found that choice is of utmost importance for the offspring: the family unconscious speaks in the language of choice. Szondi maintained that, despite the genetic inheritance that we all carry, we can freely choose part of our fates. And the greater that part is, the easier it is to carry one's own fate. Those who succumb to their genetic inheritance (their forced fate) are totally dependent on their family unconscious.

In a letter to his friend Peter Balazs in 1939, Szondi wrote that human beings must dare to be different from others—they must dare to be good despite all of the bad things that people did to them and around them. Szondi asked: "What is bad?" He answered his own question: "Bad means not yet finding the way out of the tyranny of the instincts that hold us in their clutch." For him, not yet meant that tomorrow or afterward might be different.

In fate analysis, the aim is to build bridges. This is the essence of therapy. Bridges need to be built between the various strata of the human psyche and among people in general. Szondi's basic assumption was that there is no clear border between the healthy and the sick personality and that meaning in life is dependent on the choices that we make. Fate analysis requires a solid understanding of all of the factors that shape fate, both causative and formative. Fate itself is always the result of the behavior exhibited by the subject in relation to the opposing forces; the human quest is always to attain wholeness.

Fate analysis is built on the concept of genotropism, on the attraction of the genes, which direct the individual's fate. This attraction is expressed in five areas toward which the individual's genes incline: the selection of the love partner or spouse; of friends and ideals; of an occupation and life mission; of illnesses, particularly mental illness related to a given body structure; and in the choice of death, whether by accident, incurable illness, or by suicide (Szondi, 1996a, pp. 62–65).

Evidence for the validity of Szondi's theory can be seen daily in work with the disabled and the elderly. Those who succumb to their forced fate, to injury and loss, blame fate for their situation; as long as they are unwilling to search for those doors that are still open before them, they are not subjects for rehabilitation in the psychic sense. Those who live out the role of the old and the disabled, who concentrate only on the negative aspects in their lives, find themselves in a street or road with no outlet; they are in danger of succumbing to despair or to a life lived in self-pity, which logotherapy perceives as a meaningless life.

Szondi maintained that fate analysis requires a solid understanding of all of the factors that shape fate, both causative and formative. According to fate analysis, the ego and spiritual fate together form a hand, which, to a large degree, directs the activities of the instinctual forces in human beings. These two factors in combination are capable of turning the instinctual forces against their original goals. This turning of the destructive forces, which Szondi calls the nature of Cain, corresponds, to a degree, to Frankl's concept of the human being as capable of self-transcendence.

The importance of spiritual fate becomes evident in the theory of Szondi when he speaks about those who succumb to their fate, those who suffer from fate that is forced on them. These people are incapable of resisting the opposing forces in their instinctual fate and the environmental influences acting on them.

Many people suffer throughout their lives from the fate that they have inherited from their ancestors. They lack the ego and spiritual strength to overcome what they need in order to prevail over the compelling forces in their inheritance. And they are incapable of choosing, from the many possibilities that are open before them, a single piece of individual and private life. They are sick because the functions of their faith are paralyzed.

In *Man's Search for Meaning* (1962), Frankl has shown that faith is directed toward the future. Szondi concurs with this direction. The spiritual fate of the human being is capable of turning a person into a real human being. The strength of functional faith and its quality are dependent on the strength of the ego in terms of its libido, mental energy, interests, and the social environment. If the ego disperses its energy to satisfy the instincts, its chances of getting sick are great. And, in order to prevent mental illness, the ego needs to give control to the spirit rather than to matter, and only faith can help the ego attain that function.

SZONDI'S MENTAL PICTURE OF THE HUMAN BEING

The question has been raised many times by leading depth psychologists: How does an individual become a human being, or by what process does one attain the designation of a human being in the spiritual sense of the word? Freud's discovery of the unconscious and its many manifestations—what is known today as the psychopathology of everyday life (Freud, 1991)—opened new perspectives for psychology. Psychoanalysis in Szondi's approach affects the mental picture of the human being in two ways: by discovering the irrational forces in the unconscious that, if unchecked by the ego, may cause serious harm to both the individual and the collective and by Freud's reality principle, according to which the founder of psychoanalysis tried in vain to educate people to escape the dangers that were inherent in the irrational forces that we all carry within when we lack control.

When human beings are born, they bring along the forced fate of their ancestors. Later, with development and passing through the first four phases of life—infancy, the period of being a toddler, latency, and adolescence—one may become a homo elector, that is, a person who chooses or elects his or her own fate. This election is possible only when the individual is able to use his or her super ego, what Szondi has termed the Pontifex ego. This concept is analogous to Freud's super ego. It relates to the highest aspect in the structure of the human psyche (Szondi, 1996b, p. 56).

The highest form of human being, Szondi claims, is one capable of being himself or herself, of returning to the collective, to the love of humankind. This is the main task of the homo elector. Attainment of that status is not yet the highest achievement on the way to become a human being, says Szondi. Homo liberator and homo humanisator are two concepts that, more than anything else, express Szondi's faith in humankind. Both stations can be achieved by human beings whose faith, in the spiritual sense, in a loving human collective means liberation from the confines of their instinctual nature and from the loneliness of self-love (Szondi, 1996b, p. 60). In summing up Szondi's work, one is struck by the duality of human nature: forced fate versus selected fate. Szondi claims that we can continue to adhere to our murderous inclinations, as contained in Cain's fate (Szondi, 1987), or we can use our conscience to recognize this tendency to sin and contradict it, to bring about the transformation to Moses. The tendency to kill is as old as human history, and therefore it is ever present. But the recognition of sin in the human soul has also been present from ancient times. Human beings can lead a life in which they aim to become like Moses, who struggled with his Cain's spirit and with sin and came out glorious, because he turned his murderous past into the highest achievement that a human being can attain: to become the founder of law and morals.

Szondi's theory and therapy are controversial to this day. An interesting illustration of this controversy is found in two letters that were sent to him sixteen years apart. The first letter was written by Sigmund Freud, and the second by Thomas Mann. The letters were sent to Szondi as replies to copies of his book *Analysis of Marriages* (1937). Freud's reply, two years before his death in London in 1939, was not particularly friendly and contained several objections to Szondi's book. Freud emphasized that psychoanalytic experience has brought to the surface many kinds of love; he ended his letter by stating that the factor that Szondi emphasized in his book—the genetic attraction as expressed in the family unconscious—may play a role without being exclusive or the standard.

The second letter was sent to Szondi by Thomas Mann, the famous writer, on October 23, 1953, from a place near Zurich in Switzerland. Mann perceived Szondi's book as a meaningful gift that had occupied him a great deal. On the subject of choosing one's parents, mentioned by Szondi, Mann wrote that this may be a hypothesis, and he cited Schopenhauer, who said that this could be different. Summing up the analysis of Szondi's book, Mann wrote that people's fate is what they want to become; he ended his letter to Szondi with some kind and generous words of praise.

In sum, fate for Szondi is a chain of decisions: some of them are done consciously, but the bulk of them are unconscious. Yet, even when a decision is made unconsciously, it is always a matter of choice. The essence of Szondi's theory is that we should turn our unconscious decisions into conscious ones; that is, we have to take our fates into our own hands instead of passively accepting it. One's fate is not something that needs to be accepted humbly. One can give it direction.

LOGOTHERAPY'S APPROACH TO FATE

"Destiny appears to man in three principal forms," says Frankl. "The first is his natural disposition or endowment, his somatic or biological fate. The second form, his situation, or the total of his external environments, is sociological fate, and the third is man's disposition and situation that together make up a man's psychological fate." The last form, psychological fate, is connected to taking a spiritual and free stand toward the events in one's life. Frankl wrote, "toward these man takes a position, that is, he forms an attitude. The position taken is in contrast to the basically destined position given—a matter of free choice. Proof of this is the fact that man can change his position. Man can take another attitude"(Frankl, 1986, p. 80).

This quote from Frankl underlies the concepts of forced fate and selected fate in a logotherapeutic perspective. As for forced fate, Frankl cites the case of identical twins that were separated for many years. Yet when one of them developed paranoia, the other, who lived in a distant city, sent a letter "which betrayed a delusion identical in content to his twin's paranoia." Frankl says that here was destiny indeed: the identical twins had developed from the same germ cell, had the same fundamental disposition, and developed the same mental disease (Frankl, 1986, p. 81).

There is no need to be an identical twin in order to have a forced fate. Frankl said: "The man who believes his fate is sealed is incapable of repealing it" (Frankl, 1986, p. 81). Forced fate and selected fate are issues with which we have to deal many times during a long life. Illustrations taken from Frankl's own life refer to his story as a Jew and as a human being. Frankl had a forced fate, literally, when he was sent to Auschwitz, and when his manuscript on existential analysis was forcibly taken from him and lost, along with everything else that he possessed except his life. Frankl could have resigned himself to that fate, but instead he used his own freely selected fate and reconstructed this book on scraps of paper, which later became his groundbreaking work, *The Doctor and the Soul: from Psychotherapy to Logotherapy* (Frankl, 1986).

The second story, also taken from the life of Frankl, refers to the time when he suffered a heart attack during a visit to Munich when he was old. His reaction to the situation at the intensive care unit of the hospital is a beautiful example of selected fate, as told by Lukas (1986), because he showed more than courage. Frankl showed what is written in St. Francis's prayer: "Give me my Lord that instead of being consoled, I shall console; instead of being understood, that I shall understand; and instead of being loved, that I shall love; for only in the giving we receive." Lukas recounts that Frankl, gravely ill, consoled, comforted, and gave her courage: "He didn't think of himself, he thought of me!" (p. 139). Frankl showed a personal example of logotherapy's application in real life.

THE BIOLOGICAL FATE

Logotherapy is based on the premise that human beings are capable of changing their attitudes toward the circumstances of their lives. They can turn a fate that is forced on them into a freely selected fate by the stand that they take toward a predicament. Frankl (1986) said that, only under the hammer blows of fate, in the white heat of suffering, does life gain shape and form (p. 111). This is particularly important for old and or disabled people, because the loss that they suffer tends to color their perception. It tends to alter their self-image, their attitude to self, family, work, and society. And it tends to push many such people into despair. Therefore, changing these people's attitudes—from preoccupation with their misery to a wish to be of service to others, to those less fortunate than themselves—and redirecting their mental energy to discover new meaning in life are the logotherapeutic answers for these people. Frankl wrote: "The destiny a person suffers has a twofold meaning: to be shaped where possible and to be endured where necessary" (Frankl, 1986, p. 111).

Logotherapy offers a means for attaining both. Frankl not only developed the theory and philosophy of logotherapy, he also introduced several methods and techniques to help suffering people. Two cases for illustration are briefly presented in the following discussion. The first is told by Frankl (1986) in *The Doctor and the Soul*.

A famous lawyer learned that his leg had to be amputated because of arteriosclerosis. The operation took place in the hospital where Frankl worked at that time. The healing went well, and the time came for the patient to make the first step on one leg. The patient got up from the bed and began jumping in the room and soon collapsed in Frankl's arms. He burst into tears, claiming that he would not be able to bear life as a cripple, that life had lost meaning for him in this condition, whereupon Frankl looked into his eyes and asked him if he was serious about making a career as a short or long distance runner. The patient looked at Frankl surprised, and Frankl said to him that, in this case and only then, could he understand the patient's despair, because then it would really be meaningless to live further. But for someone who has spent his life meaningfully and has gained a solid reputation in his profession to lose the meaning of life just because he lost a leg is incomprehensible. The patient understood at once, and a smile crept up on his tearful face (p. 282).

This is a case that required not only endurance, but the shaping of a new life for the patient. And to achieve both, Frankl made use of the self-distancing power of humor, the main ingredient in paradoxical intention, a technique and method of treatment that Frankl first published in 1939. This method has been used in psychotherapy ever since, with considerable success.

In logotherapy the concept of fate is exchanged for destiny. Although fate is blind to values and limited to concrete events beyond our control, destiny is connected to the way in which we respond to what happens to us. Destiny expresses the order of events and their understanding. According to logotherapy, it is possible to overcome fate by the specifically human ability of self-transcendence. This ability is part of the spiritual dimension that is unique to human beings. Fate in Szondi's theory is the opposite of freedom in Frankl's theory. The spiritual dimension signifies freedom from genetic inheritance and instincts and even from physical and social environments. It denotes the human ability to accept or to reject the limitations of those factors. In Frankl's attitude to freedom, it is up to human beings to decide how they wish to live their lives.

Instead of speaking about fate, Frankl prefers to speak about faith, for the latter is directed to the future. Without faith (not necessarily religious faith), there is no meaning to psychotherapy. A therapist who does not believe in the client's ability to change his or her attitude toward someone or something cannot fulfill the helping and caring roles and functions of a therapist. Frankl rejects a fatalistic attitude to life. He emphasizes that human beings have "response-ability"; that is, they have the ability to choose their responses to what happens to them, even in the worst conditions.

Frankl agrees with Szondi that fate belongs to all of us human beings, like the soil on which we walk, but this soil serves as a jumping board to freedom. One is not dependent on fate, and certainly not on forced fate, claims Frankl. On the contrary, one can always decide how to respond to fate. This response is dissimilar to Szondi's selected fate. One has basic freedom to take fate as a given that requires a decision, along with responsibility and determination, even against fate.

The life of a human being is a constant struggle between inner and outer powers of fate. Yet, despite the importance of fate, the starting point should be the freedom that exists even in the most severe cases of pathology. This freedom is expressed in the attitude that people take toward what is happening to them. Biological fate is like material that is open to structuring. Shaping and structuring are its aims. We can meet people who show us that it is possible to overcome biological givens and physiological shortcomings. People are capable of achieving great deeds with their spirits when they are willing to give their maximum energy to a certain cause.

PSYCHOLOGICAL FATE IN LOGOTHERAPEUTIC PERSPECTIVE

Psychological fate symbolizes things that are contrary to freedom. The neurotic fatalist always claims, "that's it" and "there is nothing I can do." The neurotic is wrong with respect to the second part of the prior sentence. For the human ego is always pushing forward and never exploited enough. A sailboat moves where it is directed by the power of the wind and by the abilities of the sailor rather than by the power of the wind alone.

Someone who really wishes to gain something must know the goal, concentrate on achieving that goal in earnest, and prepare for getting it. Someone who wishes to overcome an addiction, for example, must refrain from excuses and refrain from temptations and must decide and do what emanates from a decision such as to give up drinking completely, once and for all. In *The Doctor and the Soul* (1986), Frankl speaks of a schizophrenic woman who, when asked whether or not she suffered from weakness of her will, answered, "if I will—yes, and if I do not will—no" (p. 86).

Many people are inclined to justify their weakness of will, blaming others for their failures. Here is a chance for the therapist to bring the client or patient to understand that he or she must be free of this inclination. The neurotic fatalist prefers to escape the need to take responsibility for his or her fate, claiming weakness of will or bad upbringing. Yet, people can choose their psychological fate.

A patient who suffered from hallucinations, of hearing frightening voices, was once asked by the therapist: "How come, despite these voices, you are generally in a good mood?" She answered, "I was just thinking that it is better to hear frightening voices than to be deaf" (Frankl, 1986, p. 90).

Frankl insisted that people can oppose their psychological fate, even in acute situations; he illustrated this maxim by recalling an event from his own life. When Frankl was lying in the concentration camp with typhus, he used to overcome his delusions, the characteristic of this illness, by writing in shorthand on scraps of paper some key words for the book that he lost on entering the camp.

LOGOTHERAPY'S PERSPECTIVE ON SOCIOLOGICAL FATE

Adjustment to aging is best understood by examining the complex interrelationships among biological and social changes against the backdrop of life-long experience. In the process of becoming an adult and meeting the challenges of adulthood, each of us develops attitudes, values, commitments, beliefs, preferences, and tastes that we integrate into our personalities. As we become older, we are predisposed to maintain continuity in our personalities, habits, associations, and surroundings. The failure to preserve a sense of continuity, as occurs frequently in the transition to institutional surroundings, is one of the most common precipitators of maladjustment in the elderly (Guttmann and Cohen, 1993).

In *Man's Search for Meaning* (1962), Frankl wrote that we lost the basic instincts and traditions that gave us security. As a result, we do not know what to do and sometimes we do not even know what we wish to do (p. 106).

Sociological fate determines life only partially. Society does not prevent one from exercising freedom of will. There is always space in which to shape sociological fate. Personal freedom acts as a filter through which a decision passes and influences the final decision. Not all behavior sanctioned by society is valuable just because society has agreed to it. Sometimes the opposite is true.

Logotherapy does not condone what is right in the eyes of the public. Deeds are tested in the light of their spiritual values. Frankl (1986) illustrates logotherapy's approach to sociological fate by the story of giving the Ten Commandments to the Israelites at Mount Sinai. Accordingly, the words that the Hebrews gave to Moses—"we shall do"—should always precede the words "we shall hear," because it is possible to hear something and not do a thing about what was just heard.

Sociological fate was tested to the limit by the experiences of people incarcerated in the German concentration camps during the Holocaust. In *Man's Search for Meaning*, Frankl (1962) presented the three phases through which the victims allowed to live had to pass. The first phase included the arrival and entering the camp, when they lost all of a sudden everything that they were previously and became creatures with numbers tattooed on their flesh. In that situation, what was demanded was to cross out their previous lives and to devote all of their spiritual strength to survival. In the second phase, in day-to-day life in the camp, they were forced to participate in the struggle for satisfying their most basic needs while trying to keep their human image. And in the third phase, when the incarcerated prisoners were freed from the physical and mental pressures and from all of the fears and terrifying conditions that surrounded them, the danger that awaited was the loss of identity through an inability to be happy for their life.

Life in the concentration camp brought about the deformation of the human soul and apathy about everything, except the physiological need to eat and to find a bit of warmth. The sexual instincts did not work because of malnutrition, and lack of food caused dreams and endless talks about meals. The way to deal with these inhuman conditions was always subjective. There were inmates who were capable of overcoming their anger and apathy, who knew how to sacrifice even their last piece of bread, and there were others who became like beasts. The latter were usually the Capos—the work supervisors who were selected from among the prisoners. Thus, even in the sociological fate that was forced on the inmates, they could choose their personal reaction and attitude to the social environment in which they found themselves.

Frankl emphasized that neurotic symptoms are not only the result of something physiological or of a mental-emotional expression, but also a form of existence, and this is crucial. Hunger and lack of sleep, which are physiological conditions, and inferiority, which is a mental condition, are, in their essence, spiritual standpoints. In any situation, people are endowed with the ability to make their decisions, to decide whether they are in favor or against their social, mental, and physical environment. Only those who forwent their spiritual supports before entering the camp failed under the influence of their surroundings.

Logotherapy offers ways to cope with forced fate. These ways are based on the logotherapeutic technique called change in attitude. The purpose of this technique is to help clients gain a new attitude toward the harm done to them. The goal is to change a negative and mentally unhealthy attitude to life into a healthy and positive one.

There are four ways to achieve this goal that are offered the client: the first includes the notion that to adopt a positive attitude to the blow of fate is a tremendous human achievement. The second is to show the client something meaningful that is included in the suffering, despite the blow. The need to turn the client's attention from what has been lost to what remains—to what is whole and has not been harmed by fate—is the third way. And adopting a philosophical standpoint or a religious perspective on life that can help carry the burden of suffering is the fourth way.

An illustration is the case of a sixty-five-year-old widow who lost her husband after a long battle with cancer. She felt herself useless in the world, and she could have easily fallen into depression and despair.

The first phase in the treatment was to help her see in that forced fate had brought not only a disaster but an opportunity to discover new meaning to her life. After this phase was accomplished, the time came to find the meaning hidden in the suffering. The client was told that suffering without meaning is dangerous and superfluous, and the meaning that she could find in her situation meant seeing life in a different light, to understand that her suffering was not in vain. On the contrary; it could strengthen her spiritually and cause her to continue living for new goals, instead of the care that she gave to her husband during his illness.

The therapeutic discussion laid the foundation for the next phase in the treatment. Work in that phase concentrated on making an inventory of what has remained whole and could serve as basis for her new life: her family, her economic resources, her friends, and her own strong personality. When this client accepted the fact that she had reasons to live, she was able to free herself from her deep mourning.

People who suffer from the blows of fate can find a cure for their suffering and pain by applying logotherapy's philosophy, principles, and attitude to life, as presented earlier in this book. The human spirit is capable of remaining healthy, even in a damaged body. Those who have experienced a loss of something that was meaningful for them in their previous life can relate to the blow of fate that befell them as something beyond their control. They can change their attitude to this event and continue to move forward on the path of life, find new meaning to their existence, and be cured mentally. The specifically human capacity of saying yes to life and the defiant spirit of the human being (in the logotherapeutic sense) are two of the most important armaments in an older person's struggle for survival.

10

Despair as Mortal Illness in Aging

I knew seventy-year-old Mr. Smith (not his real name) for a long time prior to his retirement as a happy man. Mr. Smith had a good job in public service where he was esteemed and respected by his co-workers. He was also respected by his large family, his many children, and his grandchildren. His physical health was excellent also. Mr. Smith was regarded by his neighbors and many friends as an easy-going fellow and a lucky man. Then we lost contact for several years.

When I met him again, I was surprised to discover a different Mr. Smith from the one I had known. He was dejected, meek, and restless. When I asked him what happened, he could not answer my question logically. His physical health had not changed, he said, but his mental health was badly shaken since he had become a retired person. Mr. Smith could have been a happy fellow. He knew that many people would gladly change places with him. Yet, he said, something was missing. However, he did not know what was missing. Was it the work he did previously? No. Did something bad happen to the family? No, everything there was okay. Was his fortune gone? Not at all. But that something was nagging him and he felt close to despair.

Mr. Smith's case is not unique in our days. Similar cases are reported by many elderly people. People are not content with physical existence alone. They are born to work, but their work may be different from one phase of life to the next. One of the paradoxes in life is that people who are conscious of their existence and try to escape social pressures by turning to conformity, instead of being happy about their freedom, are sometimes caught by anxiety, dread, and depression and exhibit a pessimistic outlook on life.

When normal and balanced, life is a synthesis between personal and universal ingredients of freedom and discipline, spirituality and binding values, existence and essence. When this living synthesis is broken, one of the ingredients dominates the others and causes damage to the entire system.

The suffering of the individual, constant preoccupation with troubles and failures and the closeness of death, so characteristic of old age, become the yardstick for measuring existence in the present. People forget about all that was already achieved in their long lives.

In their struggle to free themselves from limitations and to care for only what is good for them, people may lose the reason for their existence. And this is what stands behind the pessimistic outlook on life that, in its worst manifestation, ends in nihilism, in negation of all moral values commonly accepted by society. It is important to remember that existence is not just a physical fact. Human existence means actualization of God-given potentials beyond the biological sphere of life.

It seems that modern gerontology has forgotten about the phenomena of despair among the aged. The same can be said about literature, psychology, and poetry. Although there are literally hundreds of studies about depression among the young and the old, many of them subsume despair under depression. Empirical research in logotherapy and meaning-oriented psychotherapy (Batthyany and Guttmann, 2005) published in the past twenty-five years has found that, among the two dozen studies devoted to depression among older people, none of the studies differentiated between depression and despair.

A computer-based search discovered only a handful of writings on despair and almost none in connection with aging. This chapter deals with the concept of despair in philosophy, relying on the writings of the great Danish writer-philosopher Søren Aabye Kierkegaard (1813–55), who devoted much effort to this subject. The chapter also presents logotherapy's attitude to coping with despair and offers ways to prevent it in old age.

DESPAIR AS MORTAL ILLNESS

The historical roots of existentialism as a philosophy are embedded in the nineteenth century. At that time the Danish philosopher Kierkegaard came to the conclusion that each individual human being is essentially alone and lacks support in a cold and meaningless universe.

Kierkegaard (1813–55) was not a philosopher in the traditional sense of this term, but rather a religious spirit, a man who struggled with the ruling philosophy and created, while struggling with the prevailing forces, his own philosophy, which later became an important factor in the basis of existentialism. His ideas and analyses of human existence were decisive for the philosophical trend of existentialism in the twentieth century. His basic interest centered on two questions: How can I as an existing subject connect with God? And how can I in my existence understand myself?

Kierkegaard was a highly productive writer, a lonely and eccentric figure, deeply sensitive and morally courageous, and one of the greatest thinkers of all times. His literary-philosophical works are paradoxical in their titles as well as their content. He bore great suspicion of both organized religion and science and maintained that human beings exist in loneliness and are connected only to God.

Kierkegaard published part of his works under a pseudonym, fearing that his attack on the Christian Church would result in very serious retaliation. The bulk of his writings revolve around the idealistic and absolute demands made of a Christian at the highest level. These demands are emphasized in his books: *Either/Or* (1971), *Fear and Trembling* (1954), *The Concept of Dread* (1991), and elsewhere. He also maintained that despair is sin, but its opposite is faith. His works became known throughout Europe thanks to two German professors, each of whom made a name for himself in philosophy: Karl Jaspers (1883–1969) and Martin Heidegger (1889–1976). These professors helped make Kierkegaard's works well-known and provided new explanations.

According to Kierkegaard (1993), lack of faith leads to despair, and this despair is a mortal illness that kills human beings. This despair is worse than any physical illness, because it involves the death of the spirit, and this death is terrible for human beings, who spiritual in their essence. Thus this illness is the illness of the self, or a pathological attitude to oneself. And this attitude to the self is known as despair, which, for a Christian, is a sin.

People fall into despair as a result of worldly, eternal, and personal factors, and the anxiety that follows despair is like the "dizziness of the heights of freedom." This despair stems from what the desperate person sees as the gap and distance between what is and what ought to be. This is a despair that resembles a deep gorge filled with depression, melancholy, and dejection. The following case illustrates this feeling.

Mrs. Leroy (not her real name), aged seventy-one, agreed to see a logotherapist mainly to "get rid of her children's nagging." She was a survivor of a great disaster and lived alone in the northern part of the country. In the discussions that she had with the therapist, she disclosed that she lived with a depressing feeling that "she had missed her life." As a young girl, she wanted to be an actress and dreamed about a great career. She was endowed with the necessary means for her wish: a slim figure, prettiness, intelligence, a quick wit, and great imagination. Unfortunately, she said, she made a big mistake. After emerging from the disaster that swept over the community in which she lived and getting back on her feet, she married a much older man, whom she adored, and had to relinquish her dream. Her marriage lasted forty years and ended in the death of her husband. During this long time she seemed outwardly happy and satisfied, but when alone with herself, she was unhappy. Mrs. Leroy was afraid to admit that she had made a big mistake when she refused to listen to her conscience, which had told her not to accept his proposal of marriage, and she suffered a lot from her "pangs of conscience." And now, she repeated over and over: "It is late. Life has passed and I am in mourning not only for my husband but mainly for myself."

DESPAIR AS FAILURE OF DEVELOPMENT

Each of us experiences situations in our lives that cause lack of tranquility or peace of mind and anxiety stemming from the unknown or from our very existence. As there are bodily illnesses that affect the human spirit, so there is also despair that is within the soul of the human being. And this despair hits us at times with an anxiety that is impossible to explain. This despair is characteristic of older people who have failed to achieve wholeness by accepting their lives. According to research in aging, many older people are living in this state.

Many older people are not aware of their spiritual condition and believe that they are in despair. Many others think that they are in despair when, in actuality, they are not. Only the well-trained professional in medicine, psychiatry, psychotherapy, or social work can differentiate between the two kinds of despair. People can pretend and play at being in despair, and they can mix despair with all kinds of symptoms, both bodily and mental. Yet, although these may pass without resulting in despair, the pretension itself is the real despair.

Despair is different from a physical illness in that there is no need to feel sick in order to be in despair. Feeling ill is a sure sign of illness, and someone who has never felt ill is the one who is in despair. Anybody can claim that he or she is in despair without playing games or pretending. Such a person is closer to regaining health than the one who says that he or she is free of despair.

The fact that this illness, this despair, is hidden is a catastrophe. Despair can dwell inside a person in such a way that it is impossible to discover. Despair can hide in people at such depths that they cannot know about its existence. On the other hand, whoever believes has the best medication against this poison called despair. This medication is the possibility that, by faith, all things are open and may be obtained any minute. The fatalist is in despair and, as such, has lost the self; everything is perceived by him or her as necessary.

Kierkegaard perceived human beings as a synthesis between the finite and the infinite, the temporary and the eternal, freedom and necessity. The synthesis is the relationship between these elements. This synthesis, however, is not the full human being. When people relate to themselves consciously, they gain their own self. And when they do not realize their synthesis or misunderstand it, they fall into despair. This despair is an indication that a person does not want to be himself or herself. This refusal to be one's own self is what Kierkegaard calls sin.

LOGOTHERAPY'S ATTITUDE TOWARD DESPAIR

The ideas of despair are dealt with differently in logotherapy. According to Frankl (1986), people have two unique traits that raise them above the level of animals: the ability to distance themselves from their symptoms and perceive themselves from the outside and the ability to rise above and beyond themselves. The latter, called by Frankl self-transcendence, is a spiritual capacity in its essence, and it verifies the fact that human existence is directed toward something different than the self. It is directed toward fulfillment of meanings. And only in the sense that human beings live their self-transcendence do they become truly human and actualize themselves (*The Doctor and the Soul*, p. 294).

Logotherapy's attitude toward despair is different from that of the existentialist philosophers: Frankl coined the concept of existential vacuum in *The Doctor and the Soul* (1986), which was originally published in 1946. What Frankl originally termed existential vacuum was the feeling of a lack of understanding and doubts about the meaning of life and lack of interest in it. This feeling of emptiness is characterized by lack of self-assurance about finding meaning in life. This feeling in itself is not an illness, but, if it persists without medical or therapeutic intervention, it may end in despair.

Existential vacuum can emerge in any individual, irrespective of social standing, gender, occupation, or religion—as opposed to an animal, which acts in accordance with its drives and instincts. These are insufficient for humans to serve as guides, because they have deteriorated in the nature of biology. Even religious tradition cannot serve this purpose, for most human beings are not religious in the traditional sense. Thus many people do not know what they want and are willing to satisfy themselves with what other people want or with what their leaders want and to follow them without thinking.

Logotherapy emphasizes the importance of gaining distance from symptoms that cause mental anguish. This self-distancing is needed to lighten the feeling of despair. Logotherapy maintains that people can distance themselves from harmful symptoms by emphasizing the values that exist, despite the despair, and these can help them overcome the loss. The mourning of Mrs. Leroy is not a mental disturbance, but a normal psychological function. At the same time, it is also an opportunity for discovering new meaning in life. We may speak of mental disturbance only in cases in which the mourning lasts too long, or at least far beyond what is commonly accepted in a given culture as normal mourning, or when that mourning prevents a return to day-to-day life.

When this existential vacuum remains empty, it may fill itself with despair, and the result may be destructive to the mental health of the individual. Frankl related to this kind of despair as one that gives preference to one value over another, so that this value gets absolute control of other feelings and values.

VALUE ORIENTATION AND MEANING

An individual's value orientation has a direct effect on mental health and outlook on the world. The Czech psychologist Kratochwill presented a theory of value orientation at a conference in London in 1968. The theory, based on Frankl's logotherapy, maintained that people can be divided into two groups: those with a pyramid-like value system and those with parallel values (cited by Lukas, 1986a).

In the first group are people for whom one value is far more important than all other values. Such a pyramid-like value system exists in people who have an extremely narrow outlook on the world and attach great significance to this value, tending to perceive it as absolute for them. And, when this world takes a negative turn—such as in loss of fortune, social status, a loved one or by way of an unwanted retirement—their world crumbles and they are left without meaning and values in life: they have put all of their eggs in one basket, so to speak, and all other values are insufficient to serve as replacements for the lost value.

These people usually fall into despair. Lukas (1986a) said that these people also tend toward fanaticism, jealousy, and intolerance toward those who belong to the other group.

People in the group of parallel values are far better equipped for living; they have many values that give meaning to their lives. And if one value should get lost or disappear, others can serve as substitutes for the lost one.

People in both groups can find meaning in their lives. There are people in doubt about the meaning of their lives without necessarily being sick. Yet, the strength of despair is greater among people in the first group, especially when the loss is perceived as a tragedy. For these people, the danger of suicide is more evident, and they should be helped by professionals.

DEFENSE AGAINST FALLING INTO DESPAIR

People are able to defend themselves against falling into despair by freeing a value from its absoluteness, by seeing it in a realistic light as against other values that also exist. This way of seeing things as they are enables people to perceive the loss or the inability to get what they want and for which they yearn—such as love—as something causing sadness, but not despair. Sadness and sorrow are inevitable in life, for almost everybody. People can usually deal with them because they are not paralyzing and are not as destructive as despair. Sometimes the sorrow can even contribute to the feeling of existence in the world. Such sorrow can provide an opportunity for reflecting on the value of life, for gaining new wisdom and a philosophical outlook on human fate.

Another way to escape despair is by commitment to life and by renunciation. Behind despair one finds the pursuit of some value, which blinds the eyes of pursuers until they can no longer see things as they really are. They give this value more meaning and more weight than it deserves beyond all proportion. This kind of behavior is more pronounced in youth than in old age. Young people tend to cling to a certain value with all their hearts and to forget the world around them. Yet older people are also caught in the same behavior. Thus those who are caught by the wheels of despair as a result of their inability to achieve their wishes must learn the secret of renunciation and sacrifice.

The best way to combat despair is by admitting that life means fulfillment of one's central task, of some concrete task that is waiting for that particular individual and nobody else. Fulfillment of the task may lead one to meaningful living. Moreover, fulfillment of the specific task means regaining self-control over one's life. It means that one no longer succumbs to the destructive forces or gives them absolute value (Volicki, 1987, p. 51).

Frankl (1986) developed a therapeutic method called dereflection for overcoming the despair that can befall a person who has lost someone meaningful and beloved. Frankl based this method on people's unique capacity to distance themselves from themselves and from the symptoms that ail them and to take a stand against external situations. They can take a stand against inner situations by using their thoughts, imagination, and memories. In this method of therapy, one disregards the symptom and uses the energy left to do or get something useful for others. The vicious circle cannot be cut by self-pity or by self-hate. Healing comes as a result of one's commitment to enlarge the circle of meaning, to enrich life.

Sometimes clients accuse others for their own failings, saying that such and such a thing happened to them in their childhood, for example, that prompted them to reject the road to responsibility and to become dependent physically or psychologically on substances and on various people. Then the role of the therapist is to turn this "because" into "despite": that is, clients must say to themselves that despite the abandonment experienced in their childhood by their parents—as a result of war, disaster, or any other calamity—and despite lack of support in their struggle for survival, they can show themselves and the world that they are capable of living normally and decently.

In cases of depression and other acute illnesses and negative life events, the role of the therapist is to help clients learn that it is possible to let the waves of life roll over their heads. As long as clients are under the waves, so to speak, they cannot see the horizon. And without seeing the horizon, they are not ready to think about the search for meaning in their life.

The importance of meanings and values in times of despair and doubt in terms of helping people withstand the vicissitudes of life has paved the way for many innovations in psychotherapeutic intervention. Among these techniques, that of appealing to the human dignity of a person has been developed and used with impressive results by Lukas (1986b). The technique rests on the power of suggestion. As such, it is contradictory to the logotherapeutic value of free will. Freedom of the will means respecting clients' rights to decide how they wish to lead their lives, to choose their own way. The logotherapist uses the appealing technique only in cases in which the noetic (spiritual) dimension is temporarily blocked.

We can stay well, Lukas (1986b) says, by using our will power to stabilize our emotional state. Psychosomatic medicine, as Takashima and Frankl have shown, contains both possibilities and explanations for getting sick or for staying healthy and well. If stress can be triggered in the psyche, it can also be prevented by the psyche. The will to live and reach a certain goal strengthens the body's capacity to withstand illness and resist the forces of destruction. Gerontology literature often includes stories of how very old and sick people cheat death by surviving "only until my granddaughter gets married" or "only until Christmas." These people exhibit strength of will beyond the ordinary; they prove the significance of self-transcendence for survival.

Ordinary people have shown repeatedly that a brave personal attitude toward death and dying is dependent only on the person, and not on his or her circumstances. The professional literature in social work and psychology is replete with case illustrations about the use of this technique when dealing with people in despair. Such people are in desperate need of a supporting hand, raising their hopes for survival. Surprisingly, however, hope has not received much attention in modern gerontology. Nevertheless, almost everybody knows that lack of hope can lead to despair and even to suicide, especially among the old. Without hope, without care, without direction, and without a reason to live for something or for someone, a human being may lose interest in life. Enhancing clients' hope and using it to change maladaptive coping behavior can help them get rid of their preoccupation with despair. The following case illustrates this point.

There are many old survivors of the Holocaust who live in despair. One of these, whom I knew and cared for, was seventy-nine-year-old Mr. Green (not his real name). He was sick with diabetes. He told me that "pretty soon" he would die. "You see," he said, "I am completely alone. My entire family perished in the concentration camp. I myself was hardly able to survive and to escape death. As long as I could take care of myself I did so, but now, who needs an old man?" Before I could reply he added, "Who cares? Who cares for one old man?"

"Yes, perhaps you are right," I said. "But, tell me, why you are still here? If you are serious in what you said, you need company. You need people to share your thoughts with, to listen to, from whom to hear that not only you had such horrible and painful experiences. There are others who have experienced even worse things and whose circumstances are more depressing than yours. It is important that you hear that there are many happy occasions which they experience and these are open for you too. Are you really serious about throwing away your life?" The old man kept silent for a long while. Then he sighed and said, "Perhaps you are right. I really didn't think about the others. I was too busy with my own sorrow. You are right. I know several survivors whose conditions are far worse than mine, people hardly alive, and nevertheless they seem to be enjoying every minute, every meeting with others. Perhaps I should join them."

Part Two

Applied Aspects of Meaningful Living in Old Age

11

The Gifts of the Gods: Sources for Discovering Meaning in Life

If many ways are closed for you, look at the vast fields of action still open before you in which you can be useful to society. (Seneca, 1997, *On Mental Calmness*, p. 22)

Logotherapy relates to the world in many ways. Each of these is built on values anchored in the culture in which one lives. In *The Doctor and the Soul*, Frankl (1986) says that our values and our philosophical attitude to life give us a limited perspective on the world, like a cross-section: The values that guide our lives are related to the tasks that we are fulfilling. Life demands the use of spiritual flexibility to use well the opportunities for finding meaning that are thrown in our path.

According to logotherapy, there are at least twelve ways in which we can discover and find meaning in our lives, some of which have already been mentioned in this book. The first three, which these constitute Frankl's original and basic ways for finding meaning in life, will be explicated in detail and the rest will be described briefly.

1. The passive way, which relies on personal experiences that one gains in encounters with nature and other human beings.
2. The active way, which relies on human creativity and actions.
3. The attitudes we take toward the inevitable events in our lives.
4. The way of symbolic growth, meaning that some special life event or experience causes us to undergo a very important change in our behavior that may result in a feeling of spiritual growth.
5. The way of discovering our real being and understanding who we are and what we want to be or to become.
6. The way of choice, meaning the use of our freedom to choose—from various alternatives—the one that can give meaning to our lives.

7. The feeling that we are unique and different from other human beings, along with the decision to use this uniqueness in the service of an ideal or for other human beings.

8. The way of responsibility, the way of our intention to accept full responsibility for our decisions.

9. The ability to transcend ourselves, above and beyond ourselves, in special situations.

10. The ability to turn guilt feelings into a lever for doing something positive and useful. (Chapter Eleven in this book is devoted to this important way.)

11. The ability to discover meaning in suffering and pain.

12. Accepting the fact that life is transitory and that we are the only creatures on this Earth who are aware of their own deaths. This discovery should lead us toward the reawakening of our responsibility toward life, rather than to the denial of death's existence.

Logotherapy has broadened the concept of meaning by incorporating spiritual meaning into its theory of human motivation. Spiritual meaning means relating to the world via the three worlds of values, each of which hold possibilities for finding meaning in life:

1. The world of experiences, or the world of experiential values, such as meetings and departures; love; hate and other sensual experiences, such as looking at nature and experiencing its beauty, enjoying works of art; listening to music; and many other emotional and sensual experiences derived from this basically passive attitude to what we get freely from the world.

2. The world of creativity, or the world of creative values, which includes all of those activities that contribute to the world. This world has almost limitless expressions. Each human being contributes something to the world, at least in theory, even if this contribution is related to procreation alone, as Nietzsche cynically remarked. Creativity is not limited to age, gender, religion, or to physical condition. It stems from the inner life, from the human imagination, spirituality, and soul.

3. The world of attitudes, or the world of human relationships, is connected to the way that people relate to their fate and destiny and to the events in their lives that cannot be changed, such as suffering and pain because of illness, accidents, terror, and death. What is especially important in this last of the three worlds is the attitude that one takes toward what happens and doing the right and appropriate thing in the situation at hand.

THE IMPORTANCE OF MUSIC TO ONE'S SOUL

The ancient Greek philosophers Plato and Aristotle saw in music the gift of the gods and connected music with *logos*, the human spirit, as divine gifts for humankind. Thus we refer to the great works of Mozart and Beethoven, for example, as heavenly music. Music uplifts the soul. It creates a quest for beauty, wonder, and grandeur that is difficult to express in words. Music fills the human heart with hope, gives strength, power, and courage, and can push us to action. It is hard to imagine someone, unless that person were completely deaf, whose eyes would not fill with tears on hearing the "Choir of the Slaves" in Verdi's opera *Nabucho*.

Music enables us to accept our existence on this Earth more easily. It reminds us that, despite everything, despite all of the troubles and calamities of life, there is still beauty in the world, sense in life, and reason and meaning in suffering and in the fight for survival. Music is the elixir for an aching heart.

Classical and popular music can awaken the heart, soul, and spirit and, via the beauty of the sound, give new meaning to life. The same applies to religious music, which can uplift the soul to heaven and fill the entire being with awe. For many older people, music, and especially religious music, can be part of the experiential world of values that Frankl described in some of his major works. Today it is almost taken for granted that music has therapeutic powers for all ages, but particularly for older people. Music can bring back long-forgotten feelings and memories, open new vistas, and suggest new areas for meaningful activities, even in advanced age.

THE THERAPEUTIC POWER OF MUSIC IN OLD AGE

A noted cantor in the Jewish religious world told this story about a ninety-year-old person—one of the greatest cantors and composers of Jewish religious music, who taught many famous performers and was a well-known conductor too—who in his old age became blind and lived in a nursing home without doing anything. This old man used to sit all day in the lobby of the nursing home and did not communicate with the other patients or the staff who took care of him diligently. The younger cantor decided, therefore, to try to move this old man by playing for him pieces of religious music that this man had known way back.

"It is impossible to describe the change that happened," said the younger cantor. The old man started to move his lips and hands with the motions of a conductor, tried to sing, and, when asked, knew exactly which piece of music was playing, who composed it, who conducted it, and who performed it. And, from that day on, this man started to communicate and collaborate with his fellow residents in matters of common interest to which he had previously been completely indifferent.

Playing liturgical music during major holy days and Friday evenings provides special meaning for the physically impaired. The therapeutic power of music for older people in particular was evidenced by this author, too. During his sabbatical year in Budapest, Hungary, he was involved, as an advisor to the director of the Jewish Distribution Committee, in setting up social, cultural, and recreational services for elderly survivors of the Holocaust and helped establish a social club based on the principles of logotherapy. The purpose was to enable the older people to use their spiritual resources: to uplift their souls, safeguard their human dignity, and strengthen their resolve to spend their remaining years in dignity and creativity.

"Café Stockholm 84" (Fried, 1989) was used as a model for this quest. This model of working with elderly survivors of the Holocaust, and with others as well, has proved to be readily applicable. It is used today in many places, including a social club for survivors in London (Hassan, 1992). The idea is to establish the atmosphere of a Central European café, such as those that were well known in pre–World War II Europe, all over this area of the world and elsewhere, with which the survivors were familiar in their youth. Music plays an important role: The participants sit, drink coffee, and listen to their favorite pieces of music. They enjoy warm and supportive attention from the staff.

Many older people could not learn music in their youth or find time to enjoy music because of the difficulties of providing for their families and growing children. A creative idea employed in this club was bringing a volunteer musician and conductor to teach the older people how to enjoy music. This musician came once a week for the entire year, taught them various pieces of music that were particularly meaningful for them, and explained and demonstrated these pieces on the piano. The result was simply great. The music brought people together and motivated them to contribute their own creativity for the same purpose. It encouraged additional musicians to come and perform voluntarily before this audience.

There were, in addition, lectures on music and singing and visits to the opera and to concerts. The high point in these activities was forming a choir, which the old survivors organized, conducted, and maintained. Participants emphasized that they had gained an important and meaningful experience. The music they heard, composed, nurtured and developed, along with the singing and the choir, opened a new world for them, the world of meaningful experiences, and it changed their entire lives.

LITERATURE AS A SOURCE OF JOY AND MEANING IN OLD AGE

One of the most pleasurable ways of finding meaning in life in old age is via literature. Older people who are able to read or have someone read to them can find satisfaction in reading the works of great writers, poets, and thinkers. Literature opens new ways for human relationships and enables the older person to sail to reality or to the world of the imagination as they are reflected in literary creations.

There are aged people who never needed books in their long lives. It is hard to imagine that these people would become bookworms all of a sudden. Those who were always attracted to literary masterpieces continue to engage in the effort, even in their advanced years, and enjoy reading their favorite books. This can be seen in the large numbers of old people who flock to book fairs, libraries, and lectures and presentations by writers, poets, and literary critics and who watch programs about books and literature on television or listen to radio presentations.

Literature in its broadest sense offers approaches to cultural, psychological, and social phenomena; it opens new ways to personal and professional connections. It enables therapists and the aged to deepen their self-knowledge and to take a stand against the variety of human problems with which it deals. Literature turns to the social reality as an integral part of living and encompasses the worlds of many generations and their relationships, including their complex perceptions and attitudes to life. Literature enlightens the connections among the generations, deals with the eternal problems of human beings, describes the struggle for survival and for preserving dignity in old age, and provides new meaning to the concept of mental health.

Literary creativity is not diminished with advancing age. Only in the romantic myths developed during the seventeenth and eighteenth centuries did some people claim that creativity weakens with advancing years. Older writers, poets, and philosophers are free of social conventions. They are aware of the opposing forces in human life; they are aware of the tragic and the comic dwelling together in the human soul. Important examples of this tragic co-existence are found in works such as Cervantes's *Don Quixote,* Voltaire's *Candide,* and Thomas Mann's *The Confessions of Felix Krull.* In each of these works, emphasis is placed on wisdom, morality, and the lessons that the young can acquire from the older generation.

Literary creations are a special art and mystery that are ageless. In many literary works, there is a revolt of the aged against the tyranny of youth. There is also a serene acceptance of the facts of life. From the poverty that accompanies the aging of many great writers and poets, great works of art are sometimes born. The artistic achievement gives impetus for further struggle with the vicissitudes of life, for creation and expression.

Many great works in literature were completed when their creators were old: Cervantes was sixty-eight years old when he finished writing *Don Quixote;* Tolstoy was eighty-eight when he wrote *What Is Art?;* Sigmund Freud was sixty-seven when he published *The Ego and the Id;* and George Bernard Shaw was sixty-eight when he completed the play *Saint Johanna.*

Engagement with literature does not need to be passive. Each older person has a fascinating life story based on the simple fact that she or he has lived a long life and has experienced many events, has had many successes and failures, illnesses and accidents. What is particularly interesting in each such life review is how the older person was able to survive and cope with difficulties.

A story based on real-life experiences is always fascinating. In such a tale, we can detect worlds that are hidden from one that has no knowledge about them, and in each there are opportunities for responding to life's demand of all of us. Writing enables people to perceive their life and the lives of others from a distance, to discover hidden elements, to gain new understanding or at least a different one. This understanding is both fascinating and painful.

LOVE'S MANY FACES IN THE SECOND HALF OF LIFE

Like the richness of life, with its never-ending changes, so are love and sex rich with change in the second half of life. Attitude to erotica is different from one individual to the next. Experience teaches that, if there are no physiological problems, illnesses, or loss of desire and interest, sexual life can go on for many years, in old age as well as in the second half of life.

Erotica continues to be a central factor, even at advanced ages. Charlie Chaplin, for example, became a father when he passed the age of eighty. There are others who are happy to end their sexual activities much earlier. Many women are happy when they become free of their marital obligations toward their husbands. These are usually women who were unhappy in their sexual lives long before they reached old age.

Many aging men are running after younger women to prove to themselves that they are still macho. They tend to relate to their sexual powers as the expression of their self-worth. Loss of their masculine power is like a death sentence for them. No wonder that they seek all kinds of medications to strengthen their self-image.

In the second half of life, when the family nest becomes empty, a crisis may happen in the life of the aging couple. All of a sudden the partners find themselves face-to-face with the new reality, and they must learn anew how to relate to each other. Therefore, it is important to learn how to awaken and to keep alive the sexual attraction that existed in the beginning of the couple's life.

In the second half of life, gradually, and, in later years, with growing urgency, the need arises to add a spiritual dimension to sexual life, in addition to its physical aspects. It is preferable that the emphasis on physical satisfaction give way to satisfactions whose sources are embedded in tenderness, appreciation of the partner's personality, and the desire to build a new co-existence based on mutual respect.

It is hard to withstand the many temptations that exist in the modern world and impossible to root them out. Desire is stronger than ability, and, when the two are not in accord, the aging individual is condemned to suffering. The beauty of youth may attract both sexes in such force that they may not withstand it at times. One can use humor and irony to combat this situation. (It is told that two old men, aged eighty-five, were walking in a park when all of a sudden a beautiful young lady in her twenties passed them. One of them said to the other with a great sigh, "If I could be seventy!") One may also use techniques of de-reflection, such as exercises, meditation, and yoga, to withstand temptation. Above all, there is a need to balance sexual life by learning anew the art of love in its broadest sense.

Love is the subject of some of the greatest novels ever written. Two love stories are provided here for illustration and for whetting the appetite of those who would like to read more about this fascinating subject: *Death in Venice* (1994), Thomas Mann's classic novel, deals with a utopian love of a middle-aged or "pre-elderly" man for a painfully beautiful young lad he meets in the city of the gondolas. The mature man is strangely attracted to the beauty, the perfection, and the art that, in his eyes, dwell together in this young creature. That beauty fascinates and enchants the older man, and, in order to be near the beautiful boy, he is ready to face ridicule, laughter, and derision. In the end, this man even falls victim to the plague that spreads through the city.

This story reminds us that each individual has a dream that combines reality with imagination, but not many older people are willing to take the risk of living their dreams in actuality. The ones who dare may gain a wonderful gift, that of discovering meaning in their lives.

A literary hero endowed with a courageous heart for realizing his dream and erotic love for his beloved is the eighty-four-year-old "King of the Confection." Roman Gary's (1980) unforgettable book *The Dread of King Solomon* describes the old hero's great love for Cora, his companion before the Nazi invasion of Paris, and his search for her after the war ended. Cora was a well-known singer during those times, but because of her association with a Nazi officer, she was shunned and forgotten. Now, at age sixty-five, she lives in destitute circumstances. The King himself—as is commonly known in the city—became rich from his thriving confection business after the war and devoted his life to charity. He meets Jan, a young taxi driver and jack-of-all trades and occupations, who serves as messenger for the King and as deliveryman of the gifts and presents that the King sends regularly to many needy aged people.

Gary describes the old man beautifully, with much love, as a forceful older man, dressed in an elegant suit made of durable long-lasting cloth, who defiantly visits the fortune teller to prove that he still has a future, exercises regularly, and is looking in a matchmaker's office for a long-lasting marriage, a partner in life.

Both elderly heroes are lonely people. Both are unhappy and suffering and they desperately need each other. Jan, with his realistic attitude to life, understands their loneliness and longing and arranges a meeting between the King and Cora. This fateful meeting leads to the reunion of the former lovers and to the blossoming of a great and enthusiastic love.

Love's great power can withstand all of the vicissitudes of life and the vagaries of fate. It is strong enough to hold during even the greatest storms and trials in life. The hero is equipped with a strong yet sensitive character and is wise enough to do good things for others while he is still able. The old hero in this moving book understands that his wealth can buy almost anything, except what he yearns for—love.

The King is a model of healthy old age, the living example of logotherapy's attitude to life, a hero who Gary's talent has breathed life into. This man exemplifies Frankl's own attitude to life, of saying yes to life despite all of the limiting circumstances. This "despite" has great value for survival in old age, as Gary tells us via his hero; he calls on all of us to emulate him.

MEANINGFUL INTERGENERATIONAL RELATIONSHIPS

Grandfathers and grandmothers serve as important models for their grandchildren. They are necessary links between past and future. The stories they tell about places, events, and people; the photos they show; the sayings they repeat; the advice they give; and the love and kindness they bestow on the young generation work in two ways. For their own children and grandchildren, they enliven meaningful life events in the past. They also refresh family traditions and enable the next generations to take part in their experiences, feelings, and memories. They get recognition that they have something of value to pass on to the younger generations.

Although some aging people are convinced that their children and grand-children have no interest in those memories, because they are connected to a different historical time, research on the next generation, and especially on grandchildren, has shown that this is not true. Many elderly people kept their memories hidden deep inside their souls. Today they know that they made a mistake. Adult children and young grandchildren are interested to learn from the past, especially about events related to their own extended family.

Oscar Wilde (1856–1900) wrote a beautiful story for children and adults called *The Selfish Giant* (1990). In the story a giant chases away the children who are playing in his garden and even builds a high wall to keep them out so that he can hide from the world. But the giant gets punished; the garden remains empty and forlorn. Without the children, spring refuses to come to his place. When the children sneak back to the garden, everything fills with joy, laughter, and life.

The behavior of the giant resembles many aging people who, in their old age, search for a place to stay alone and even erect walls around themselves. These walls are not made of bricks and stones, yet, like real walls in the physical sense, they are built for the same purpose—to keep others from entering their inner lives. When people keep on building walls and strengthening them, there is a danger that they will indeed keep the spring away, keep the joy of life away. In order to pull the lonely old person out from his garden, physically and emotionally, there is a need to renew his or her connections with the human (social) world.

The connection between the children and the giant resembles the connection of the aging individual with the younger generations as it gradually turns into a con-nection of mutual love. In a beautiful passage in the story that touches the heart, Wilde tells us how the giant arrived at the decision to destroy the wall and let the children freely enter the garden: When a small boy tried to climb on a tree and did not succeed, the giant helped him, lifted the small boy, and placed him on a branch, and suddenly his heart was filled with joy and love. This feeling was intensified when the small boy put his arms around the giant's neck and kissed him.

Generations are social units connected in a given historical time, in which there are changes and continuity. Today there are many opportunities for finding meaning in life by fostering better connections among the generations. Yet not every individual knows how to use the opportunities that are open.

In the work of the South African writer, Ran Jacobson, for example, *The Zulu and the Zaide* (Brody, 1995), the story focuses on an older white parent whose son disregards his father's need for love and care, and his place in the family is taken over by a young black servant from the Zulu tribe. This servant is endowed with wonderful sensitivity and tact and cares for the old father with devotion and kindness. The connection between them becomes stronger and stronger with each passing year until the old man dies. The son learns too late what he has missed and must live with his bad conscience throughout his life.

Love of a small child for an old man, not his grandfather, is the subject of a story by the Israeli writer Nira Harel (1981). "Koby Knows" is a story about an old man who cannot find the house he lives in and cannot remember the family name of his son, who has changed his name from Polish to Hebrew. This old man is called by the children in the neighborhood "Hayim Eyeglasses." Koby is a lonely child, the only son of a divorced mother who came to live in this neighborhood not long ago and who, so far, has not adjusted to life in the new environment.

Hayim Eyeglasses has no grandchildren. Koby sees him as an old, weak, and lost man. The old man arrived by mistake at the apartment of Koby. This mistake created new meanings in the lives of these heroes in the story. The child adopts Hayim Eyeglasses as his grandfather, and the old man gains a grandchild. They need each other and together they complete each other's lives.

Each generation must transfer to the next the strength for dealing with its own aging. The strength of the old is expressed in wisdom, beginning with the knowledge that has accumulated and ending with good judgment. When this wisdom is spiced with spiritual energy and joy of life and combined with voluntary renunciation of all superfluous things, such as vanity and honors, some old people can teach the younger generation how to age with dignity, without falling into despair.

In the second half of life, Erikson (1964) says that people close the circle of their life. This closing is not done linearly. Thus it points to the possibility of a new beginning, to renewal. That renewal can happen in the second half of life. Sometimes the same beginning is expressed as a return to the wonderful traits of childhood: curiosity, joy of life, search for the magic and wonders of nature, and discovery of their meaning. Some people may return to other traits, to the childish ones—to dependency on others or to helplessness.

DISCOVERING MEANING IN OLD-AGE HOMES

The world of an old-age home, with its intricate human relationships, is well known to millions of people in the West and other industrialized countries. Old-age homes contain a cargo of human lives. Each individual is a world in himself or herself, and each world develops its own unique approach to the place and to the people who live there. Many of the new residents in such places live in anxiety about the unknown environment with which they have to cope or, at least, come to terms. Yet even in this world, people can use their unique capacity to rise above and beyond the surrounding physical and social circumstances and conditions and to discover new meaning to their old age.

This world is the subject of great literary creations. One of these I wish to present here for illustration. The famous writer Bohumil Hrabal, winner of the Nobel Prize for literature, whose attitude toward meaning in life has been presented earlier in this book, describes with humor and irony the relationships among the residents of an old-age home and their offspring in his novel *The Millions of Harlekin* (1997).

Hrabal uses an old-age home as an allegory for life itself. A young physician on the premises serves as son and grandson for the residents, bringing new spirit and joy to the lives of the people there by playing classical music and songs that they all know and are familiar with. They can even hum this music together. This music, the "millions of Harlekin," is played all day long, over and over, in every room of the old-age home, and the young doctor recites some words from the poem of Franz Liszt, the composer: "be careful with your words, for a rough word truly hurts; and when you these pronounced; you already regretted. And your heart aches, for you didn't mean" (p. 140).

People can discover meaning in life and enjoy life in many ways: in work, including volunteering, hobbies, and all kinds of creative activities. They can find meaning in travels and hikes in nature, in gazing at the sunrise and the sunset, in the stars and the sea, in lakes and forests. They can find meaning in the many forms and expressions of art, music, dancing, drawing, sculpture, and writing. And above all, they can find meaning in humor and laughter, of which more will be said in the next chapter.

12

The Importance of Humor and Laughter in Old Age

An old man was asked by his friend: "Tell me, what do you do now that you've retired?" His friend answers, "Each morning the maid brings me a cup of tea and the papers. I drink the tea very slowly and read all the obituaries. If my name is not listed, I get up and go for a walk." (Cohen, 1994, p. 368)

The power of humor and laughter as primary means for survival was already noted by the ancient Greeks and Romans in many humorous plays, satires, and poems used on various occasions in the theater and elsewhere. The Bible also contains humor and laughter, but these instances are different from what is commonly perceived as humor and what scholars see as such. In the Bible humor is literary, circumscribed, assumed, and delicate; it requires the reader's use of imagination.

Humor and laughter are seen today as therapeutic, relaxing, and enjoyable values that help people face difficulties, hardships, distress, stressful life situations, and even calamities and traumas.

Attitude toward humor and laughter is always individualistic and subjective. What makes one person burst into laughter is not necessarily so funny to another human being. Cultural background, intellectual level, personal mood, and social attitudes influence the perception of what is humoristic and laughable and channel humor in commonly known and accepted ways in a given society, giving it special character and characteristics.

Some people are quick witted and get the point of a joke in an instant. Others need some time before they perceive what is so funny, and still others need an explanation before they can understand the same joke. And there are the serious ones who will not descend to this level because they have no sense of humor and are afraid to admit it.

Having a sense of humor is such an important personal characteristic that people are willing to accept many weaknesses and shortcomings—except the lack of a sense of humor. A well-developed sense of humor occupies an honorable position among all human values.

There are three areas of creativity that do not contradict themselves: humor, revelation, and art. Karl Marx saw in humor an important factor in the historical development of humankind: "History passes many phases until she puts an old design to rest; and the last phase in that process is comedy." It seems that Marx had a good sense of humor when he added, "Why does history go this way? To let the human race leave the past with a good feeling" (Szalay, 1983, p. 160).

Of the considerable literature on the importance of humor and laughter, this author has selected what he subjectively thinks is relevant and directly connected to the main thrust of this book. In general, there are five groups of theories that deal with humor and laughter—theories that deal with the psychoanalytical perspective; emphasize comical, mismatch, discrepancy, incompatibility, and maladjustment; legitimize the worlds of adults and children; support self-worth and liberation from anxiety; perceive humor and laughter as social roles and stress social communication and critique of society; and emphasize the creativity vested in humor and its symbolical meaning (Cohen, 1994).

Humor as it is perceived today is a relatively new phenomenon. It surfaced mainly during the past three hundred years. The ancient Greeks, for example, perceived humor as a bodily fluid or physiological phenomenon that influenced mood.

Socrates, the wise philosopher in Athens, saw in humor a mixture of what is beautiful and painful in the human soul, and he thought that many human characteristics and traits are connected in this mixture. Even the most tragic thing can create a sense of beauty, as in the ancient Greek tragedies.

Although humor is an abstract concept, its expression in the form of a joke is a kind of art or artistic creation. Humor, as the psychologist Reuven P. Bulka (1989) has said, is one of the most useful ways for the individual to gain distance from a given situation. By laughing at fate, people can get out of themselves and look on fate as if they were watching it from the outside. Humor enables people to gain an ability to rise above and beyond the circumstances in which they live in reality (Bulka, 1989, p. 51).

THE VALUE OF HUMOR IN THE SECOND HALF OF LIFE

Humor's therapeutic value has been known in all cultures for thousands of years, as the literature on this subject indicates. Each nation has its own collections of humorous stories, plays, sayings, proverbs, and so on that show the importance people everywhere attach to humor and laughter.

Modern medicine has also made good use of this human ability. For example, the American writer Norman Cousins (1981) gave an illuminating account in *Anatomy of an Illness* of how he treated himself with laughter after he was sentenced to death by several physicians. Cousins had included in this book the results of a survey involving thousands of doctors as to the therapeutic power of humor and laughter, and the results indicated that laughter is indeed the best medicine.

With its many sides and forms, humor has a direct influence on the physiological and mental functioning of the human being. Mother Nature saw to it that we should relieve ourselves from harmful stresses via laughter, which speeds the functioning of the hormones in our bodies.

Laughter can ease pain or, at least, lets us forget it for a time and thus brings relief to a suffering individual. Almost all physiological systems are influenced by humor and laughter. The latter strengthens the immune system, improves the quantity of oxygen in the blood, activates muscles, relaxes stress, and even helps against constipation. Laughter serves as a proven medication against bitterness, frustration, and despair by breaking the pattern that is characteristic of an ailment.

The special value of humor in old age is vested in its ability to help the aged to cope successfully with the vicissitudes of life. Freud (1982) discovered the importance of the psychological defense mechanisms against the urges of the biological instincts with which we are endowed.

Researchers in gerontology found that, in old age, emphasis should be placed on the mechanisms of coping with physical and mental losses that nobody can escape (Cohen, 1994). These mechanisms are behavioral, emotional, and mental reactions, and they have a two-fold function: they help older people solve problems that cause tensions and they diminish emotional unease that accompanies a stressful situation. Therefore it is important to include humor and laughter, jokes and wittiness, funny stories, anecdotes, play on words, and other literary and poetic content that can cause enjoyment for students and learners in the helping professions, particularly in teaching gerontology, medicine, and geriatrics.

The application in the field of various forms of humor, in appropriate quantity and at the right time, can advance and enhance the health of an older person, spread a good atmosphere in the classroom, raise awareness and creativity in the use of humor, and put a therapeutically useful and enjoyable tool in the hands of the therapists who are working with older individuals.

Humor is one means that can be used in actively fighting tensions, as well as in the search for knowledge to understand a situation and act for change. This form of coping with problems and stresses that are acting on an older person is of utmost importance; it is the best and most useful strategy for achieving this purpose.

Humor is equal to the enjoyment that people feel when they stumble into a ridiculous situation; it is the ability to laugh at what is hidden in the message for that purpose. Humor is a cognitive ability to perceive human relationships and ideas in an uncommon way.

The social value of humor and laughter is well known. They serve as the glue that promotes feelings of solidarity and internal cohesion, relieves tensions and conflicts, helps overcome crises, and creates a pleasant atmosphere. An older person with a sense of humor is better for a group than an angry and quarrelsome one. People who know how to keep their sense of humor and use it wisely are more readily accepted by their peers and by the younger generation. Humor can change a person's attitude to the world and to the reality in which he or she lives; its therapeutic value is priceless.

Laughter enables us to escape from the humdrum activities of daily life. This is most probably the reason why most people turn first to the daily comics and cartoons in the newspapers. Laughter permits the renewal of strength and powers. It also has practical aspects: it brings a good feeling in its wake and helps us overcome boredom and fatigue. Its main benefit is in the mental tranquility that it causes. Laughter has a positive influence on human physiology.

The famous philosopher Immanuel Kant (1724–1804) placed laughter next to hope and sleep as the most beneficial means of renewing the soul. There are educational results, too, that are connected to laughter. People learn more easily and with greater joy and enthusiasm when the material for learning is offered in a humoristic way. Laughter enables people to escape the burden that they feel in situations that involve a feeling of inferiority. When we laugh at something or someone, we feel, at least temporarily, superiority over the one at whom we are laughing.

FREUD'S ATTITUDE TOWARD JOKES

Freud first published his serious work "The Joke and Its Relationship to the Unconscious" in 1905, after he had systematically collected Jewish jokes since 1897. This collection represents a much-respected contribution to the prevailing social, cultural, and worldview of those times. This book was a serious analysis of the joke's technique. Freud was not only a master of the human psyche, but he also showed his serious attitude to jokes in general and to their importance in the psychological lives of human beings.

The essence of a joke is to enable one to find hidden meaning in two opposing things. The joke may be defined as giving meaning to what appears to be lacking meaning. It is based on surprise and on instant insight. The body and soul of the joke are the brevity with which it achieves its point.

The joke is always aimed at unity, yet in a humoristic form. For example, people's lives have two parts: in the first part, they say to themselves, "I wish I were already living in the second part." In the second part, they say, "I wish I were living in the first part."

Another example is a joke attributed to Lichtenberg as told by Freud (1982, p. 82): "The month of January is the month in which man sends cordial greetings to his friends; and the rest of the months are spent wishing that they will not materialize."

What is common to both jokes is that they use the same material—the first part of life as opposed to the second part, or the month of January as opposed to all the rest of the months—that is, known materials, but in a different and original form that unites the content and forms humor and laughter.

As for the means that the joke uses, Freud made a comparison of the joke with the dream and saw that they have similar lines, despite differences. The similarities include concentration and reduction, transference (in the Freudian sense), a mistaken argumentation and reasoning, absurdity, double meaning, a multitude of meanings, contrariness, and repeated use of the same material in its entirety or partially (p. 58).

Freud also differentiated between naïve and purposeful jokes. The latter he described as expressing forbidden contents, hostility, and vulgarity and as enabling the satisfaction of an instinct, passion, or hostile feeling toward something that blocks the way for these to act. They circumvent the block and, along the way, produce enjoyment from the same source—access to which the block has closed.

Freud was aware of the importance of logical mistakes included in the joke, and he used these to show the unconscious intentions in human behavior. The source of producing pleasure by humor is in the emotions. In his important essay on the joke and its relationship to the unconscious, Freud presented many illustrations from the treasury of Jewish jokes, particularly some of the comical characters and situations that characterize these jokes.

Of the many characters in Jewish humor, Freud emphasized four that represent the special ability of this much-persecuted people to find laughter even amid terrible situations: the luckless, the beggar, the matchmaker, and the naïve. They serve as inexhaustible material for jokes.

The following is an illustration of the many jokes on the matchmaker: A matchmaker offers a bride to a young man, but he finds all kinds of shortcomings in her and in his future mother-in-law. The young man says, "I don't like my mother-in-law. She is an old and stupid woman." The match-maker replies, "But you don't marry her, only her daughter." "Yes," says the young man, "but the bride is no longer young and is far from being beautiful." "So what?" says the matchmaker, "she'll be more faithful to you." "But she has little money," says the young man. "Who is talking here of money?" asks the matchmaker. "Do you want money or a wife?" "But she is a hunchback, too, in addition to all the rest," says the young man. "So what do you think, young man?" asks the matchmaker, "that she will be without blemish?" (Freud, 1982, p. 78)

Freud investigated the unconscious elements included in the joke, the hoax, and anecdotes in his cultural environment and found that the joke is the most popular. Jokes provide opportunities for more meaningful enjoyment. They enable one to express unconscious emotions, attitudes, and thoughts; only a joke can make the point and, without the point, there is no joke. The joke tries to give the most laughter and happiness to the second party. We cannot laugh at our own jokes. When we tell a joke or anecdote to another person, we enjoy it ourselves, and we laugh with that person, even if to a lesser degree.

THE JOKE AS A MEANS FOR SURVIVAL

Freud (1982) wrote that humor is the opposite of acceptance. Humor is teasing that promises the victory of the ego and the principles of pleasure that can express itself in this form, despite the distress or hardship. Freud saw in humor medication against pain. He wrote: "As a means of defense against pain, humor occupies a place in the long line of methods that people have built and used to free themselves from the tensions that the pain creates" (p. 163).

The joke opens the door to unconscious energies and enables them to escape from repression. The dream and the joke use similar ways to overcome the barriers that the human consciousness erects to prevent unwelcome and forbidden thoughts from entering the consciousness. Although this clearing or elimination is done by a complex and masked process in the dream, the process used in the joke is less serious. The joke is able to express its real content directly and openly, and the censor (the super ego) has less control of the joke than of the dream.

The joke is the most social of the psychic processes. It needs other people in order to exist. It must be understood by people, despite all of its camouflage of words, in order to cause laughter and joy from the original thought. The joke is a game that, like all games, aims at releasing repressed energy to be used in the service of happiness. It is aimed at the satisfaction of a need via a sly detour of its purpose. It wishes to cause delight. Both of these actions are joined together in mental activity (1982, p. 194).

Only a healthy psyche is able to enjoy humor, and only a healthy individual can laugh without restraint. Laughter heals the soul and defends against sickness. Jewish humor, for example, is aimed at one who has experienced loneliness as a result of his or her faith and religion. Such humor is historically connected to the fate of the Jewish people, the eternal victims of jealousy and persecution. They have shown the world an ability to survive, to rise from the ashes, to blossom, and to resist all attempts to oppress them.

Bulka (1989) tells the classic joke of those four hundred Jews who suddenly died during a pogrom and were rushed up to heaven. The gatekeeper was slightly unprepared and asked a compatriot in hell to take care of these people for one day while arrangements were made to give them proper habitat in heaven. About half way through this period, the gatekeeper of hell called up to his colleague in heaven and said that he could not keep those people there any longer. "What's the problem? Why can't you keep them a little longer?" asked the gatekeeper of heaven. "You see, these people have only been here for less than a day and they have already raised half a million dollars to install an air-conditioning system" (p. 51).

Mobilization of the individual's sense of humor can be used for a host of problems, as Bulka (1989) has stated: "When one is mired in a situation, which taken seriously would lead one to becoming depressed or almost suicidal, then laughing at fate becomes a survival tool par excellence" (p. 51).

Even prisoners in Nazi concentration camps developed humor and used it to survive all of the horrors, atrocities, and dangers in their lives. This kind of humor is called gallows humor. It became an integral part of life in the camps. It protected the courage of the prisoners and raised their morale (Cronstrom-Beskow, 1991).

Humor enabled the prisoners to break the pattern of fear and the expectation of anxiety that enhances it and to control their own destinies to some degree, rather than to remain victims of the instincts that push them to obsessive behaviors. Frankl personally experienced that no amount of persuasion, force, explanation, or guidance suffices for people who are mired in their own fear. Only turning to the human capacity to laugh via humor gets the sought-after result.

APPROACHES TO HUMOR AND JOKES IN LOGOTHERAPY

In his autobiography, *What Isn't Written in My Books* (1995), Frankl said that, for a long time, he toyed with the idea of writing a book about the metaphysical aspects of jokes. To the chagrin of those who knew firsthand his enormous ability to erect and develop new and bold ideas on human behavior, this wish of his did not materialize.

Frankl loved jokes. He had a strong sense of humor, and he used it in social and professional occasions in his lectures and discussions. As a master of humor, Frankl also had a wide range of jokes that encompassed many areas of life and made each meeting with him delightful. His very good sense of humor was known and appreciated all over the world. Frankl knew how to time the punch line of the joke to make listeners laugh with a roar and leave the meeting holding their stomach in laughter.

Here is one joke that Frankl told to friends and family on a joyous occasion: "An old Jewish man who had immigrated to Berlin is walking in the park when a bird overhead lets loose its droppings and they land right on the old man's hat. He takes off his hat, looks at it, and says: "For the gentiles, you sing" (Klingberg, 2001, p. 242).

Humor enables one to emphasize a certain point that otherwise would get lost. Frankl made good use of this in relation to all of the exaggerations that people tend to use because of jealousy, hatred, prejudices, greed, stinginess, and intolerance. Jokes have no limits. They can be used in professional work, too, in medicine and in psychotherapy, as well as in attitudes to politics, nationalism, and in many other areas of social behavior. Frankl used his sense of humor even in the concentration camps, as discussed later in this chapter.

Recruiting one's sense of humor can do miracles, beginning with the use of humor against stuttering, insomnia, facial tics and twitches, uncontrollable shaking, and even, in some cases, impotence. As an example, a man sent to Frankl for help suffered from chronic pain in his hand that was diagnosed as writers' cramp. This man had been an accountant for many years. The pains in his writing hand became more and more bothersome until it became almost impossible to read his handwriting. When Frankl heard this man's story about his untenable and sad situation, he advised him to approach his new job by saying the following: "Now I will show my supervisor what a good scribbler I am. I will have such terrible pain that nobody will be able to read what I write." The first reaction of this man to Frankl's advice was to smile and nod his head in wonder. After a while he agreed to try what Frankl has advised him to do. The result was amazing: the pain disappeared in a few days and did not return, even after a long time during which this man was in follow-up treatment (Bulka, 1989, p. 50).

There are several important differences in the attitude to humor, particularly to jokes, between Freud and Frankl. Freud's interest was motivated mainly by a wish to understand the mechanism of the joke in terms of its physiological and psychological characteristics. Frankl, on the other hand, wanted to understand why the joke can serve as a roadblock to anxiety.

In Frankl's *Man's Search for Meaning* (1962), he emphasized that humor was one of the most important means for survival. It served as a spiritual victory over the persecutors and murderers. Humor protected the sanity of the prisoners and turned their minds away, even if for a few minutes, from the inhuman conditions in the camps. Derision and laughter helped, even in the hardest and cruelest hours, to ease the suffering and torture of the prisoners.

Frankl wrote that he practically trained a friend who worked next to him on the building site to develop a sense of humor. Frankl suggested to him that they would promise each other to invent at least one amusing story daily, about some incident that could happen one day after their liberation (p. 42).

Frankl realized those elements that make laughter such a valuable medicine in the hands of a quick-witted and well-trained therapist: the surprises contained in turning the same objects that the patient fears into tools to heal him; exaggerating the fear to the extent that it becomes laughable, while maintaining a serious attitude; the willingness of the therapist to take an active part in the humorous situation to bolster the patient's self-confidence; and the enabling function, so that the client discovers and realizes that fear can be controlled, even extinguished, by the power of laughter.

Frankl's discovery of the mechanism by which underlying anxiety can be turned around and used for the treatment of neuroses is truly a testimony to his creativity. As soon as the patient stops fighting his or her obsessions and tries instead to ridicule them by irony and by applying paradoxical intention, the vicious circle is cut, the symptom diminishes, and the obsession finally atrophies.

Confronting fear is the best medicine to overcome a phobia, Frankl declared. He cited his own encounter with such a situation: On a mountain climbing occasion that happened on a rainy day, Frankl witnessed the fall of one of the climbers into a ravine some 200 yards below. The man miraculously survived. Two weeks later Frankl climbed along the same steep path, and once again it happened to be a rainy day. Yet, despite the psychological shock that he had experienced two weeks earlier, he was able to overcome his fear and the mental trauma that he had suffered.

Frankl (1985) stated that it is important to assess when to use logotherapy and paradoxical intention and in which cases their use may bring about unwanted results. For example, Peter (not his real name), a sixty-eight-year-old man, came to logotherapeutic treatment on the advice of his friend. The latter was a former client and had known the therapist a long time. Peter was constantly in fear of making mistakes in his work as an accountant in a large corporation. The sense of fear had spread from the workplace to his home. He was particularly afraid of his supervisor, who used to derogate, tease, and plot against him. Each time the supervisor appeared, Peter was flooded with anxiety and dread of meeting that man.

Peter had had an unhappy childhood. His father demanded that he excel in his studies and in sports, and, when Peter could not deliver good results, his father would despise him and say that he was no good and would never succeed in life. It seems as if Peter had internalized the warnings of his father and became slow, lacked self-assurance, and could not trust his intelligence to understand even simple stories and facts. His mind was occupied with thoughts that tortured him, especially with his father's prophesies about the fate waiting for him. Even though he had an aptitude for numbers and mathematics, Peter was not able to concentrate on his work. The fear of making mistakes would paralyze him sometimes for a long time, and his failure to cope with this fear only emphasized the predictions of his father.

The treatment of his fears concentrated at first on strengthening his self-worth and dignity as a human being and enhancing his self-image. There was a need to change his attitude toward the prophecy of his father by concentrating on what he had achieved so far in life despite that prophecy. This required repeated discussions and simple exercises that helped him see that, in several important areas of life, such as work and family life, he had not failed. Peter could find solace by understanding that he knew how to help his children when they needed help. Strengthening his sense of security in himself helped him relax. Now he began to concentrate on the present and the future, rather than on reviewing the past. Also, Peter was able to develop a change in attitude toward his supervisor by using paradoxical intention. Learning this technique taught him to laugh at his fears and to mock and ridicule them.

Lukas (1986a) maintains that the formulations that the patient learns to use must be humorous enough to eliminate serious misgivings and to defuse the fear. (The same technique is detailed on p. 108 in the Hebrew translation of this book by Elisabeth Lukas [1988] *Meaningful Living: A Logotherapy Book.*) At first patients practice these formulations with the therapist. Later, alone, they face the feared situation. Lukas also said that what makes us smile and laugh cannot cause horror.

At the first encounter with this technique, Lukas's client failed to perceive the humor behind the words of the therapist. His sense of humor was weak. Yet he was determined to master the homework that he was given at each session until his efforts were fruitful. As a result he gained greater faith in his ability to deal with fearful situations at the workplace and at home.

Breaking the pattern of fear by an exaggerated wish for the very same thing that is feared and replacing it with a healthy attitude to life may bring about a new sense of self and well-being. The unique capacity of human beings to laugh at themselves has been found to be of great importance for survival, in both the clinical and the community sense. As Bulka (1989) stated: "By laughing at defeat, we transcend it; by jesting in the midst of our predicament, we transcend it; by smiling in the midst of depressing circumstances, we retain our individual and group sanity" (p. 58).

13

Dealing with Guilt and Remorse

A seventy-eight-year-old businessman, whom we shall call Mr. Smith, was sick with an incurable illness. He lay in his bed, day after day, and waited for his death. While he waited, he had plenty of time to review his life. He remembered those years in which he was the manager of a large chemical plant. He remembered the effort he invested in the development of the plant that gave him much pleasure and satisfaction. Yet, these could not stop his heart from aching. He became aware of the price he paid for his success: His wife had to give up a career as a gifted teacher to share the burden of managing the business with him, and his three sons gradually became strangers to him.

Mr. Smith was musing to himself that he had lost the opportunity to really know his children, for he had never had time for them. The business absorbed all his energy and interest. Sometimes he had felt pangs from his conscience and could sense that it demanded a change in his behavior, but he didn't listen to these warnings. Now lying on his deathbed, so close to his end, he thought that it was too late to change. He fell into a mood of great dissatisfaction with himself. He felt that he had failed as a father and as a husband.

The philosopher Eva Ancsel (1995), in *Life as an Unknown Story,* states that one's motivations may remain hidden to the extent that sometimes one cannot differentiate between what is real and what is an illusion, between the true and the false. Human beings, and only human beings, have a tendency for self-deception. Animals, by nature, simply cannot do it. This tendency is expressed in wishful thinking, and in harboring the thoughts we wish to believe, regardless of what is true. A human being can cheat, and yet believe his or her actions are right and honest. This self-deception is usually connected to the wish to gain something without paying its price and without carrying responsibility for it.

People are not transparent. We cannot see through them and know what they really feel, think, and imagine. Therefore we do not know whether or not they are sincere with themselves and with the social worlds that encompass them. This lack of transparency gives an individual his or her inner freedom. Only those who are mentally sick wish to and are able to express their inner thoughts without control and without consideration for other people's feelings (Ancsel, p. 39). The lack of transparency is a privilege, says Ancsel, even if it makes cheating possible, for there are times when the cheating and misleading of others are necessary.

In *The Devil in Moscow* Bulgakov (1993) describes an imaginary discussion between Jesus and Pilatus, the Roman Governor of Judea. When he sentences Jesus to death for lack of respect for the Emperor Tiberius and for teaching revolutionary and dangerous ideas, Pilatus is attracted in a strange way to the human quality of Jesus. Pilatus experiences a feeling that what he should do, what is right to do, what is meaningful in this situation is to release this man as one who is not at all dangerous to the people. Pilatus understands that this is the meaning of the moment, yet he listens to the high priest and sentences Jesus to death.

Immediately after the sentencing Pilatus's conscience begins to nag him, yet he disregards his inner feeling; he disregards what is just and true. Pilatus knows that the accused is innocent, yet he acts contrary to his conscience. When Jesus is taken to the place of execution and the sentence is carried out, Pilatus understands that only death will end his pain and suffering. A heavy sadness falls on his soul and pierces his heart. Pilatus has a vague feeling that he missed the opportunity to ask Jesus an important question, and this feeling accompanies him for the rest of his life. In his musings he knows that he has forfeited his responsibility to maintain just relationships with all the citizens in his care, and therefore he will continue to suffer throughout his life because of this failure.

This work is valuable to all therapists due to the insight it provides into the heart and soul of a person. Many older people today can attest to the truth contained in this literary work. The suffering caused by guilt can embitter the lives of those who bear it, and extinguish the joy of life for them.

In the therapeutic work I did with many people who were in the latter half of life, with elderly widows and widowers in particular, I found a phenomenon that was present in almost every case. Each individual tried to explain his or her mental distress by stating that he or she did not listen to the voice of his or her conscience, and did not heed the meaning of the moment when it came. These individuals were afraid to leave the path of social conformity. They did not allow themselves to live their lives as they really wished. They renounced their own wishes in order to please their families, relatives, and friends. Their social standing was more important for them than their own peace of mind.

Giving permission to one's self to behave in accordance with one's unique way of being authentic, to express one's unique personality—without deviating from the right path—is essential for mental and spiritual health for everybody, including old people. It is imperative for therapists. This permission is the basis for good therapy, while for the client it is an achievement. Giving permission to the client to be unique and authentic is the first step in the client's long journey to become a really authentic individual. The following case is presented for illustration:

A woman we will call Mrs. Cahn, aged sixty-nine, recently became a widow and complained of headaches, dizziness, and a dull feeling of anxiety and depression. These symptoms were familiar to her. During the forty-two years of her marriage she had experienced similar feelings rather frequently, but she used to ignore them as by-products of the tensions of modern living. When her husband died, she lost interest in her grandchildren, and didn't want to participate in social gatherings. When her children insisted she be present, she would sit in a corner in complete passivity, withdrawn, and told her family that life had lost interest for her.

At the repeated requests of her children, she agreed to see a therapist. In the first session she said that she had been angry at herself for many years. "You see", she said to the therapist, "I know exactly when I started to have my headaches. The first time it happened was two years after my marriage. At that time we lived in a large city in which I had a good job and many friends, and I was liked by all. I had a dream of being an actress at the local theater. But my husband urged me to move to a smaller place where he could be near his friends. He also had ambitions for a career in politics, and he thought that in that smaller city he could succeed better and more easily than in a bigger one. I had my chances to object to these ideas, but I didn't use them. My heart told me to stay where I felt good, but I gave in and agreed to move. Since then my life has lost its meaning: Outwardly I remained the same and did what was expected of me, but inside I felt frozen. Many times I have felt that I am doing things against my real wishes; that I am sacrificing myself and my dream. I heard my heart telling me to demand that my husband change this situation, but, instead, I escaped to these headaches and depressions. I continued to ignore my real self, my inner self, and see what has become of me."

GUILT AND REMORSE

The sense of guilt constitutes a frequent subject in many works of literature, philosophy, music, religion, and ethics. Guilt and atonement occupy a central role in the courts, in lawmaking, and in the punishment of crimes committed against society. Nevertheless, it is hard to define exactly what is meant by guilt, or wherein its source lies.

According to religious teaching, the tendency to sin is an integral part of life. It is based on human conscience and consciousness, for only human beings can sin. Other creatures lack this ability. A human being who sins generally experiences feelings of guilt. Each sin contains both physical and spiritual dimensions. These indicate that the human being is a spiritual entity. Spiritual sins, if they dominate an individual, are far worse than the physical ones.

The concept of guilt and guilt feeling are usually tied to a certain deed that is perceived by society as bad. When an individual understands that he or she did what was prohibited or bad, as in the Biblical story about eating from the Tree of Life, or the killing of Abel by his brother Cain, then the person who committed the crime feels guilty.

A human being always has a choice to act in the right way. Departure from that way and doing a bad deed, whether by intention or by mistake, brings in its wake a feeling of guilt. Yet whether we choose the right way, or ignore it and engage in bad deeds, there is no way to escape the responsibility that accompanies the choice. The one who chooses the wrong way is punished by a feeling of guilt which is hard to bear. This feeling can be so intense that it can drive the sinner to suicide, as in Tolstoy's novel *Anna Karenina*.

John Lukacs (2001), the well-known historian and philosopher, differentiates between sin and taboo. Sin as a phenomenon is dependent on social relationships. It cannot be erased from one's consciousness. When we sin, we know that we have sinned, but do not necessarily feel guilty. Yet sooner or later the sin causes us to feel sad and to regret what we did, and even feel responsible for our deeds. These feelings are what we call *guilt feelings*. Taboo, on the other hand, is a strong social prohibition against words, objects, actions, discussion, or people that are considered undesirable or offensive by a group, culture, or society.

Sigmund Freud (1950), in his classic book on *Totem and Taboo*, traced the origin of the taboo to the fear of the presence or return of the dead person's ghost among the savages. This fear leads them to various ceremonies aimed at keeping the ghost at a distance. Freud also has shown that there are many similarities between taboo-holders and obsessive neurotics that point to a psychological condition that prevails in the unconscious. According to Freud, there are two *universal taboos*, incest and patricide (Freud, pp. 26–30).

As in many other areas of human behavior, the subject of guilt and guilt feeling must begin with the attitude of Freud toward these concepts, for he paved the way to modern psychology and psychotherapy. Freud coined the term *super-ego* to explain the concept of conscience. This psychological mechanism represented for him the moral demands society makes of its members. It was perceived as a father figure that commands individual behavior in accordance with the demands of religion and society. According to Freud's theory, disregard for the rules and demands of society causes guilt feelings. His concept of the super-ego was based on the mythological figure of Oedipus; guilt and guilt feelings derive from the psychological complex associated with this figure in the well-known myth. The *Oedipus complex* derives from an old story in ancient Greece about a king whose fate was to kill his father and marry his mother. Oedipus tried to escape this cruel fate, but could not. After he unwittingly committed these terrible crimes, he punished himself with blindness. His mother objected to the investigation of her son-husband and insisted that many men dream of sexual relations with their mothers, yet there is no need to attach much importance to dreams. Freud (1994), in *Introduction to Psychoanalysis*, said, "But we do not disdain the dreams, and especially not typical dreams, those that happen to many people, and we do not doubt that the dream Iokasta [Oedipus's mother] mentions is connected in a strong connection to the horrible content of this myth" (p. 270).

This severe super-ego dictates to the ego its standards of behavior, disregarding the pressures that come from the *id*—the drives and instincts—and from the outside world, meaning society. If these standards are not heeded, then the super-ego punishes the individual with a strong feeling of inferiority and guilt.

Not every leading psychologist in the Viennese schools of psychology agreed with Freud's attitude toward the task of the super-ego, nor with Freud's division of the human soul into three parts, in which only one part controls morality and the deeds considered bad by society. Alfred Adler (1994) thought that man's style of living can be good or bad, but there is no need to connect it to guilt feeling. We are born with an inability to solve all the problems life brings to us, Adler said, and our task is to develop a socially responsible lifestyle, and to accept responsibility for our failures.

Carl Gustav Jung refrained from speaking about guilt and guilt feeling. Jung based his approach to the concept of guilt largely on the concept of the *collective subconscious* that exists in the human soul—in which guilt is always connected to the first sin of man and woman as described in the Bible. This sin is connected to the oppression of the sexual drives of the id by the super-ego.

Today we have a different social attitude toward sexual urges and their satisfaction, and toward guilt feelings. Yet the concept of guilt continues to serve as a subject for much discussion and debate (Kalmar, 1997). Whereas in Freud's time, in the Victorian era, many people experienced guilt feelings due to giving freedom and expression to their sexual urges that in those days were prohibited, today the opposite is true; today the repression of those urges and drives are the sources of the guilt feelings.

GUILT IN RELATION TO THE FIFTH COMMANDMENT

The Fifth Commandment in the Old Testament teaches that one should honor his or her father and mother. The sixth through tenth commandments deal basically with what is prohibited in human behavior according to Jewish and universal ethics. The Fifth Commandment is the only commandment in the Bible that has a reward for its fulfillment in the form of a long life upon this earth—indicating perhaps the fact that honoring and caring for an old parent is a difficult and complex matter. Caring has both physical and emotional aspects.

In caring for an elderly parent when he or she becomes ill, and especially when the parent has to be placed in an institution, one seldom escapes feelings of guilt. Such feelings are heightened when expectations either on the part of the parent or the adult child cannot be met. Guilt may be experienced by the siblings of the caretaker who do not involve themselves to the extent they could in caring for their aged parents.

There are many stresses involved in parent-child relationships that produce guilt feelings: Role reversal and feelings of dependency that may be rejected or resisted by both parent and child; loss of roles, and strains associated with shared households when the sharing is not done out of choice. The caretaker's competing claims of work and career, and the needs of his or her children, can be another source for feelings of guilt for the adult child. Many women in their middle years look forward to the joys of the *empty nest*, meaning the freedom from the parenting functions and pursuit of individual goals and dreams—only to find themselves burdened with new responsibilities in caring for their own parents. Many such caretakers resent the fate that forces them to postpone, or to give up completely, their dreams.

Professional literature in gerontology contains many studies that deal with the relationships between elderly parents and their adult children in the industrialized world (Olson, 1994). For example, Volkov (1992), in *To Be Son to an Elderly Parent: A Phase in the Family's Life Cycle Crisis*, presents many cases that illustrate the crisis in the relationships between elderly parents and their adult children within Israeli families. Her book describes situations in which there is no escape from placing an elderly parent in a nursing home.

According to professional literature in gerontology, family members are not the only ones who take care of old, frail, sick, and mentally deficient people. A system of community services and institutions of all kinds provide service at various levels of quality and quantity in accordance with the economic situation of the elderly people and their families, both in private and in public and/or government sectors.

It is a well known maxim that elderly people as a whole prefer to live in their own homes, apartments, and neighborhoods as long as possible. The same applies to their adult children who provide the bulk of services for their parents in the parents' home. They resist the temptation to transfer the old parent to a nursing or an old age home as long as possible. They see in these institutions the last resort, a most unwanted solution.

Many researchers in gerontology have found that the majority of elderly parents are transferred to an institution only when the main caretaker becomes ill, or has exhausted him- or herself. Even then, they see in this transfer one of the saddest events they have experienced in their lives (Olson, 1994). For example:

A woman we shall call Mrs. Brown, aged eighty, suffered a sudden deterioration in her health and could not remember when she had last taken her medications against high blood pressure. Mrs. Brown was caught time and time again leaving the gas open after she cooked something for herself. Sometimes she was also found in a ditch near her home after she lost her balance and fell. There were black and blue bruises on her body from bumping into the furniture in her apartment. In addition, several times Mrs. Brown forgot the address of her home and was seen searching helplessly for someone to tell her.

Mrs. Brown's family did what they could to lengthen her stay at her apartment, but they were not able to cope with her need for twenty-four-hour care and supervision. This situation caused many ambivalent feelings for her children. On the one hand, they saw the need to place Mrs. Brown in a nursing home where she would get proper care; on the other hand, they were suffering from the emotional conflict of choosing one of the two alternatives when both were seen as bad. Volkov (1992) wrote that the daughter, usually the main caretaker, suffers more than the other siblings, for she is torn between her personal and family's needs and the needs of the parent. Volkov emphasized that the emotional support the main caretaker needs is no less important than the concrete help the family should get from a professional worker (p. 74).

In this catch-22 situation, it is impossible to escape feelings of guilt that emanate from caring for an aged parent in need of institutional placement. Parents may also have guilt feelings. These are expressed in declarations such as, "I don't want to be a burden for my children." Many suffering and frustrated parents cite the well-known proverb: "One parent can care for ten children—and ten children can't care for one parent."

The professional literature in gerontology has passed over the guilt feelings of the elderly parents toward their offspring and deals mainly with the opposite situation described above. The non-professional literature, on the other hand, describes many cases in which guilt feelings of old parents serve as motivation for regret. An illustration of such a case is found in Tamaro's (1997) book *To Follow Your Heart,* in which the heroine, an elderly Italian woman who feels that her days are coming to an end, writes a long letter to her granddaughter. This letter is a confession and life review. When the woman confessed to her daughter that the man whom the daughter thought of as her father was not her real father, the daughter ran away in a car and was killed in an accident (p. 68). The woman raised her granddaughter after her daughter died in this accident.

The old woman feels guilty for never telling her granddaughter how the accident really happened. In the letter, she speaks about the hard life and suffering she has experienced because she was a smart and curious child. In her youth, those traits were not welcomed by society. The grandmother hopes that the losses she has experienced in her long life will help the granddaughter to develop a healthy approach to life. She gives her granddaughter the following advice: "When there will be many paths before you and you will not know which to take, then don't choose one at random, or by chance, but sit down and wait . . . Sit in your place, quietly, and listen to the voice of your heart. And when it will speak to you, get up and go where it will lead you" (Tamaro, p. 65).

This old and intelligent woman is able to understand that it is impossible to run away from guilt feeling, and it is impossible to accuse others. The grandmother knows that one has to be brave to carry guilt and to accept responsibility for one's failings. She understands that the only way to cope with guilt is by continuing to live, by moving forward, and by trying to prevent its recurrence. The old woman wants to help her granddaughter not to repeat the mistakes she made in her youth.

LOGOTHERAPY'S ATTITUDE TOWARD GUILT

Logotherapy has invested much effort in trying to approach guilt from a different and new angle. Frankl coined the term *the tragic triangle*, of which guilt is one part. Suffering and death are the other two parts. Frankl maintained that to find meaning in life, one has to cope successfully with each part of this triangle, for each part contains opportunities for finding new or renewed meaning for living.

Guilt occupies a central role in logotherapy. Frankl used to tell his own story, detailed in this book in principle number eleven, to illustrate this concept. The lesson learned from this dramatic and true story is this: If Frankl had chosen to go to America, rather than staying with his elderly parents, he would most likely have been punished by his conscience with guilt feelings for abandoning them to their fates. In the long run, escaping one's responsibility always leads to neurosis, or to a life without meaning. Logotherapy characterizes such life as *living in an existential vacuum.*

Frankl viewed guilt connected with suffering and death as a phenomenon that everybody will encounter in his or her life. Yet, he did not attach the same value to guilt as to the other two sides of the tragic triangle. He wished to emphasize that meaning can be squeezed even from guilt, by turning it into an opportunity to change and to make one into a better person. *Existential guilt* is embedded in one's soul, said Frankl (1982), and he cited the words of the philosopher Scheler, who said that man has a right to be guilty and to be punished. "When we try to nullify his guilt by seeing him as a victim of circumstances, we take away his dignity as a human being. I tend to say, one of the privileges of man is to feel guilty. But it is also true that his responsibility demands of him to overcome his guilt" (Frankl, 1982, p. 58).

Logotherapy differentiates between *real, neurotic,* and *noetic guilt. Real guilt* emanates from a real event, due to some act that was basically wrong. This is *guilt by commission.* There is also a guilt which is felt for something that was supposed to be done and was not. This is *guilt by omission.* For example, lack of attention to the needs of an old and frail parent for security is guilt by omission. When the parent falls and gets hurt, then the party who failed to act feels remorse and guilt.

Neurotic guilt is felt by someone who did not actually perform a wrong deed—only wished for it to happen. The most dramatic illustration of neurotic guilt was given by Shakespeare in his play *Macbeth.* The intention or wish to do something bad has deep roots in the human soul. Lady Macbeth is very ambitious to become Queen of Scotland. This ambition leads her to wish for the death of Duncan, the king. Lady Macbeth manages to persuade her husband to commit a horrible crime, killing King Duncan and blaming the servants for his death. When the plot succeeds and Lady Macbeth becomes queen, she is assaulted by strong pangs of her conscience. She develops insomnia, and obsessively washes her hands to get rid of the blood she imagines to be on them—to no avail.

In a similar vein, when someone wishes in secret for the death of his or her aged and sick parent, and when the parent suddenly dies from natural causes, then the person who wished for the death begins to feel guilty for having killed the parent. This feeling of guilt has no real basis, yet the person cannot get rid of it. Often this person spends the rest of his or her life tormented by thoughts that he or she caused the tragedy.

Noetic, or existential and spiritual guilt, is different from the other two. We feel its influence in behavioral disturbances expressed in confusion, discomfort, and dissatisfaction with self, as if something is not in order and needs to be corrected.

Preoccupation with disturbing thoughts continues to nag the afflicted until he or she is forced to do something to get rid of this feeling. At times, however, the sufferer prefers to repress or to ignore the urging of this feeling for action, and develops neurotic guilt or depression. In its most severe form, lack of response to the demands of life can bring the sufferer to lose interest in life, to become cynical, or to fall victim to uncontrolled anger and hatred. However, when one recognizes the reason for the guilt feeling, when one acts against it, when one fulfills one's responsibility and invests the mental energy in the action, then one gains mental tranquility and satisfaction, as well as a feeling of freedom and well-being (Sternig, 1984, p. 47).

What is existential guilt, and how can one cope with it according to logotherapy? Frankl (1962) coined the term *existential frustration* and has defined it as a situation in which one's search for meaning is frustrated or blocked. Sternig (1984) has stated that existential guilt is so different from real guilt and neurotic guilt that it would have been better not to call it guilt at all. This guilt is not something that can be looked at from judicial or religious perspectives. It is a kind of feeling that something is not in order, without really knowing how to define what that something is. Yet this something requires attention (p. 47). Frankl and Sternig claim that we must learn how to respond to the demands of life to the best of our ability, for our welfare and well-being are dependent on it. Our happiness is tied to the responsibility we take toward the demands of life. Who does not respond to these demands will pay a price—the torments of conscience.

Overcoming feelings of guilt is necessary in cases of real and neurotic guilt, says Frankl (1962). As for existential guilt, Sternig (1984) thinks that we can relate to it differently, for it works in our souls for a certain purpose or goal. Therefore we do not have to overcome it, but to learn how to live with it.

Lukas (1986b) referred to the concept of guilt in two ways: as justified or not justified, and has claimed that the two should be separated. We must ensure that guilt is anchored in reality and is not some imagined matter, as in neurotic guilt. In cases where guilt feelings stem from mistakes—justified guilt—therapy must include an explanation of the mistake. The therapist should turn the client's awareness to his or her unwillingness, or lack of free will, to take responsibility for the results of the action. When the feeling of guilt is unjustified, as in an illness, the therapist could help the client to get rid of the feeling by turning it into something ridiculous, or by ignoring it altogether. The following case illustrates this attitude.

An eighty-five-year-old man we shall call Jacob, a retired professor from a well-known university, was lying on his deathbed, suffering greatly from an incurable disease that attacked him in the last two years of his life. As he was lying in the bed unable to read or to watch television, he had plenty time to think about his family, the successes and failures of his children and wife, and about his relationships with them. Jacob had three grown sons. Two of them followed in their father's footsteps and became respected in the academic world. The third son did not want to do likewise. He said that he was free to make his own decisions about his life, and to spite his father, he became a mechanic, an occupation that his father considered beneath the family's dignity. This choice angered and saddened Jacob. There were many loud debates and quarrels between them every time the son visited his parents' home, until one day Jacob, who in the meantime had become ill, told his son that he would disinherit him. From that day on the son would not come to see his father.

When Jacob was nearing his death, he was tormented by his rashness and by the manner in which he told his son about the decision to disinherit him. Jacob consulted with the therapist how to restore the relationship with his son. The therapist suggested that Jacob express true and full regret and correct his will. Jacob, however, did not have the courage to do as advised. Nor did he do what could have eased his torment and give justice to his son. Jacob died shortly afterward with a heavy feeling of guilt.

14

Coping with Loneliness

A great spirit has an opportunity for development even in a lonely life. (Seneca, 1997, *On Mental Calmness*, p. 20)

Although the Bible says "It is not good for man to be alone" (Genesis 2:18), more and more elderly people live alone and suffer from loneliness. Community leaders, policy makers, gerontologists, and demographers consider loneliness—which will grow as technology advances—a major problem in aging. Surprisingly, however, this subject is among the least discussed in professional literature.

LONELINESS AMONG THE PRE-ELDERLY

Miriam, age fifty-two, is a social worker and mother of three children, ages fourteen to twenty-three. I met her in a conference on welfare and well-being of the aged. Three years ago she found herself without her husband, who simply disappeared leaving their youngest son with her. The other children were grown-ups, and they had already left home. One son was serving in the Army, and the other was studying in a faraway college. Miriam said,

At first I was completely stunned and didn't know what to do. Until this happened to me I thought that our lives were in order. I simply could not imagine that my husband would be unhappy with me. He didn't give any sign about his dissatisfaction. I've learned about it later, after he left home. My husband was a psychiatrist in a private office. There was a young secretary, and he fell in love with her. When he disappeared I finally understood what had happened, a rather banal case. I didn't expect such a thing from a professional supposed to control his feelings. Later we quarreled about our joint resources and the divorce, and these left me exhausted and hurt. At the end of all this I was left alone. I was fortunate to have sufficient resources for a decent living in economical terms, so that I could devote time for studies. I

133

became a social worker to help other women in similar situations. This gives me strength to live as a divorcée. But I feel that I have no chance for a new beginning. There are no eligible men around me, and those who could qualify are "taken" already. I will have to succumb to a life of loneliness.

Miriam's situation is similar to that of many housewives in their midlife and beyond, even when they remain married. The children have grown up and left home, and the husband is busy with work. Thus they find themselves alone in the house. The movie *Shirley Valentine* depicts such a woman, who in her solitude speaks to the wall in her apartment. When her husband comes home, he grabs the newspaper and a bottle of beer, sits at the table without saying a word, and waits for his dinner. But one day this woman revolts against him and leaves for Greece, where she slowly begins to build a new life. After learning the hardships of managing a home, the abandoned husband renounces his masculine pride, travels to Greece, and hopes to earn forgiveness. Now he is ready for a new life with his wife based on mutual respect.

The philosopher Schopenhauer spent most of his life in solitude, and he emphasized that we must learn early to cope with solitude and loneliness so that we are prepared when these come later in life. The ability to deal with loneliness may help us find solace, and people in midlife and beyond should be ready to accept that aging makes us lose people close to us, family members and friends.

People must learn to trust and to believe in themselves and in their abilities. It is important to arrive at old age aware of our strengths and weaknesses. We must trust this strength and use it in accordance with the opportunities available in the social environment. We must be aware that it is possible to develop mental and spiritual strength in the second half of life, as in the first one, especially those powers that were hidden until now.

This idea was eloquently expressed by the psychoanalyst Carl Gustav Jung in his *Memories, Dreams and Thoughts* (1997). Looking back, Jung tells the reader that his loneliness started early in life as a result of knowing things that people in general refused to hear about, such as his dreams and his interpretations of them. Jung said that one who knows more than others is prone to become lonely. His loneliness was not related to opposition to the collective. Rather, it resulted from his uniqueness and his refusal to become part of the herd.

"The older I became," Jung said, "the less I was able to understand myself, the less I recognized myself; I am disappointed in myself, and I am happy with myself. I am sad, and I am enthusiastic. All these are me. I can't summarize myself" (Jung, p. 451).

Jung (1998) stresses that as we advance toward the second half of life, and the better our social and economical standing become, the more we tend to conserve. We tend to hold on to what has been gained so far, as if it will stay forever, and as if there is no need for changes. Alas, human beings forget that refraining from change means diminishment of the personality, because many aspects of life are neglected.

Jung tells the story of a Native American chief and warrior who in his second half of life saw a great spirit in his dream. This spirit told him that from that moment on he must wear women's clothes, sit among the children and the women in the tent, and eat with them. The chief fulfilled the command of the great spirit without losing his honor and social standing. This story is intended to teach us about the changes in us that may happen in the second half of our lives—if we are open to face them. Sometimes these changes include preparation and readiness for a life of solitude (Jung, 1998, pp. 452–455).

There are many elderly and young people who did not learn to deal with loneliness because they always ran away from it. They forget that it is impossible to learn something when one runs away. Loneliness may be seen by many people in the second half of life as emptiness. This is why parents call their homes *empty nests* after their grown-up children leave.

Many people are afraid of looking at themselves, concentrating on and listening to their hearts' desires, and hearing the voice of their conscience. They refuse to get over the barrier of fear that prevents them from accepting loneliness in a positive way. They imagine that loneliness means not only emptiness, but also lack of experiences. They need to learn not to be afraid of loss—even if it is sudden, hard, and unexpected—and not to sink into self-pity. Children leaving home or the dissolution of a marriage may contain new opportunities for self-fulfillment—even when such opportunities involve a lot of effort.

LONELINESS AMONG THE ELDERLY

Loneliness may be defined as lack of company; remoteness from human habitation; seclusion from others; a state of dejection or grief caused by the condition of being alone; or a deliberately selected state of solitude (*Webster's Dictionary*, 1986). Loneliness—which is closely related to loss or its opposite, failure to gain significant human relationships—is tied to stages of development during the life course (Rubinstein, 1986).

In discussions of loneliness we have to differentiate between **voluntary loneliness and forced loneliness**. The former refers to individuals who find solace in solitude and/or to those for whom loneliness is a long-standing way of life. These individuals usually don't constitute a social problem, whereas the latter do. The following case refers to voluntary loneliness.

Judy (fictitious name) was forty years old when her husband was taken to forced labor in the last year of World War II. She miraculously survived the war, and when it was over, she immediately started looking for her husband, whose whereabouts became unknown in the fall of 1944. Alas, all her efforts were in vain. Judy turned to various organizations (including the International Red Cross), institutions, and associations representing prisoners of war, but none could provide her with reliable information. After many years of waiting and hoping, she was officially recognized as a widow by the religious court. Despite her new status, she continued to wait for her husband and did not marry again. Judy would not heed the advice of her grown-up children to begin a new life. Loyalty to her husband was more important than anything in life, and she preferred to remain a widow, waiting and hoping for a miracle.

This is a case of voluntary loneliness based on cultural, religious, and traditional values, the result of a conservative education handed down from one generation to the next, mainly within Eastern European Jewish religious circles.

Loneliness may be felt more or less intensely. It may lurk as a nagging reminder of the state a person wishes to forget or deny. The elderly have a rather stereotyped image of being lonely. This image was highlighted by the findings of the Harris Poll in a national survey completed in 1975: Although only twelve percent of the aged in this study thought loneliness was a very serious problem for them personally, sixty percent considered the phenomenon to be very serious for most elderly people.

In the most recent study conducted by the National Council on Aging, called "The Myth and Reality of Aging in America" (March 2000), the percentages were similar to those in 1975. Furthermore, loneliness among the young aged eighteen to twenty-four was found to be more pronounced than among the elderly. Nevertheless, loneliness is a serious problem in old age among the noninstitutionalized elderly living in the community.

THE MANY FACES OF LONELINESS

There are many types of loneliness connected to various degrees of feeling alone and estranged from the world. The first one refers to **loneliness in the physical sense**, which is a feeling of being alone and far away from other people in the vast expanse of the universe. This type of loneliness is usually psychologically harmless for most people.

The second type of loneliness is **a feeling of being rejected** by other people. This is more pronounced than the former among old people because they are very sensitive to interactions with the younger generation. When the feedback they receive is one of rejection and when this rejection causes too great a suffering, they may react by sinking into mental disturbance, depression, and more loneliness.

The third type of loneliness is connected to **feelings of being left behind.** Many elderly people feel that they are not well equipped to compete with the younger generations in conquering the marvels of technology; that they don't have the "right personality" to understand the special language used in technology; or that they can't communicate easily in this new world. Others may feel rejection because of their personal characteristics—such as race, color, values, and lifestyles—and experience loneliness and despair.

Gibson (2000) discusses two additional types of loneliness: **trait and state.** The first one refers to an individual's basic personality. Some people are lonely all their lives irrespective of their living conditions and social environment. The second can happen to any person experiencing a temporary period of being cut off from regular social interactions. Such is the case with people who are temporarily unemployed, sick, or injured in accidents. This type of loneliness usually disappears when people return to their normal functioning. In general, human beings are more vulnerable to ill health in their later years. They are also more prone to loneliness due to loss of family members and close friends than are younger people.

Baziz (1997) perceives loneliness as a separate psychological situation that stands alone among other psychological situations even in the midst of such feelings as enthusiasm, joy, and elation, which are usually shared with someone or with many people. Loneliness in old age is seen by Baziz as a situation that causes great anxiety and sadness for the individual involved in that situation. The strength and quality of this feeling change from one individual to the next, depending on the life experiences he or she has had. For the lonely elderly, memories of times past—if they were good—only strengthen the suffering caused by loneliness because they bring with them sad reflections on the present situation. The following case illustrates such a situation.

Suzy (fictitious name) was seventy years old when she lost her husband, who had been gravely ill with an incurable disease for more than six months. Because Suzy did not believe she was going to lose her husband, she did not prepare herself to become a widow and thus to be alone. At first, she said, loneliness was not a problem. There were so many things to do and to take care of that she would come home exhausted, which prevented her from feeling lonely. Her children and friends helped her forget what had happened prior to her husband's death. But this period came to an end rather soon, and she found herself more and more alone, as the sense of loneliness began to creep more and more into her consciousness.

Sometimes Suzy felt happy about her newly found freedom; sometimes she had a feeling that she could take on the whole world; sometimes she thought that she could respond well to the demands of life; sometimes she sank back to old habits of dependence on her husband in making decisions about important things, but the husband was not around; sometimes she found herself enclosed in her loneliness like a pearl in an oyster, shying away from people and the world, mourning the death of her husband and her fate. These feelings came over her like the waves of the sea and flooded her with sadness, raising unknown anxieties. Then she would weep and cry a lot because she lost her former way of life.

LONELINESS IN THE LITERATURE ON AGING

Cohen (2003) discusses loneliness—with its varied manifestations in literature, art, and poetry—and its influence on the human psyche from many perspectives in a series of articles. These works are based on his own struggle with loneliness and on his scientific approach to the subject.

Cohen conducted a series of interviews with 376 subjects representative of the adult population in Israel in terms of various age groups, gender, social backgrounds, and life experiences. One of the shortcomings of theoretical and empirical approaches to the study of loneliness, Cohen concluded, is their inability to encompass the experience of loneliness with its myriad expressions and the whole gamut of feelings connected to it, as well as the many coping mechanisms that people use.

Cohen thinks that the best and most meaningful attitude to loneliness is found in literary creations, poetry, and short stories. These are relevant for therapeutic work with the elderly who suffer from loneliness. In his books on this subject, Cohen brings many personal stories that enliven and illustrate not only subjective feelings about loneliness, but also its existential manifestation and its influence on the mental health of the individual experiencing it.

As mentioned before, results of the survey conducted by the National Council On Aging indicate that the old are by and large less lonely than the young. One can live alone without being lonely. Most elderly people live their lives along with others, both old and young, and continue to be involved in social affairs. However, this finding cannot repeal the persistent myth about the loneliness of most old people. Another myth equally popular among many older people suggests that in former times the aged lived in harmony with their families and kin, enjoying much honor, dignity, and reverence, and not suffering from loneliness. Alas, reality is quite different. In all historical times the aged experienced abandonment and, consequently, loneliness to greater or lesser degrees.

The literature on loneliness is enormous. Some of the best-known literary and philosophical works focus on loneliness. Among these are Defoe's *Robinson Crusoe,* Swift's *Gulliver's Travels,* and Shakespeare's *As You Like It.* Many great writers have written about their own solitude. Søren Kierkegaard's *The Mortal Illness* (1993) and Arthur Schopenhauer's *Life Wisdom* (2001) discuss loneliness from a philosophical perspective.

Loneliness in later life was described by Dickens (1974) as being connected to some moral fault. One of the famous characters in Dickens's *Oliver Twist* is Fagin, an avaricious man who recruits street boys and teaches them how to steal. Dickens's contempt toward Fagin is revealed in his description of that character: "[Fagin] was a very old shriveled Jew, whose villainous-looking and repulsive face was obscured by a quantity of matted red hair" (p. 50).

Fagin is not the only Dickensian character depicted as a horrible old person. Lonely old people in Dickens's books are often ugly, vicious, repulsive, deformed in body and spirit, and evil. The few exceptions to this rule are old people whose ages aren't noticeable through their physical appearance and who consequently are free of the faults of old age.

It seems that Dickens was not only an ageist but an anti-Semite as well. Gibson (2000) writes, "The writings of Dickens with their popularity and unforgettable characterization have undoubtedly been one of the factors that have helped to maintain this negative stereotype" (p. 78).

Another great novelist who made a remarkable contribution to the literature on loneliness is Joseph Conrad (1857–1924). In his novels and short stories this famous writer concentrated on loneliness as a grim phenomenon in an individual's life. Conrad did not find any dignity in solitude, which he viewed as unpleasant loneliness and a product of some moral weakness and guilt. In

Conrad's novels each man is alone, a stranger to himself, and fully aware of his isolation from his fellow human beings.

A moving literary description of loneliness was presented by the great twentieth-century philosopher Bertrand Russell in his *Autobiography* (1967). Russell (1872–1970), recipient of the 1950 Nobel Prize in Literature, spent eighty years in loneliness and unhappiness, longing for love and knowledge, and struggling with his "unbearable pity for the suffering of mankind"—until he married once again and lived happily another eighteen years (p. 13).

The lesson learned from all these literary works is rather simple: successful aging requires courage and stoic acceptance of the vicissitudes of life, including loneliness.

JEWISH PERSPECTIVE ON LONELINESS

Jewish traditional sources have not paid substantial attention to the subject of loneliness in old age. Neither the Jewish (1907) nor the Talmudic (1978) Encyclopedias discuss this topic. This omission leads to two assumptions or possibilities: (1) loneliness in old age was not a major problem before the beginning of the industrial era or (2) loneliness was always a problem, but the issue was subsumed under more pressing matters, such as religious and ethical behavior, and family and community affairs.

In Biblical and Talmudic times the aged controlled the family's fortune. They were considered wise and experienced, and their longevity was seen as a blessing rather than a curse. Emphasis used to be placed on marriage and on family life to avoid a state of loneliness among the aged. Old Jewish tradition saw marriage as necessary for men. In the Babylonian Talmud (Yebamot 62:72 and 63:71), the Sages said: "It is not good for a man to be without a wife, for a man without a wife is like a person without joy, without blessing, without a wall (the woman is like a wall which guards someone against sin), without peace, and in fact such a man is like a nobody" (Solomon et al., 1989).

The second assumption is that old age was always a problem and all societies struggled with it according to their values and ethics. The loneliness of the very old was echoed throughout the ages in the book of Psalms. Here we find the cry of all lonely elderly: "Do not forsake me in my old age, when my strength fails" (Psalms 71:9; 71:18).

According to the Talmudic Encyclopedia (1978), "the transition from the position of the powerful elder to an aged pauper, requiring special assistance outside the frame of the family, is an outcome of the heritage of Judaic-Muslim-Christian civilization" (p. 346).

LONELINESS IN SPECIAL GROUPS OF ELDERLY PEOPLE

Loneliness can exist in social settings that were created precisely to provide their members with security, companionship, and social involvement. Take for example the kibbutzim (collective settlements), in which about two percent of the

Israeli population live. Since its beginnings in 1910, the kibbutz movement has romanticized community living as well as the idea of sharing resources and work. And one of its goals was the creation of opportunities to attain a meaningful existence in a society in which they are masters of their own fates and destinies.

Those living in kibbutzim have higher longevity than the other Israelis. According to various researchers who specialize in studies about living in kibbutzim, higher longevity is associated with life in the kibbutz. Opportunities for lifelong employment, rotation in jobs, higher levels of education, intensive cultural life, and comfortable living conditions all increase one's life span.

Today the problem of loneliness among the elderly has taken on frightening proportions. It is no secret that the kibbutz movement is in serious trouble. It has become an aging society undergoing rapid changes in its composition, purpose, economic activities, and attitudes to the aged. Privatization is now widespread in all Israeli kibbutzim, and in many of them such privatization has resulted in the break-up of families, loss of values, and a different outlook on life.

Aged members who are seventy-five years old or older constitute almost three-fifths of the population in the more established kibbutzim, whereas the average proportion of those who are sixty-five years or older is fifteen percent. A heavy sense of loneliness is felt particularly among the old widows and widowers who find themselves alone after tens of years of married life in the kibbutz. This feeling is intensified especially in the evening, when the elderly are usually alone in their rooms, and during holidays such as Passover and New Year's.

Many elderly widows say that they feel lost and unhappy. One of them said, "It is true that we have a social club for the members where we can listen to lectures. We can join therapy groups in the nearby city, go on sightseeing tours, and engage in many other activities; but when darkness falls, everybody is closeted in his or her room, and then we feel the full burden of loneliness. Sometimes I want to cry out aloud my sadness and unhappiness." The following case illustrates this situation.

Sarah (fictitious name), age seventy-two, has recently become a widow. She has lived in an older kibbutz for over fifty years. Sarah has a relatively large family in the kibbutz, and she is regarded as one of the more fortunate members because she has children and grandchildren living in the same place as she does. In the kibbutz, many of the widows without a family are envious of her.

Sarah is aware of her fortune. "You see," she told her group worker, "it is true that objectively speaking I am in a better situation compared to many other widows in the kibbutz, but they don't know how much I suffer from loneliness. When I come home after a visit with my children and grandchildren the walls close and suffocate me, and I want to scream! And when I sit to eat my meals alone, without having a soul with whom to share, I feel so sad. It is hard to describe. The monotony of each day resembles another, like two drops of water. This simply makes me mad. Sometimes I invite a stranger, one with whom I never had any social relationships in the kibbutz, to share a meal with me just to escape being alone."

Although the loneliness Sarah is experiencing is well known from many studies, not every widow sinks to the depths of despair, and not every widow looks upon her widowhood as a disaster. Yet, despite the efforts of many kibbutzim to take care of their older and frail members, loneliness among them is inevitable.

At kibbutzim, or outside in the villages and cities, physical needs can be met more or less satisfactorily. This is not the case with emotional needs. You cannot force people to express kindness, to treat others with consideration, and to care for the lonely even in the kibbutz. Many old-timers confess that loneliness is much more prevalent and harder inside the kibbutz than outside it. Many elderly members lack mobility and have no children living there to turn to. Privatization carries a heavy price especially for the elderly members in the kibbutzim lacking support from their families. It is well known that over fifty percent of the children born in the kibbutzim leave their homes after their military service and a large number of them live outside the country thus leaving the elderly parents behind.

PROGRAMS FOR ALLEVIATION OF LONELINESS IN OLD AGE

Many industrialized countries have programs to ease the loneliness of the elderly. The goal of these programs is to include the elderly in voluntary activities that will allow them to develop new social relationships with other people, old and young alike. Such interactions create new opportunities for the elderly to find meaningful connections to the outside world.

Social clubs and day centers for the aged are places where new friendships can be created and maintained, new skills acquired, new activities enjoyed, and many services provided. These and other social institutions offer opportunities for the elderly to engage in voluntary activities with their peers.

One of many innovative programs for the alleviation of loneliness in old age has recently been implemented in Jerusalem, Israel. A housing project was built in which the ground floors were designated for lonely elderly residents, whereas the top floors were rented out to young couples with children, thus creating opportunities for frequent contact between the generations.

Another successful program for the same purpose is called *A Grandparent for the Kindergarten*. Elderly and usually lonely people "adopt" a kindergarten in their neighborhood, where they do volunteer work such as helping with various chores, supervising the children, and acting as surrogate grandparents to children with special needs.

Religious institutions—such as the Church or the Synagogue—brotherhoods and sisterhoods, religious schools and colleges are other important sources for alleviating loneliness in old age. Many studies on the impact of religion on life reveal a significant correlation between life satisfaction and religious activity. In Israel, for example, orthodox Jews adjust better to aging than the nonorthodox because of the formers' strong belief and faith in God, which helps them to overcome grief, loneliness, and despair.

LOGOTHERAPY'S PERSPECTIVE ON LONELINESS IN OLD AGE

Despite the many innovative programs currently in use in the world to help older lonely people cope with the sorrows in their lives, there is still a need to create new and positive attitudes and approaches to this malady. Logotherapy is particularly well suited for this role.

Frankl characterized our times as lacking meaning. Today more and more people feel that they live in a world that lacks sense. This world was foreseen by Freud, who in *Civilization and Its Discontents* (2002) said, "The life imposed on us is too hard for us to bear; it brings too much pain, too many disappointments; too many insoluble problems" (p. 13).

Freud also said that to endure life we must take palliative measures. These he listed as "powerful distractions which cause us to make light of our misery; substitutive satisfactions, which diminish it; and intoxicants, which anesthetize us to it" (Freud, p. 13).

Loneliness in old age was not directly addressed by Frankl in his final work, *Man's Search for Ultimate Meaning* (1997a). Instead, Frankl addressed the problem of "lack of meaning in life." Lack of meaning in life in logotherapy means living in an existential vacuum, without a sense of direction and a clear goal that one intends to accomplish. This situation in its severest form may become an emotional disturbance or neurosis.

Logotherapy emphasizes a different approach to the troubles of human beings. The purpose of this approach is to elevate man to a higher level of existence. Logotherapy intends to help elderly people living lonely and forlorn lives to attain a dignified old age.

Logotherapy is aware of the suffering of many people, and especially of the suffering of former prisoners in concentration and prisoner-of-war camps, the mentally sick, and those who suffer from various ailments. Many of these people were not as fortunate as Frankl in living a long and fruitful life within a loving and caring family, surrounded by many friends, and enjoying the adoration and gratitude of millions all over the world. But Frankl didn't forget the lesson learned in the German concentration camps in which he spent three and a half years. He said, "[W]henever one is confronted with an inescapable, unavoidable situation, just then one is given a last chance to actualize the highest value, to fulfill the deepest meaning, the meaning of suffering. What matters above all is the attitude we take toward suffering" (Frankl, 1962, p. 112).

Gibson (2000) refers to cases of individuals who toward the end of their lives experience a sudden loss of faith in the values by which they have always lived. He calls this loss of faith "existential loneliness." For example, many older members of Israeli kibbutzim experience "existential loneliness" because of loss of lifelong ideals and values. This loss may come suddenly or develop slowly over the years. Some writers associate this loss with religion, and they claim that it is basically a thirst for God.

Gibson (2000) cites the theologian Ronald Rolheiser, who characterized this loneliness as "one that is not caused directly by our alienation from others, but from the very way our heart is built, from our structure as human beings" (p. 18). When such feeling of loss pervades the human soul, it can result in the feeling that one's life was wasted, and this may contribute to a strong feeling of loneliness.

Loneliness does not need to be like this. An older person does not need to see his or her loneliness as immutable fate. On the contrary, one must remind him- or herself of the original words Frankl used in his famous book *Man's Search for Meaning* (1962): "Despite everything else say yes to life!" The word "despite" is the key to changing the situation.

Logotherapy maintains that a human being is a choosing creature, that is, a creature that chooses the attitude toward what happens to him or to her. And there is no situation, however difficult, that doesn't offer more than one choice. One does not need to accept without revolt or protest what life and fate throw in one's path, but one can always take a stand.

Research in gerontology has shown that aged people close to death, who made special efforts to "survive until Christmas," or "until the wedding of my granddaughter" did in fact survive (Olson, 1994).

Coping with loneliness, as with any other situation in life, is dependent on one's resources. Coping with loneliness is not different from coping with other emotions in life. The greater the resources available to human beings, both internal and external, the more human beings are able to diminish the effects of the harms and losses that befall them, for the resources act as a shield against the tension and stress that accompany the losses.

Coping requires a change in attitude to what happens to the person. Changing a person's attitude from preoccupation with his or her misery and loneliness to one of service to the less fortunate as well as redirecting the mental energy to discover new meaning in life are imperatives in logotherapy's attitude to loneliness.

Life is full of wonders, miracles, and surprises. We only need to open our eyes to discover all that it entails. Each human being is given opportunities to find something meaningful during the second half of life. Each human being is blessed with the ability to love ideas, nature, as well as other human beings. Such love may become a source of satisfaction even in loneliness. For example, in an Israeli kibbutz there was once an old man who lived a life of solitude. His behavior was eccentric too. He used to get up early in the morning to walk in the fields, listen to the singing of the birds, and enjoy the fresh air and the beauty around him. At the end of his walk, he would return to the settlement, and with his eyes glued to the ground he would look for old and rusty nails around the various workshops, garages, and factories. The ones he found he would take to his little workshop. There he would straighten and hammer and keep them in boxes marked according to their sizes. This habit was a never-ending source of jokes and laughing matter for the young members of the kibbutz. They saw in him the epitome of stinginess and strangeness characteristic of old people. Yet, these nails helped a lot in the war of liberation, when the kibbutz came under siege and there was a need to erect barricades. They literally saved the kibbutz from being overrun. Then all the people in the kibbutz became aware of the contribution this old man had made to the defense of the settlement with his nails. Those nails in fact expressed his love for life in the kibbutz.

Many great philosophers found power and strength in loneliness, something good and advisable for aging people. They chose loneliness not to escape reality or to avoid the hatred of others. They were not secluded as monks in a monastery and did not preach refraining from the pleasures of life. They saw in loneliness an opportunity for spiritual enrichment, an opportunity for creating something that can be created only in solitude.

Even an ordinary person—someone who is not a philosopher or a great scientist such as Einstein—may aim at learning and creating something. One cannot expect someone else—other than oneself—to free him or her from the oppressive feeling of loneliness, if such a feeling persists. Our children can't do such a miracle—even if they would devote all their time and energy to that purpose. When we learn how to deal honestly and earnestly with this feeling, we will be able to attain mental tranquility.

The psychoanalyst Carl Gustav Jung (1993) wrote that if we shall walk in the paths of the depth of our souls; if we shall discover what is hidden inside our psyche and free it from all the hard layers that were erected on top of it during many years of existence, we shall free the divine spark enclosed. That spark, when freed, will ignite a flame that will illuminate the darkness. This way we will be able to look at the face of loneliness bravely, without fear, as an integral part of life.

15

A Logotherapeutic Perspective on Death

In November 2004 I was invited to give a seminar in Mexico City on logotherapy to a group of professionals that included teachers, physicians, psychologists, and social workers. I arrived exactly on the Day of the Dead, which is an important date in that country. The huge city was decorated with gay colors. At the National Museum, there were exhibits celebrating death in all types of artwork. In the middle of the main hall were huge statues adorned with mosaics in every imaginable color and material, and the ceilings were decorated with skeletons made of wallpaper.

Plates and baskets full of fruits, crops, and foods, as well as jars containing drinks for the dead were placed in front of the statues. Children were running happily, playing games with the skeletons without any sign of fear, and adults were singing songs for the deceased. Fine works of art hung among the offerings. It seemed as if all Mexicans were eager to express their culture's best aspects. Outside the museum bands of mariachis played various instruments to the happy crowds, and the streets were filled with joy and laughter. I was fascinated by what I was seeing, and I thought to myself that the Mexican attitude toward death was very different from that of the West, where there is still denial of death and even avoidance of its mention.

Mexican people's approach to death is perhaps the closest to the one dreamed by the ancient philosophers. The great Roman philosopher Cicero (1909) said, through his protagonist Cato the Elder, that an old man who is afraid of death is a wretched creature. For what is there to fear? One will either stop suffering or perhaps even be happy! And who can be so foolish to think that he or she will surely be alive tomorrow, even if he or she is young?

Cicero wrote, "When death comes, then everything disappears. What remain are the memories of your brave deeds. The best way to die is when your faculties are still intact, your thoughts are clear, your senses function well, and suddenly comes 'mother nature' and liquidates by her own hand what she has built" (1909, p. 76).

The death of the ancient Roman philosopher Seneca could serve as a model for all of us. When he was commanded by the Emperor Nero to put an end to his life, Seneca sat calmly and stoically in his bathroom, took a knife, and cut the arteries in his ankles. Then he waited patiently until life slowly left him and he died.

A healthy individual accepts death as something healthy, as part of nature and life. Therefore, an old man who doesn't learn, in the course of his life, to accept death calmly, without complaint or fear, is indeed foolish. Cicero said that old men and women must accept the fact that nature has its own way. All things in accordance with nature are good, including death. The little time left to old people should not be spent with greedy eagerness or abandoned without cause. "To disregard death is a lesson which must be studied from our youth and up; for unless that is learnt, no one can have a quiet mind" (Cicero, p. 73).

HOW TO ACCEPT DEATH?

There are four approaches or attitudes to death: The first is a stoic attitude toward death. It means accepting it without illusions about life in another plane. Such an attitude was exhibited by Sigmund Freud who detested death and kept his scientific detachment until the end of his life.

The second approach to death is seeing it as something impossible to grasp, something to which people return, continuing to exist in spirit, thanks to the good name they made for themselves while living, which enables them to achieve immortality.

The third approach is to relate to death as a friend that one is happy to greet, and the fourth approach is to be cognizant and open about the end of life and to talk about the meaning of life in the face of death.

We can change our attitude toward death in accordance with the circumstances of our life and self-understanding. The four aforementioned attitudes on death are based on philosophical perspectives on life gained in childhood, and they accompany us throughout life. From the age of seventy and up, there is little difference between men's and women's death rates. And it is no surprise that this subject occupies a greater deal of time for people when they are old than it did when they were younger. Nevertheless, old people are not constantly preoccupied with death. In fact, they are more open to this subject than are the younger generations. What really interests people in their midlife and beyond is not when death will come, but how and where.

For most older people the fear of death includes three elements: sadness for knowing they must leave the world; lack of security in life after death, and the process of dying itself. Most people perceive this process as connected to lots of suffering, pain, and feelings of helplessness. The last element, the process of dying, occupies the thoughts of aging people. Woody Allen has said that he is not afraid of dying, but he wouldn't like to be there when it happens.

As we get older, we must consider that dying becomes more likely. Several factors influence one's longevity, some of which the individual can control—such as smoking and drinking; one's genetic inclinations and heredity, marital status (better married than single), and lifestyle in terms of nutrition, engagement in physical exercise and sport, and investment in spiritual matters.

There are three main causes of death for people in their sixties and up: illnesses related to blood circulation; illnesses affecting breathing, and cancer. If it were possible, all of us would like to die as Moses in the Old Testament. It is written there that he was 120 years old when he died; his eyes were not dim, his strength was not abated, and the "kiss of death" took him.

Even illnesses that quickly bring about death can be desired as a means for dying. Everybody would like to die in such a way that all others left living would say that he or she died in an instant. And even if pain is not the factor that makes death fearful, most people see pain as something undesirable, and they are afraid of it.

There are other experiences connected to death—such as depression, dependence on others, confusion, loss of dignity and mobility, difficulty in breathing, constipation, and apathy—that make it so hard to bear even in thought.

Aged people everywhere would like to extend life as long as possible without losses in physical and mental health, and to die without too much suffering or pain. Older people prefer to die in their own homes and own beds, surrounded by a loving and supportive family. But the chances for attaining this are not very good. Only one-third of all elderly people have this wish fulfilled; the others die in nursing homes and in hospitals. All human beings would like to die in accordance with the etymological sense of the word *euthanasia,* which means *good death,* that is, death with dignity and without suffering.

If aging were perceived by older people as a happy period in their lives, and if there were satisfying living conditions for old people in general, then it would be possible to approach death without fear and to perceive it as an opportunity to greet the dead as we do when someone goes on a holiday, as if he left for a life of eternity and thus there is no need to cry for him. Then there would be no need to think of the dead as a loser in the game of life.

In an idealistic and utopian attitude toward life older people should have waited for a time when death would be perceived as something positive, when people could be happy for the departed as one who has fulfilled his mission in life and who can now expect new adventures that we cannot even imagine. Such an attitude to death was exhibited by the famous Hasidic Rabbi Simcha Bunam. When he was lying on his deathbed and his wife was crying bitter tears, he said, "Why are you crying? Don't you know that my whole life was in order to learn how to die?" (Buber, 1976, p. 31).

MIDLIFE AS A TURNING POINT

If we were to compare human life to the sun, then we would discover the spectacle of the circle. In the morning the sun rises and gathers strength until noon, when it reaches its greatest warmth. And then the crisis begins. From here on, the sun doesn't gather any more strength. From here on, it begins to sink slowly until the end of the circle. The same thing happens with people. As children and teenagers, their parents and teachers help them develop and advance in life, until they reach the zenith of their careers in accordance with their talents, perseverance, and a bit of luck. And in the second half of their lives the task is to concentrate on easing the descent. Many young adults mistakenly think that life has value only during the ascent, when one is on the move toward greater achievements.

The psychologist Carl Gustav Jung perceived the second half of life as no less rich in terms of development than the first one. Human beings have natural and cultural goals. A young man is busy with creating a family, looking for a job, and securing his social standing. When this phase is over, then he begins to pursue his cultural goal, which is to enrich the overall culture of human beings. Unfortunately, he has no help from his parents or from others for achieving this second goal.

One must engage in this process by his own effort. If in one's childhood and youth the fear of life was an obstacle for fulfilling the natural goal, in the second half of life the obstacle is the fear of death. Yet, despite what has been said above, there is help for the interested. This help is religion, but this is relevant to only a small part of mankind, those we call believers. For these people the belief in their religious values serves as preparation for old age, death, and life in the world to come.

Many people live with a feeling that they have missed the boat, that they have missed many opportunities; they thus start the second half of their lives looking back, or even worse, standing paralyzed in one place, rather than advancing with time.

The Hungarian poet George Faludy wrote a ballad about such a person. Charley Null, Faludy's protagonist, looks back at his life at the age of sixty and decides that he must write down what he has done in those sixty years. But he doesn't know if he should begin with his youth, which now seems to him empty of content, or with his adulthood, which went by without great experiences. Charley remembers those years that were full of boring work and insignificant events. Now he feels he's aging, and he becomes angry at himself for having missed all the opportunities to make his life meaningful. He wants to get back all the dreams he had, all the passions he never fulfilled; he wants to know his real self. He thus decides to put his reflections and thoughts on paper. He goes to a store, buys 100 sheets of paper, and sits at his desk to write. The next day at noon, when his daughter comes to visit him, she finds him dead, bent over his desk. A hundred sheets of paper were neatly arranged, and at the top of the first one was written *My Life*, and nothing else. No lines, no words; only the empty pages: these were his life.

In the second half of life the goal should be to make the descent meaningful. Death should be meaningful to man in the same way as birth is. And whoever is not making the necessary preparations resembles a young man running away from life as an adult.

In *On the Paths of Our Depths* (1993), Jung emphasizes that an aging person must remember that his life will not reach new heights, for an irreversible inner process narrows it (p. 17). Death indeed can be horrible; yet, it can also bring ease and the means to another existence that we cannot fathom at this time.

DEATH AS A CONCEPT

In the second half of our lives, we become more and more aware of the finality of life and of death, which is waiting for us all. We feel that the time left is decreasing. This feeling varies from one individual to another, for each human being lives and dies in his or her unique way. The literature dealing with the subject of death shows that, in general, we can approach death from four perspectives: (1) as an entrance into eternity; (2) as a phenomenon in accordance with the rules of nature; (3) as an event to be accepted quietly; or (4) as a friend one greets happily, for it comes when one is ready, and it helps one depart with a feeling that one has done his or her share and lived a meaningful life. Therefore, one is not afraid of death. One perceives dying as a task to be fulfilled decently.

DEATH ACCORDING TO GREAT WRITERS AND SPIRITUAL LEADERS

The Russian writer Lev Tolstoy had a unique approach to death. In his well-known book *The Death of Ivan Illich* (1992), Tolstoy's belief that a man's attitude can change and make life meaningful when he faces death is made clear. In this novel, whose hero is a clerk in governmental service, insight and death are intertwined. When the hero becomes ill, he realizes the meaninglessness of the life he has had prior to his illness. Now that he is on his deathbed and in relentless pain, he has time to ponder over his life. Tolstoy characterizes this man's life in the following way: "The life of Ivan Illich was simple, ordinary and horrible . . . He knew that he was dying. In the depth of his heart he knew that he was dying, but he wasn't used to the thought. He simply didn't understand and wasn't able to grasp that it is possible" (Tolstoy, p. 225).

The dying man suffers without respite; he remembers happiness and love, and his pain disappears as soon as he stops clinging to life. Suffering brings insight into his life: he makes peace with his family and with himself.

Ivan Illich develops spiritually beyond what was expected of him by his society and becomes a man of inner greatness. This greatness makes the last days of his life meaningful. These are offered as compensation for all the trouble he caused until this change. Ivan Illich is an example of Frankl's concept of self-transcendence, that is, of a man who could transcend himself to achieve a great human accomplishment.

Both Tolstoy and Schopenhauer thought that the fact that life ends in death forces us to speak about its meaning. Others think that this awareness about the end of life in death destroys the happiness of the individual and his search for meaning. Belief in God can relieve to a certain extent the anxiety over death, and the promise of an afterlife enables one to work hard in this world, so that he or she could gain entrance to the heavenly world. Yet, if God doesn't exist, as so many scientists and atheists claim, then our whole world is absurd and life too is absurd.

A most moving and poetic description of death is found in Hrabal's (1994) previously mentioned book *Too Noisy Silence*. The hero in this book loses his job at the mill after thirty-five years. His machine is replaced by a modern compressor that can produce ten times as many packages as the old one. Lonely and forlorn by his friends and acquaintances, he sits down on a bench in the park and imagines how his old machine will make a nice package for his body. The hero imagines meeting the little gipsy girl who used to sneak into his small room and share her life with him— until she was taken by the Germans to a concentration camp and never returned.

Hrabal wrote, "I was sitting on the bench, smiling an innocent smile; I didn't remember anything, didn't hear anything, for I was already in the midst of the 'Garden of Eden' and thus I couldn't see or hear my two gipsy women [being] hugged by two gipsy men passing me in a hurry like in a dance and disappear beyond the bushes" (p. 77).

A LOGOTHERAPEUTIC ATTITUDE TOWARD DEATH

Almost 2,000 years after Cicero's book *On Old Age* (1909), Viktor Frankl (1962) developed a philosophy toward dying and death that has gone far beyond the ideas presented by that philosopher of antiquity. The main element in Frankl's philosophy is a psychological and philosophical alternative to the perception of death as meaningless.

The unconditional meaningfulness of life, even with the reality of death, is based on Frankl's analysis of the meaning of death for all human beings. Frankl claims that we are the only creatures on this planet who are aware of their own death. This discovery should reawaken in us a sense of responsibility toward life, and not lead us to deny death. This point is illustrated by the case of an old physician who went to see Frankl to ask for advice. His beloved wife had died the previous year, and he couldn't overcome that loss. As a physician, he could easily prescribe himself a tranquilizer to calm down, but he knew that this would not help him, and thus he decided to ease his suffering by turning to Frankl for help.

Frankl asked this physician what would have happened if he had died before his wife. "I can't even think about it," the old physician said, "how she would have suffered!" At that point in the therapeutic session Frankl said to him: "You see, she has been spared such suffering, and it was you who have spared her this suffering, but now you have to pay for it by surviving and mourning her."

The old physician understood at once the meaning of his suffering and the meaning of the sacrifice he had to make. He understood that it is impossible to change fate, but it is possible to change one's attitude to fate. Fate has robbed the old physician of his wife but left in his hands the ability to discover meaning in suffering by having a positive attitude to death. Then he calmly shook Frankl's hand and left the office (*Man's Search for Meaning*, 1962, p. 113).

What is the attitude of logotherapy to death, suicide, euthanasia, and immortality? Logotherapy has developed a psychological alternative for those who think that death has no meaning. Frankl (1962) emphasized that logotherapy's main purpose is to help people attain their potential by making their lives meaningful. Frankl wrote that "those things that seemingly take away meaning from one's life are not only suffering, but dying too, not only distress, but death too" (Frankl, p. 120).

Therefore, instead of being preoccupied with death, one must occupy himself with life, even if he is suffering from a deathly illness. Those who don't learn to live with ill luck—that is, illness—only wastes the little time left. A wise attitude to life compels us to accept that life is transient.

Frankl has personally demonstrated this attitude to death in 1970, when he suffered a heart attack and was taken to a hospital's emergency room. When Elisabeth Lukas, a former student, called and asked how he was feeling, he said that his condition was serious and that his heart could stop beating any minute.

In *Meaning in Suffering* (1986b), Lukas wrote that she very much wanted to talk to Frankl to help him, but she couldn't find words. Frankl then calmed her down and said that death for him was not frightening at all, for he had completed his task; responsibility for his life was taken from him, and he would accept fate's decision.

Frankl asked Lukas to remain calm when she faces her own death in the future. "There is no need to be afraid," he said. "He didn't think about himself," Lukas wrote, "he didn't think about his heart attack, he thought about me" (Lukas, p. 139).

Empirical research conducted in the past twenty-five years supports Frankl's attitude to death (Batthyany and Guttmann, 2005). Findings in more than twenty studies indicate that people over fifty, who are motivated by their inner forces, exhibit less fear of death than those whose attitude to life is pessimistic.

Preoccupation with death, and constant reflection on it, prevents people from doing their immediate tasks. Thoughts about death have a negative psychological impact on them. On the other hand, an optimistic attitude to life and setting realistic goals in the short run lessen the anxiety caused by the idea of death. Women exhibit greater anxiety over death than men do. Contrary to expectations, religion and spirituality do not significantly affect fear of death.

In *The Doctor and the Soul* (1986), Frankl speaks of two types of people regarding attitude to death, the pessimist and the optimistic. The former is an individual standing before a calendar and anxiously watching each day that passes away. Such a person compares his or her life to the pages in the calendar and notes anxiously how these are getting closer to their end. The latter is a person who removes from the calendar the day already lived, writes on it what he or she has accomplished that day, and adds it to the pages already lived. Such a person doesn't occupy him- or herself with thoughts of getting old, and he or she doesn't envy the young for having a long life before them. Instead, such an individual is happy with the knowledge of having already lived a long life. And now he or she can look back on it and see all achievements, love, and suffering experienced in a long life. These fill his or her heart with pride.

Frankl compared human life to a work of art. Similar to the sculptor who takes a block of stone and works it with a hammer and chisel to give it form and create a statute, without knowing when he or she will complete it, so is a person's life, for one never knows when one will be called. Thus he or she must use the time available to move forward with his work—even if his creation will not be finished.

Sometimes an unfinished work is the most beautiful, as are the symphonies of Schubert and Mozart. The fact that a work is not finished does not necessarily mean that it has no meaning and value. The richness of one's life, not its length, is what enhances life's worth.

The finiteness of life can be a reminder that we should use the available time and opportunities in the best possible way. Therefore, we must be aware of and responsible for our own lives. This attitude to life and death is available to everybody, irrespective of one's level of education and social standing.

The therapist may ask a client to imagine that he or she is old and pondering over the pages of his or her life. Then a miracle happens and the client can choose what to change in the last chapter of his or her life. If the client is able to imagine such a situation, then he or she could grasp the weight of the responsibility for his or her life in a given moment and understand what this responsibility demands of him or her each and every day.

Frankl used to emphasize a maxim of logotherapy: live as if you were living your life a second time and avoid the mistakes you did the first time. He used to ask his clients to imagine their lives as a movie, but without being able to reverse what has been recorded. Thus they could see their own responsibility for what had happened and was happening, and correct what may still be possible to correct in the future.

Frankl was asked whether life should be preserved at all costs. He replied that when life is no longer fit for human beings—that is, when the lives of human beings become similar to those of lower animals or vegetables—they live such horrible lives that it would be better to die, for any human being would refuse such a life. Each individual would like to live a meaningful life irrespective of its length. A short life can be full of accomplishments, such as the lives of many great composers, and a long life can be without value.

Death gives value to life. Without death people would postpone doing everything and disregard all commitment and responsibility toward their time. Life itself would thus be without value and meaning.

Klingberg (2001) wrote a biography of Viktor Frankl and his wife, Eleanor. Viktor used to say that the greatest value and honor that had been bestowed on him was a certificate attesting that on his ninetieth birthday ninety trees were planted by students of a high school in Canada, one tree for each year of his life. And every time Viktor passed by this certificate he used to say, "Whenever I see this certificate, I am ready to die" (p. 319).

LOGOTHERAPY'S ATTITUDE TOWARD SUICIDE

Logotherapy's attitude to suicide is based on the ethical principles derived from the Hippocratic Oath, which is commonly attributed to Hippocrates, the great physician of ancient times and the founder of scientific medicine. In its modern structure and content, this oath serves as a guide for the ethical behavior of a physician anywhere in the world. This oath is the basis of the ethical codes in the helping professions despite the many changes that have happened in the profession of medicine during the past 2,500 years. The Hippocratic Oath is still important today, and not only from a historical perspective.

Among the main elements of the Hippocratic Oath is respect for the patient (this means refraining from engaging in sexual relations with the patient and keeping confidentiality—except when the courts order otherwise), respect for the teachers who taught this profession; respect for one's colleagues; obligation to participate in consultations and in the development of medical science and technology; prohibition against accepting bribery and issuing false documents; and dealing with the consequences in case the oath is violated.

The Hippocratic Oath forbids the killing of a fetus (abortion) or giving assistance to anyone wishing to commit suicide. But what can be done in difficult situations, when life and its meaning for the individual are at stake—as in cases of endless suffering from an incurable disease, total limitation in mobility, loss of self-respect or a great love, and economic or moral bankruptcy? Should the command to save life be valid in these cases too? And how to reconcile the Hippocratic Oath with modern societies' new concepts of quality of life, life in dignity, or dignified death? Each doctor must answer the questions above in his or her own way, in accordance with his or her conscience.

The medical oath in all its versions and details has kept alive the social mission of physicians for thousands of years. The Hippocratic Oath is even more significant today than it was in the past, for debates about beginning and ending a life not only cause controversy among cultures and within religions but also affect medicine's attitude toward these critical issues. It is indeed possible to refer to the Hippocratic Oath to justify a certain position in medical practice for good or bad, but one cannot avoid the central message contained in each of the recent versions of that oath, its most important command: *Primum, non nocere*—that is, before all else, do not harm!

Serving human beings as a physician is a privilege. Doctors must keep and safeguard the physical and mental health of patients, ease their suffering—irrespective of gender, religion, political belief, or economical status—and refrain from using professional knowledge for purposes other than what is included in the Hippocratic Oath.

Frankl, as a physician and psychiatrist, was of course aware of what was expected of him; he knew well the demands and obligations toward society emanating from this oath. For this reason, Frankl based logotherapy's attitude to suicide and euthanasia on the ethical principles stemming directly from the Hippocratic Oath.

Research in logotherapy and meaning-oriented psychotherapy reveals that out of a total of fifty-two studies examined, only four dealt directly with suicide or thoughts of suicide among the aged. The other studies investigated suicide among teenagers and young people—particularly students in colleges and universities—or among mentally sick patients. According to studies carried out worldwide, suicide is much more frequent among the young than among people who have entered the second half of their lives (Batthyany and Guttmann, 2005).

An older person who loses belief in his or her values often feels that it's time to die, that there is no meaning in continuing to live or in continuing to suffer. These feelings are accompanied by thoughts of death. A person entangled in a crisis of values often thinks about death; however, these thoughts are seldom followed by acts, for the person involved is afraid of death.

Even if we can understand the wish to die in certain situations, suicide is not accepted by many religions or by modern psychology, including logotherapy. The sacredness of life, of keeping it under the most trying conditions, is based on the understanding that only in life is it possible to correct mistakes, find meaning, and achieve goals. And only by living can one reach the highest spiritual level of existence.

Finishing life untimely meant for the psychologist Jung ending an experiment before it has begun. Jung thought that when we were born, we found ourselves in the midst of an experiment that we have to conclude. Jung's attitude to suicide is close to that of Frankl, who developed logotherapy while serving as a physician and psychiatrist during the first half of the twentieth century.

Frankl's approach to suicide became a principle of logotherapy. Frankl was convinced that even in situations that seem hopeless, there is an outlet. Suicide always causes suffering to another human being. The one who commits suicide can never annul or correct this suffering. Therefore, suicide is never an honorable act. Those considering suicide should be warned that no problem can be corrected by such an act.

No physician, psychiatrist, or social worker can protect another human being from unhappiness, but it is possible to help people have meaningful lives even when not all of their wishes can be fulfilled. Meaning can be acquired by overcoming negative feelings and by learning. Suffering can make one more mature and able to cope with fate.

A would-be victim of suicide can be assisted in the discovery of new goals and new tasks that answer the question of why. Knowing why helps one to carry the how. This knowledge has great therapeutic value when one is in a mental crisis. One can be taught that one's life has a unique purpose, a purpose which only he or she, and no one else, can or should accomplish. If one is aware of this uniqueness and perceives life as a mission, then one is able to grasp its value and to use the opportunities life would bring in the future.

In *The Doctor and the Soul* (1986), Frankl compares a victim of suicide to a chess player who, when he is about to lose the game, sweeps all the figures off the chessboard; but to no avail, for he can't thus solve his problem. People can't solve real problems in life by throwing away life itself. And in the same way that the chess player is not acting according to the rules of the game when he sweeps off the figures, one who commits suicide is violating the rules of life when he chooses suicide as solution to his problems. These rules do not demand being victorious all the time and at all costs. They only ask that we do not give in and leave the battlefield without a fight (p. 53).

In his work with people contemplating suicide in Vienna's Steinhof Hospital for the mentally sick, Frankl helped some 1,200 women to avoid suicide. His method consisted of the following: First he would familiarize himself with the personal background of the patient and then he would ask the patient whether she still had suicidal thoughts. The patient would answer no, for she wanted to leave the hospital to commit suicide. Then Frankl would ask why she no longer had suicidal thoughts. If the patient was nervous, she would try to avoid eye contact with him, and she couldn't offer any reason why not to commit suicide Frankl knew then that she posed a danger to herself. But if the patient answered the same question by saying that she had a family to take care of, or that she had a task to fulfill, then Frankl knew that this patient saw meaning in life and thus posed no danger to herself.

When Frankl was incarcerated in a concentration camp, he realized that his method worked well, for as long as prisoners attached meaning to their suffering, as long as there was a loved person or an important goal that the prisoner wanted to achieve, he or she would not commit suicide. Of course, any prisoner could die in many different ways in a concentration camp, but discounting misfortune or bad fate, such a prisoner was among the survivors (Klingberg, 2001, p. 78).

EUTHANASIA FROM A LOGOTHERAPEUTIC PERSPECTIVE

In 1987 the world was shaken by the news of the murder of helpless old people in a hospital in the city of Vienna, Austria. The murders were committed systematically by three young nurses and by a forty-nine-year-old head nurse. In the investigation following the discovery of the murders, the nurses stated that they had killed forty-eight old and sick patients in cold blood. The head nurse was responsible for killing thirty-nine of the victims, by giving them lethal doses of insulin and by strangling them. These nurses were known in the hospital as industrious and kind people, and their colleagues and patients could not believe their confessions published in the newspapers.

The four nurses accused of murder claimed in their defense that they committed those acts to ease the suffering of their victims. They tried to escape punishment by saying that they had simply performed euthanasia. This event was an isolated case in the nursing profession at that time, but the potential for repeating it exists everywhere. Therefore, it is important to understand the concept of euthanasia.

Many members of the helping professions have power over those in their care. This power could be misused with fatal consequences. Although the great majority of these professionals are decent and law-abiding people, some of them may think like the "good nurses" from Vienna.

Sometimes a patient may ask a nurse or a doctor for help in ending his or her life, and the request sounds reasonable, for the patient can't bear the suffering. The patient is fully conscious, has control over his or her mental power, and understands the meaning of the request—to die with dignity. Yet, even if the request sounds reasonable, the helping professional must abide by the law. Euthanasia is rejected almost universally. But beyond the written law, the Hippocratic Oath, or the Code of Ethics of a given helping profession is the sixth commandment in the Old Testament: "Do not kill"(Exodus 20: 13).

There have been heated debates about the rights of a terminally sick person to be euthanized. In the center of this debate are questions such as: Isn't it better for a terminally sick old person to die, instead of suffering from untreatable illness? Does this person have a right to ask a physician to end his or her suffering and help him or her to end his life? The request by such a patient is an expression of the age-old human quest to die with dignity and without suffering. This is the real meaning of euthanasia today. Logotherapy does not accept "mercy killing" for any reason.

Euthanasia in its original meaning means this attitude toward death. The author of this book has no interest in delving into issues of active or passive euthanasia, or into issues of whether or not a patient has a right to control his or her death. These issues are too complex for analysis in this book. Therefore, he only wishes to concentrate on logotherapy's attitude toward euthanasia. Let us begin with an example from Frankl's *Psychotherapy for Every Man* (1971).

An old and very industrious nurse in a hospital was sick with incurable cancer. She was in despair for not being able to carry on her work and wished to die. Before she could do any harm to herself, Frankl visited her to find out what he could do to ease her suffering and despair, and to tell her that any person can work hard, but not everybody can suffer with dignity. Frankl told her that now she had been given an opportunity to show the other patients that the meaning of life is not dependent on hard work alone, for if this were true, then none of the helpless patients and disabled people had the right to live. There was still one thing that this nurse could do: to serve as a model for others on how to die with dignity. The nurse died a week later from natural causes.

Euthanasia in its narrowest sense means easing one's suffering by taking medications. The practice is treated as a "matter-of-fact" by all physicians and, as such, does not cause any controversy. The problem with euthanasia centers on ending a life considered not worthy of a human being by the doctors. Logotherapists do not consider doctors the only authorities for decisions about life and death. No doctor is God! If doctors are given the right to decide when another person's life becomes worthless, even if that person is considered medically untreatable, then doctors have power that does not belong to the medical profession. That is why logotherapy vehemently opposes any form of euthanasia.

Some politicians, journalists, and experts in public relations try to justify euthanasia in cases of severe mental illness, by saying that it is better for them to die than to suffer, and it is better for society to use the resources allocated for the care of those people in a more useful manner. Frankl rejects such claims altogether. He emphasizes more convincing reasons for their rejection by logotherapists.

First of all, what does it mean to say that a patient has an incurable illness? He presented a personal experience with the following case: a gravelly ill young man was lying in a hospital for a long time, being fed through a tube in his nose. What could be expected in this situation? Wasn't it better for the patient to be euthanized? The future provided the answers to these questions.

One day the young man sat up in his bed, asked for food, got out of bed to exercise his legs, and behaved normally. Pretty soon the muscles in his legs had strengthened so much that in a few weeks he left the hospital and returned to his previous occupation. This patient, now cured, began to give lectures on his experience in the hospital where he had spent five years. During those years he observed human behavior, especially the behavior of doctors, nurses, and other patients. If he had been "sentenced" to euthanasia, he would have missed out on his new life.

What is considered today an incurable illness may become routinely cured tomorrow with the help of new medications. And who could say with certainty that there is nothing to do in a given case? Who would have imagined 100 years ago that certain forms of mental illness can be cured or at least palliated?

Frankl objected to using illnesses that were incurable as justifications for performing euthanasia It was his contention that we have no real knowledge about human beings or about illnesses to claim with certainty that a patient cannot be cured. And who gives the doctors the right to play God? Who gives them the right to be the judge?

Since the days of Hippocrates a physician has had two purposes: to cure when possible and to ease the suffering when curing was not possible. Therefore, a doctor has no right—in fact, he or she is forbidden—to decide whether a person's life is worth living or not—even if this person suffers from an incurable illness.

Many doctors can testify about cases in which old patients in acute pain begged them to end their suffering through euthanasia, only to return home happily and full of plans after the crisis had gone by. If those patients could hear themselves when they were brought to the hospital in dire condition, they wouldn't believe their own ears. They wouldn't agree that they were the same people who cried bitter tears and wanted to die by all means.

ATTITUDE TOWARD IMMORTALITY

Man takes into consideration immortality and forgets to take into consideration death. (Kundera, 1990, p. 74)

No one could begin life anew for we can never discover the sponge with which we could erase the table of our life. (Ancsel, 1999, p. 128)

Jonathan Swift (1667–1745)—satirist, essayist, poet, and writer of political pamphlets—is best remembered perhaps for his wonderful book *Gulliver's Travels* (1962). In his third voyage, Gulliver encounters some strange creatures called Struld-Brugs. These are human beings with a special mark on their foreheads, born in the land of the Log-Nogs. This mark, a red circle above the left eyelid, attests to their immortality. The color of this mark changes with development: when a Struld-Brug reaches the age of forty-five, the red circle becomes black and grows to the size of a coin.

The children of these creatures resemble other children. There are no more than 1,100 immortals among them. When Gulliver tells his hosts that he wishes to become one of the immortals to gain eternal life, to accomplish great deeds, and to teach future generations about the wonders of nature, the universe, and history, his hosts hasten to correct his mistaken thoughts.

The Struld-Brugs tell Gulliver they act like all other people until the age of thirty. Afterward they gradually become melancholic and depressed until age eighty, which in Gulliver's times was the longest age a man could reach.

Gulliver's hosts show him all the shortcomings the aged Struld-Brugs have to face, along with all the pain and suffering that endlessly burdens their existence, for they can't die. They can't experience any feeling of kindness, friendship, or mercy.

The Struld-Brugs are full of envy, passion, and longings for pleasures that they cannot have. They are envious of those who can die, because they no longer suffer. Their memory is limited to what they have learned in their childhood. They are incapable of learning new things. The least miserable among them are those who lost their memory altogether. These get some help out of mercy because they lack the bad traits evident in the others.

The Struld-Brugs cannot get married for fear of continuing the suffering of their race in the world. When they reach the age of eighty, they are considered dead. They lose their properties to their heirs, except for a small pension for a meager existence. They can't hold any public position or office, buy land, or serve as witness in any civil or criminal dispute or trial. At the age of ninety, they lose their teeth and hair, and the sense of taste, and they eat and drink without wanting to. They are vulnerable to many illnesses, and they forget the names of people (even friends and relatives) they come in social contact with. They can't even get in touch with other Struld-Brugs of another generation for they don't remember their language, and they can't speak with people who have been living for 200 years. They seem to Gulliver horrible and unhappy creatures, especially the women, who have lost their human form.

Swift laughs at the human quest for eternal life and says that the reader has undoubtedly understood by now that what he has heard or seen did not wet his appetite for eternal living. Gulliver adds that no cruel tyrant or dictator could invent a more horrible death that he would not happily accept in order to escape from such a life.

Lengthening life beyond what nature has devised is a stupid thing, he tells his readers. Instead of trying to achieve eternal life, we should concentrate improving the living conditions of those who lack the resources for a dignified human existence.

Longevity, which has doubled in the past 100 years, is a blessing for those who are able to enjoy the benefits of modern medicine, science, and technology. As for the others, longevity means adding years to their suffering and pain.

Swift's book warns us against the endless pursuit of eternal life and advises that we should devote our energies in living a good life, no matter if our life is short or long.

The subject of immortality continues to occupy an important place in human endeavors. The mystery of life after death is part of all major religions. For these the issue is a matter of belief, reward, or punishment.

The mystery of death has been the subject of many great works in literature, music, and cinema. The Czech writer Milan Kundera, for example, has devoted one of his works to this subject. His witty book *Immortality* (1990) attests to his sense of humor, intelligence, and sharp eye. This work criticizes Western culture's perception of metaphysic existence.

In a most entertaining imaginary conversation between the philosopher and poet Goethe, and the famous writer Ernest Hemingway, Goethe says that human beings know that they are mortals; they know that there is death, and nevertheless they are unable to accept it, to understand it, and to behave accordingly. A human being does not know how to be mortal or how to become dead. Kundera adds, "Now that he is already dead some one hundred fifty-six years, the time has come to laugh at immortality and to use his being dead to go to sleep" (p. 291).

The immortality Kundera refers to in his book is not connected to the eternity of the soul. For Kundera this concept has no religious connotations. Kundera's notion of immortality is interested only in what will remain in the memory of future generations after one's death. "Each human being can attain great or small immortality, a short or a long one," says Kundera (p. 49). There is a difference between "small immortality—defined as the memory one leaves in the hearts of those who knew him or her—and "great immortality"—that is, the memory one leaves in the hearts of those who didn't know him personally.

Great immortality, or eternal glory, is the domain of famous artists, military leaders, and politicians. Kundera presents a third type of immortality, which he calls "ridiculous," and in which a famous person is caught in a ridiculous situation. Of the three types of immortality, the last one is the one famous people want to avoid.

A man's life is like a clock, says Kundera: until a certain time death seems far away and unworthy of thoughts, for it cannot be seen. This is the first and best period of our lives. But then, all of a sudden, we begin to see death right before our eyes, and we cannot stop thinking about it. Death remains with us. And since immortality is inextricably connected to death, we can say that immortality, too, remains with us, at least in thought. And as soon as we know that it is with us, we begin to prepare ourselves to greet it. This is the second part of our lives. There is also a third part, short and most mysterious, and about which we know very little. The strength and vigor we used to have diminishes, and we tire easily. This is the period in which immortality of an old man or woman plays an important part. When old people get closer to death they usually give up their preoccupation with mundane matters and concentrate their efforts on securing for themselves some form or measure of immortality. For example, a known artist who has to admit that he or she can no longer paint may ensure that his or her creations will end up in a museum or gallery and that they are exhibited long after his or her death.

There are, however, some exceptional old people—such as the poet, playwright, and philosopher Goethe, who at the age of seventy-five was able to come to life once again when a young and attractive woman knocked on his door. Although he knew that the real reason for the unexpected visit was the woman's interest in his immortality and glory, this knowledge didn't prevent him from becoming a victim to her charm over and over again.

In a hilarious passage in his book, Kundera arranges for Hemingway and Goethe to meet. The two talk about the great sadness that had befallen them for being immortal. They talk about their inability to escape from public admiration and about their real selves, as opposed to their public personae. Their real selves are very different from their public selves. They also talk about what they really desire: to rest.

The literary legends created by poets, writers, journalists, and historians never match reality. One can plan his or her immortality, even prepare for it, but there is no guarantee that it will last as planned and wished by the planner. It is impossible to determine ahead of time what meaning future generations will give to the immortality of great people.

"When I understood one day that the subject is immortality," Hemingway tells Goethe, "I was scared to death. Since then I asked everybody a thousand times to leave me alone. I moved to Cuba to escape from their eyes. I don't give a hoot about immortality. A man can end his life, but he can't end his immortality" (Kundera, p. 82).

Goethe comforts Hemingway with a personal story about the troubles of immortality. He describes in vivid colors the way Bettina, the young woman supposedly in love with him, pursues him. And when Hemingway remarks that Goethe is dressed ridiculously, the latter bursts into laughter. "The immortals have a right to dress as they please," Goethe tells Hemingway. "I got dressed like a scarecrow because of Bettina. She speaks of her great love for me everywhere and I want people to see the subject of this great love . . . an old and bald man without teeth, wearing some transparent green piece of cloth tied with strings over his forehead. I wear it for my eyes hurt a lot" (Kundera, p. 85).

When the psychologist Carl Gustav Jung was asked about life after death, he answered that so far he didn't know it, and when he died, he would be able to say, "now we shall see." But as long as he was around and living, he could only talk about what he had to do here and do it the best he could (1997).

Many people are not interested in the subject of immortality, and they get horrified by the idea that they will be sitting on a cloud and playing the harp for 10,000 years. Others get so sick of life that they prefer nothingness over any other form of existence after death. Yet, in most cases the longing for immortality is immediate.

If there were a conscious existence after death, Jung said, it would develop like human consciousness toward greater heights. Many people, those who didn't achieve in their lives what others did, wish to attain immortality after death as a compensation for this deficiency in their lives (Jung, *Memories, Dreams and Thoughts*, p. 382).

Frankl agrees with Jung's attitude to immortality and claims that human beings do not want to accept that with death everything will cease for them. Human beings can't accept that one day they are here, and the next they are gone, or that there is no answer to the question of where the dead have gone. Immortality cannot be grasped by contemplation, the same way that one cannot decide whether a pair of glasses is good by only looking at them: one can find out only by looking through the glasses.

A spiritual personality remains accessible to others during his life and afterward by his voice. Even someone who died a long time ago—a great artist such as Caruso, for example—remains immortal through recordings of his voice. A great scientist such as Einstein remains immortal through his invaluable scientific contributions, which remain after his body no longer exists.

In death we lose our consciousness and the sense of time. A spiritual existence is possible only in the spiritual dimension, not in the temporal one. And where there is no time, there is no past, no present, no future, and no existence. Therefore, all hypotheses about existence beyond the physical, the here and now, are groundless.

Logotherapy recognizes the importance of the values explicated in this book. It recognizes and emphasizes first of all human beings as the supreme value. Logotherapy insists that each human being is a world in itself—special, unique, and unable to escape loneliness in the face of death. Yet every human being can cope with death through love and choice. According to this philosophy of life and theory of motivation, a human being can choose how he or she wants to live and die.

Logotherapy's insistence on the unconditional meaningfulness of life; on turning suffering into a human accomplishment; on deriving from guilt the opportunity to change for the better; on seeing life as transitory and thus requiring one to take responsible action; and, above all, on a person's freedom to choose a meaningful life, can all be helpful in alleviating fear of death in old age.

This idea is eloquently expressed by the poet Hayim Motalis (1996, p. 90), whose poem I wish to present here (in my translation from Hebrew to English) to sum up this book:

Say yes to life
> Say yes to life,
> And good morning to a new day,
> Begin your day
> In your old age
> In hope and strength, without fear!
> Memories and pictures

Of hours and days,
Of lovely minutes
Pass in procession;
Despite wrinkles and gray hair,
Despite losses and aches,
Good morning to a new day
In hope and strength, without fear!
Look around you, everything's blooming
Enjoy the golden lighting, sun's ray
That dance around your porch,
Awaken you from your dream
With good morning to a new day;
With flowers,
With colors,
With fragrance,
Even for an old man.
Say yes to life
And good morning to a new day
In hope and strength—without fear!

Bibliography

Adler, A. (1994). *What Life Should Mean to You?* Translated by S. Nyiro Jozsef, Budapest: Kossuth Publisher. In Hungarian.

———. (1996). *The Meaning of Life.* Translated by S. Nyiro Jozsef. Budapest: Kossuth Publisher. In Hungarian.

Agnon, S. J. (1960). "Hamalbush." In *Ad Hena.* Jerusalem: Shoken Publisher, pp. 305–332. In Hebrew.

Ancsel, E. (1995). *Life as an Unknown Story.* Budapest: Atlantisz. In Hungarian.

———. (1999). *All Her Prefaces.* Budapest: Kossuth Publisher. In Hungarian.

Ankori, M. (1991). *The Heart and the Spring. Hasidism and Analytic Psychology.* Tel Aviv: Ramot Publisher. In Hebrew.

Balzac, H. de. (1991). *Father Goriot.* Translated by Lanyi Viktor. Budapest: Europa Publisher. In Hungarian

Barker, R. L., (1999). *The Social Work Dictionary.* (4th ed) Silver Spring, MD: National Association of Social Workers.

Batthyany, A. and Guttmann, D. (2005). *Empirical Research in Logotherapy and Meaning-Oriented Psychotherapy, an Annotated Bibliography.* In collaboration with PsychINFO (American Psychological Association). Phoenix, AZ: Zeig, Tucker &Theisen, Inc.

Baziz, O. (1997). "The Loneliness of Woman in the Works of David Shachar." *Moznayim* 71(8): 11. In Hebrew.

Botton, de, A. (2000). *The Consolations of Philosophy.* London: Hamish Hamilton.

Brecht, B. (1990). "The Undignified Old Lady." In *Aging in the Mirror of Literature.* Translated by David Atar. Ramat Efal: Yad Tabenkin. In Hebrew.

Brody, S. (1995). *The Zulu and the Zaide.* Johannesburg: (Mimeo).

Buber, M. (1975). *Between Man and Man.* New York: MacMillan Publishing Co.

———. (1976). *The Way of Man according to the Teaching of Hasidism.* Secaucus, NJ: The Citadel Press.

———. (1994). *I and Thou.* Translated by Biro Daniel. Budapest: Europa Publisher. In Hungarian.

Bulgakov, M. (1993). *The Devil in Moscow.* Translated by Szollosy Klara. Budapest: Europa Publisher. In Hungarian.

Bulka, R. P. (1989*).* "Jewish Humor—a Logotherapeutic Tool for Survival." *The Proceedings of the Seventh World Congress of Logotherapy,* pp. 50–58. Berkeley: Institute of Logotherapy Press.

Camus, A. (1955). *The Myth of Sisyphus and Other Essays.* Translated by Justin O'Brian. New York: A. Knopf. In French.

———. (1991). *The Plague and the Myth of Sysiphus.* Budapest: Europa Publisher.

Cicero, M. T. (1909). *On Old Age.* New York: P. F. Collier and Son.

Cohen, A. (1994). *Homour-therapy.* Haifa: Amatzya Press. In Hebrew.

———. (2003). Chained to the Rock of their Loneliness. *Nefesh,* Vols. 13–14, April, pp. 5–24. In Hebrew.

Conrad, J. (1990). *Heart of Darkness.* London: Hoddler and Staughton.

Cousins, N. (1981). *Anatomy of an Illness as Perceived by the Patient.* New York: Bantam Publisher.

Cronstrom-Beskow, S. (1991). "Coping Strategies in Death Camps." *The International Forum for Logotherapy, Journal of Search for Meaning,* pp. 92–96.

Dalai Lama (His Holiness). (1999). *Ethics for the New Millenium.* New York: Riverhead Books.

De Botton, A. (2000). *The Consolations of Philosophy.* London: Hamish Hamilton.

Dickens, C. (1974). *Oliver Twist.* Oxford: Oxford University Press.

Einstein, A. (1934). *The World as I See it. (Mein Weltbild).* Translated by Szecsi Ferenc. Budapest: Gladiator Publisher. In Hungarian.

Ellis, A. and Velten, E. (1998). *Optimal Aging: Get Over Getting Older.* Chicago: Open Court.

Erikson, E. H. (1959). "Identity and the Lifecycle." *Psychological Issues* 1: 1. New York: International Universities Press.

———. (1964). *Insight and Responsibility.* New York: Norton and Co.

———. (1968). *Childhood and Society.* New York: Norton and Co.

Frankl, V. E. (1962). *Man's Search for Meaning, an Introduction to Logotherapy: A Revised and Enlarged Edition of From Death Camp to Existentialism.* New York: A Touchstone Book.

———. (1971). *Psychotherapie für jedermann.* (12th ed) Freiburg: Herder Publisher.

———. (1978). *The Unheard Cry for Meaning.* New York: Simon and Schuster.

———. (1982) *Trotzdem ja zum Leben sagen: Ein Psychologe Erlebt das Konzentrationslager.* München: Kosel Verlag. In German.

———. (1985a). *The Unconscious God: Logotherapy and Religion.* New York: Washington Square Press.

———. (1985b). *The Will to Meaning.* Tel Aviv: Dvir Publisher. In Hebrew.

———. (1986). *The Doctor and the Soul: From Psychotherapy to Logotherapy.* New York: Vintage Books.

———. (1995). *Was nicht in meinen Buchern steht: Lebenserinnerungen.* München: Quintessenz. In German.

———. (1996). *Der Mensch vor der Frage nach dem Sinn, 1989.* Translated by Maria Molnar and Schaffhauser Ferenc. Budapest: Kotet Kiado. In Hungarian.

———. (1997a). *Man's Search for Ultimate Meaning.* New York: Insight Books, Plenum Press.

———. (1997b). *Viktor Frankl Recollections, an Autobiography.* New York: Plenum Press.

Freud, S. (1950). *Totem and Taboo: Some Points of Agreement between the Mental Lives of Savages and Neurotics.* Translated and edited by James Strachey. New York: W. W. Norton & Company.

———. (1982). "The Joke and Its Relationship to the Unconscious." In *Essays.* Translated by Bart Istvan. Budapest: Gondolat Publisher. In Hungarian.

———. (1991). *Zur Psychopathologie des Alltagslebens.* Budapest: Cserepfalvi. In Hungarian.

———. (1994*). Introduction to Psychoanalysis.* (2nd ed) Translated by Hermann Imre. Budapest: Gondolat Publisher. In Hungarian.

———. (2002). *Civilization and Its Discontents.* New York: Penguin Books.

Fried, H. (1989). "Café Stockholm 84: A Unique day Program for Jewish Survivors." In *Aging in the Jewish World,* Jerusalem: Brookdale Institute for Research in Aging, pp. 163–167.

Gary, R. (1980). *The Dread of King Salomon.* Translated by Inbar Avital. Tel Aviv: Am Oved. In Hebrew.

Gibson, H. B. (2000). *Loneliness in Later Life.* London: MacMillan Press.

Gray, R. (1965). "Goethe's Faust Part One." *Cambridge Quarterly* 1(2): 125–143.

Green, M. (1990). *The Robinson Crusoe Story.* University Park, PA: Pennsylvania State Press.

Gullan-Whur, M. (2002). "Struggling to Be Happy—Even When I'm Old." *Journal of Applied Philosophy* 19(1): 17–30.

Guttmann, D. and Lowenstein, A. (1992). "Psychosocial Problems and the Needs of the Elderly in Mental Health." In F. J. Turner (Ed.) *Mental Health and the Elderly.* New York: The Free Press, pp. 478–502.

Guttmann, D. and Cohen, B. Z. (1993). "On the Relationship between Meaning-in-Life and Excessive Behaviors among the Active Elderly in Israel." *Journal des Viktor-Frankl-Instituts* 1(2): 38–55.

Guttmann, D. (1994). "Meaningful Aging: Establishing a Club for Survivors of the Holocaust in Hungary." *Journal des Viktor-Frankl-Instituts* 2(1): 67–73.

———. (1996). *Logotherapy for the Helping Professional: Meaningful Social Work.* New York: Springer.

———. (1997). "Homo Elector and Homo Patiens: Fate, Choice, Suffering and Meaning in the Works of Szondi and Frankl." *Journal des Viktor-Frankl-Instituts* 5(1): 66–81.

Harel, N. (1981). "Koby Knows." *Stories from the Collective House.* Jerusalem: Keter Publishing. In Hebrew.

Hassan, J. (1992). *Creative Approaches to Working with Holocaust Survivors.* London: (Mimeo).

Hemingway, E. (1995). *The Old Man and the Sea.* New York: Charles Scribner & Sons.

Hrabal, B. (1994). *Too Noisy Silence.* Translated by Ruth Bondi. Tel Aviv: Aked/Gvanim Publishers. In Hebrew.

———. (1997). *The Millions of Harlekin.* Translated by Detri Zsuzsa. Budapest: Europa. In Hungarian.

———. (2001). *Memories of a Class Repeater.* Translated by Kortvelyessy Klara. Budapest: Europa. In Hungarian.

Jacobson, S. (1995). *Toward a Meaningful Life: The Wisdom of the Rebbe Menachem Mendel Schneerson.* New York: William Morrow and Co.

Jewish Encyclopedia. (1907). New York and London: Funk and Wagnalls.

Jung, C. G. (1954). "The Practice of Psychotherapy." (Vol. 16) In *The Collected Works of C. G. Jung.* London: Routledge.

———. (1993). *On the Paths of Our Depths*. Translated by Bodrog Vilmos. Budapest: Gondolat. In Hungarian.

———. (1997). *Memories, Dreams, and Thoughts*. Translated by Kovacs Vera. Budapest: Europa. In Hungarian.

———. (1998). "The Stages of Life." In *Aging Concepts & Controversies* (2nd ed), ed. Harry R. Moody. Thousand Oaks, CA: Pine Forge Press, pp. 452–455.

Kalmar, S. (1997). "About Guilt and Guilt Feelings." *Journal des Viktor-Frankl-Instituts* 5(1): 101–108.

Kierkegaard, S. (1954). *Fear and Trembling and the Sickness unto Death*. Translated by Walter Lowrie. Garden City, NJ: Doubleday. In Danish.

———. (1971). *Either/Or*. Translated by D. F. Swenson and L. M. Swenson. Princeton, NJ: Princeton University Press.

———. (1991). *The Concept of Dread*. Translated by Racz Peter. Budapest: Goncol Publisher. In Hungarian.

———. (1993). *The Mortal Illness*. Translated by Racz Peter. Budapest: Goncol Publisher. In Hungarian.

Klingberg, H. Jr. (2001). *When Life Calls Out to Us: The Love and Lifework of Viktor and Elly Frankl. The Story behind Man's Search for Meaning*. New York: Doubleday.

Kundera, M. (1990). *Immortality*. Translated by Ruth Bondi Tel Aviv: Zmora-Bitan Publishers. In Hebrew.

Leibovits, Y. (1999). *I Wanted to Ask You, Professor Leibovits: Letters to Professor Leibovits and from Him*. Jerusalem: Keter. In Hebrew.

Lukacs, J. (2001). *Confessions of an Original Sinner*. Translated by Barkoczi Andras. Budapest: Europa. In Hungarian.

Lukas, E. (1986a). *Meaningful Living: A Logotherapeutic Guide to Health*. Foreword by V. E. Frankl. An Institute of Logotherapy Press Book. New York: Grove Press.

———. (1986b). *Meaning in Suffering: Comfort in Crisis through Logotherapy*. Translated by Joseph B. Fabry. Berkeley, CA: Institute of Logotherapy Press.

Mann. T. (1955). *The Magic Mountain*. Translated by Mordechai Avi-Shaul. Tel Aviv: Sifriat Poalim. In Hebrew.

———. (1994). *Death in Venice*. Translated by Lanyi Viktor. Budapest: Europa Publisher. In Hungarian.

Motalis, H. (1996). "Say Yes to Life." *Gerontology* 75: 90. In Hebrew.

Nagy, E. (2000). *Guide for the Aged*. Budapest: Noran. In Hungarian.

Nietzsche, F. (1997a). *Ecce Homo: How One Becomes What One Is*. Budapest: Goncol Publisher.

———. (1997b). *The Gay Science*. Translated by Torok Gabor. Budapest: Holnap Kiado. In Hungarian.

———. (2004). *My Sister and Me*. Translated by Yeshayahu Yariv. Tel Aviv: Yediot Ahronot Publications. In Hebrew.

Olson, L. K., ed. (1994). *The Graying of the World*. New York: The Haworth Press.

Raz, S. (1986). *A Very Narrow Bridge: The Sayings of Rabbi Nachman of Breslav*. Jerusalem: Keter. In Hebrew.

Rubinstein, R. L. (1986). *Singular Paths: Old Men Living Alone*. New York: Columbia University Press, pp. 181–192.

Russell, B. (1956). *Reflections on My Eightieth Birthday*. New York: Simon and Schuster.

———. (1967). *The Autobiography of Bertrand Russell*. Vol. 1. London: Allen and Unwin.

Scheler, M. (1960). *On the Eternal in Man*. London: SCM Press Ltd.

————. (1973). *Formalism in Ethics and Non-Formal Ethics of Values*. Evanston, IL: Northwestern University Press.

Schopenhauer, A. (2001). *Life Wisdom*. Translated by Dr. Kelen Ferenc. Budapest: Szukits Kiado. In Hungarian.

Schweitzer, A. (1999). *Honor of Life*. Translated by Dani Laszlo. Budapest: Ursus Publisher. In Hungarian.

Scully, M. "Viktor Frankl at Ninety: An Interview." *First Things The Journal of Religion, Culture and Public Life* 52: 39–43.

Seneca, L. A. (1997). *On Mental Calmness and on the Brevity of Life*. Translated by Bollok Janos. Budapest: Seneca Press. In Hungarian.

————. (2001). *Letters on Morality*. Translated by Kurcz Agnes. Budapest: Europa Publisher. In Hungarian.

Shakespeare, W. (1947). *As You Like It*. III, 2. The Works of William Shakespeare, London: P. J. Basil Blackwell.

Solomon, D., Weinberg, J., Slaigh, M., and Ilani, Z. (1989). *Aging according to Israeli Sources*. Jerusalem, Israel: Jewish Torah Publisher. In Hebrew.

Sternig (1984). "Finding Meaning through Existential Guilt." *The International Forum for Logotherapy: Journal of Search for Meaning* 4: 79–82.

Swift, J. (1962). *Gulliver's Travels*. New York: MacMillan.

Szalay, K. (1983). *Komikum, Szatira, Humor*. Budapest: Kossuth Publisher. In Hungarian.

Szondi, L. (1937). "Analysis of Marriages. An Attempt at a Theory of Choice in Love." *Acta Psychologica* 3(1): 1–80. The Hague: Martinus Nijhoff.

————. (1987). *Cain the Offender of Law, Moses the Creator of Law*. Budapest: Gondolat Publisher. In Hungarian.

————. (1996a). The Languages of the Unconscious: Symptom, Symbol and Choice." *Thalassa* 96(2): 61–82. In Hungarian.

————. (1996b). "The Way to Manhood." *Thalassa* 96(2): 39–60. In Hungarian.

Takashima, H. (1984). *Humanistic Psychosomatic Medicine. A Logotherapy Book*. Berkeley, CA: Institute of Logotherapy Press.

Talmudic Encyclopedia (1978). Jerusalem: Talmudic Encyclopedia Institute. In Hebrew.

Tamaro, S. (1996). *To Follow Your Heart*. Translated by Anat Spitzen. Tel Aviv: Modan. In Hebrew.

Tolstoy, L. (1992). *The Death of Ivan Illich*. Translated by Gellert Gyorgy. Budapest: Europa Publisher. In Hungarian.

Volicki, M. (1987). "Despair—An 'Absolutization' of Values." *The International Forum for Logotherapy Journal of Search for Meaning* 5(1): 50–51.

Volkov, L. (1992). *To Be a Son to an Old Parent: A Phase in the Family's Life Cycle Crisis*. Tel Aviv: Ramot Publisher. In Hebrew.

Webster's New Universal Unabridged Dictionary (2nd ed.) (1986). Cleveland: New World Publication.

Wiesel, E. (1993). *Souls on Fire*. New York: Touchstone.

Wilde, Oscar. (1990). *The Selfish Giant,* cited in David Atar's *Aging in the Mirror of Literature*. Ramat Efal: Yad Tabenkin. In Hebrew.

Yalom, I. E. (1980). *Existential Psychotherapy*. New York: Basic Books.

Index

About the Author

DAVID GUTTMANN is Emeritus Professor and former Dean of the School of Social Work at the University of Haifa in Israel. An internationally known expert on logotherapy, and personal friend of the late Viktor E. Frankl—the famed founder of logotherapy—author Guttmann received the Grand Award for lifetime achievement in logotherapy from the Viktor Frankl Foundation and the City of Vienna in 2003. In other roles that helped fuel the issues raised in this book, he served as Presidential appointee to the White House Conference on Aging, Founding Member of the Southern Gerontological Society of America, Academic Advisor to the Golda Meir International Training Center in Community Development, and Director at the Center for the Study of Aging at the National Catholic School of Social Service at Catholic University of America. He has authored, co-authored, or edited twelve earlier books.